THE PRIVATE LIFE OF PARENTS

THE
PRIVATE LIFE
OF
PARENTS

How to take care of
yourself and your partner
while raising happy, healthy children
—a complete survival manual

Roberta Plutzik and Maria Laghi

Illustrations by David Hatfield

NEW YORK   EVEREST HOUSE   PUBLISHERS

LIBRARY OF CONGRESS CATALOGING IN PUBLICATION DATA:

Plutzik, Roberta.
  The private life of parents.

  Bibliography, p. 259
  Includes index.
  1. Parenting. 2. Adulthood. 3. Family. 4. Social
role. I. Laghi, Maria. II. Title.
HQ755.8.P59   1982   649'.1   82–11750
ISBN 0–89696–119–2

For reprint permission grateful acknowledgment is made to:

Julie Armstrong, Judy Edmundson, Jane Honikman, and Judy Mrstik for
their chart, "Common Post-Partum Feelings," Copyright © 1979 by Julie
Armstrong, Judy Edmundson, Jane Honikman, and Judy Mrstik.

Pennwalt Corporation for the "Calorie Substitution Chart" from "Are you
really serious about losing weight?" Copyright © 1979 by the RX Division
of the Pennwalt Corporation.

Dr. Gabriel Smilkstein for the "Family Apgar Questionnaire," Copyright ©
1979, 1980 by Dr. Gabriel Smilkstein.

FOR OUR MOTHERS
Tanya Plutzik and Fritzi Garner
AND OUR HUSBANDS
Neil Baldwin and Jay Laghi

CONTENTS

ACKNOWLEDGMENTS   xi

INTRODUCTION   xiii

1   YOU   1
    The Private Doubts of Parenthood ⁊ The Search for
    Parental Wellbeing

2   INITIATION   10
    Getting Through the First Six Weeks: A Parent's
    Survival Manual ⁊ Coping with Post-Partum Emo-
    tions ⁊ Parent and Pediatrician ⁊ Colic: A Parent's
    Perspective ⁊ Feeding Your Baby ⁊ Parents and Hos-
    pitals ⁊ If Your Baby is Handicapped ⁊ If You Adopt
    ⁊ If You Are an Older Parent

3   MARRIAGE AND SEX   38
    Recapturing the Style of Your Relationship ⁊ Parents
    as Partners: Evolving Contracts ⁊ Coming to Terms
    with Conflict ⁊ Communication: The Missing Link ⁊
    Eight Questions That Can Save Your Marriage ⁊ Sex
    after Baby ⁊ Some Physical Aspects of Sex after
    Childbirth ⁊ Sex and Your Psyche: An Interview
    with Dr. Shirley Zussman, President, American So-
    ciety of Sex Educators, Counselors, and Therapists
    ⁊ Marriage as a Framework for Sex

4   SINGLE PARENTS, STEPPARENTS   64
    Acknowledging the New You ⁊ Divorce and Small
    Children ⁊ How to Break the News to Your Kids ⁊

Telling Family ⁄ Telling Friends ⁄ The Decision to Separate: Evolving Patterns ⁄ When Child Custody Disputes Escalate ⁄ Tips for New Singles from Veteran Singles ⁄ Romance and Remarriage ⁄ Becoming a Stepparent ⁄ The New Adult Relationship ⁄ What Stepparents of Preschoolers Should Know ⁄ What the Kids Should Call You

5 LIFESTYLE   85
Getting Out of the House ⁄ The Peripatetic Parent ⁄ Having People Over ⁄ The Gourmet Toddler: Or, How to Eat Out Successfully with a Small Child ⁄ Traveling with Kids ⁄ The Home Front ⁄ Moving

6 FAMILY AND FRIENDS   126
The Post-Partum Family ⁄ Handling Help and Advice ⁄ Recognizing *Real* Family Danger Zones ⁄ Loyalties and Rivalries ⁄ Family Gatherings ⁄ Rules of the House ⁄ Allowing Our Parents to Grow ⁄ Friends ⁄ Why Friends Go ⁄ Making New Friends ⁄ Avoiding Obnoxious Behavior ⁄ Coping with Awkward Moments

7 WORK   151
Careerism ⁄ Work: The Guilt-Edged Sword ⁄ Overload ⁄ Home Sweet Home ⁄ The Changing Workplace ⁄ Going Back to Work ⁄ The Two Dust-Rag Family: Or, Sharing Housework ⁄ Taking the Big Step: Hiring a Caregiver ⁄ Pros and Cons of Individual Home Care ⁄ Daycare Centers ⁄ Parent Cooperatives ⁄ Nursery Schools

8 TIME   185
Time Management for Parents: Shaping Your Day and Beyond ⁄ Where Does the Time Go? ⁄ Organizing Your Time ⁄ Parallel Time ⁄ Making Decisions

9   MONEY   194
    Who Needs a Budget? ⟋ Families and Houses ⟋ Con-
    dominiums and Cooperatives ⟋ Life Insurance and
    the Young Family ⟋ Wills ⟋ Money and the Two-
    Career Family

10 NUTRITION AND EXERCISE   210
    Nutrition and the Expanding Family ⟋ Self-Aware-
    ness: First Step to Good Nutrition ⟋ The Parent's
    Survival Exercise Program ⟋ Fitness ⟋ Spot Reducing
    ⟋ Before You Exercise ⟋ How to Stretch ⟋ Do It To-
    gether: Exercises for Parents ⟋ Strengthening Exer-
    cises

11 THE DEVELOPING FAMILY   230
    Power and Responsibility ⟋ Growing Pains and Sepa-
    ration ⟋ Have We Done a Good Job?

12 HELP   239
    A Directory of Parent Support Groups, Services, and
    Resources

APPENDIX: The Questionnaires   255

BIBLIOGRAPHY   259

INDEX   271

ACKNOWLEDGMENTS

SINCE 1978, when we first thought about collaborating on a book for parents, many people have helped us in many ways, from taking care of our children to free us to write, to being available for interviews in their subjects of expertise. As the book became longer, so did the list of professional and personal friends to whom we're grateful. In alphabetical order, they are Andrew Baldwin, Dr. David Baldwin, Halee Baldwin, Neil Baldwin, Elaine Berry, Robert Blood, Heather Brenzel, Karen Brody, Dr. Martin Cohen, Cheryl Corbin, Katie Dyer, Michele Fairchild, Dr. Martin Finkelman, Richard Gatley, David Giveans, Judith Glickstein, Susan Goldstein, Blair and Dawn Gorsuch, Paula Gritzer, Doris Haire, Susan Hinkle, Jane Honikman, Valerie Howard, Suzanne Jones, Carol Kirsch, Jay Laghi, Jules and Norma Laghi, Helen Lazar, Martin Lieberman, Jeanette Lofas, Dottie Mandlin, Dr. Alicejane Markenson, Illona Maruszak, Eucklyn McCrae, Denise McLaughlin, Janice Miller, Dr. Robert Morris, Susan Muenchow, Jean Nassau, Pamela Newman, Deborah Paley, Jonathan Plutzik, Tanya Plutzik, Terri Raphael, Barbara Root, Dr. Clifford Sager, Nancy Sahlein, Dr. Gabriel Smilkstein, Mary Stanton, David Stiles, Delia Tedoff, Thomas Tilling, Kathy Weingarten, Bernice Weissbourd, Barbara White, Dr. Leonard Wolf, Dr. Shirley Zussman.

Special thanks to our agents. Gayle Benderoff and Deborah Geltman. From the very beginning they believed in us, lifted our spirits when we thought the book would never end, and went far beyond the business relationship in the quality of their moral support. We thank our editor, Jerry Gross, and his assistant, Mike Cantalupo, for their constructive criticism and enthusiasm for our project.

INTRODUCTION

THE PRIVATE LIFE OF PARENTS is *not* a child care book. It is a unique guide to *parent care*. Plenty of books tell you how to feed, diaper, and otherwise keep up with the growth of your young child. However, you also need a practical, down-to-earth resource book for coping with the basic challenge of contemporary parenthood: how to integrate your new life as parents into your *continuing* lives as spouse, worker, friend, relative, adult.

The joys of parenthood may be timeless, but the work of combining parenthood with adulthood is harder than ever. Those of us who begin a family today feel more isolated than ever, both spiritually and geographically, from the extended family, from other parents, and from the American mainstream. Where support structures once existed ready-made, we now have to construct or discover our own—someone to babysit, someone to advise us, someone to pass down baby clothes, and someone to share our coffee, our triumphs, our complaints.

The very idea of a nuclear family has become something of a curiosity in American society. Mom, dad, two kids, and a spaniel look great in those TV reruns, but may not exist on your block. And those of us who do begin family life in the traditional way—man, woman, baby—must wrestle with serious questions of Who's going to do What, and to Whom. Role-sharing ideals, and the wonderful challenges of the women's movement, have forced us to set our sights beyond the traditional mommy-daddy structure, making even greater demands on the parental partnership.

Within the society of parents, we are both inspired and confused by the variety of lifestyles among us, including single-by-choice, blended families, late first-time parents, divorced, teenage, dual-career, adoptive, traditional, and non-traditional. If we have kids later in life, it's tougher to break old habits, from reading the morning paper to having time and money to ourselves. Also, many of us were nurtured by the "challenge" decade of the sixties and coddled by the "Me" thinking of the seventies. Suddenly, in the eighties, we become parents. And it isn't easy.

There *is* a happy medium between child-centered and self-centered. *The Private Life of Parents* will help you find it for yourselves.

This book began as a conversation between two women. At 32, Maria Laghi was a young mother thinking about becoming a writer. Roberta Plutzik, then 29, was a successful freelance journalist thinking of becoming a mother. Our first conversations were a gentle tug-of-war between two topics—work and parenthood. Roberta was wrestling with the questions of how a baby would fit into her life and marriage. Would she be able to continue writing? Would she and Neil manage financially? Would their theoretical parental role-sharing arrangements survive the test of reality? Would they be resilient enough to be good parents without losing sight of their own identities? Unspoken was Roberta's worry that she wasn't patient enough, or committed enough, to have a child. Both Roberta and Neil worried that having a baby would deprive them of choices about where to work and live, choices they had made freely in the past. In short, Roberta had a thousand private questions, from how to reorganize their small apartment to how to reorganize their lives.

Maria had felt, in her own words, "totally out of it" since the birth two years earlier of her son, Jud. She'd gone from a ten-year career in publishing to full-time motherhood, and, although she'd intended to complete the unfinished novel in her desk drawer, she hadn't written a word, or even found time to read for pleasure. In their six years of marriage before the baby, Maria and Jay had talked a lot about what kind of parents they wanted to be and the family lifestyle they wanted to live. They were still firmly committed to their earlier decisions, but there was much they hadn't anticipated. Because of the single income, Jay felt breadwinner pressures he had never experienced before. Jud slept little in his first, colicky months, leaving both Maria and Jay too exhausted to go out or invite people over. Maria, who had always made friends easily, found herself in solitary confinement that first winter. How could she feel so lonely and strange in such a bustling, familiar neighborhood?

To combat her feelings of isolation, Maria organized, with another new mother, an informal family support center in her community. She put notices up on local bulletin boards and took a small ad in the neighborhood paper. The headline read: DO YOU FEEL STRANDED WITH YOUR SMALL BABY OR TODDLER? WANT TO MEET OTHER NEW PARENTS? Seemingly from nowhere came about three dozen new mothers, fathers, even full-time babysitters who became the Brooklyn Heights Family Center, an indoor playground, support group, and clearinghouse for local family goods and services in Brooklyn, New York. The Family Center, which flourished for over three years in a small second-floor room of a local church building, served another valuable function unforeseen by its founders. It offered new parents a chance to air and share their private doubts, questions, complaints, ideas, and experiences in a supportive, non-judgmental atmosphere.

The Private Life of Parents draws on three perspectives. Much of the material is distilled from our own experience. (Yes, Roberta and Neil did opt for parenthood.) We drew in many other parents—friends, neighbors, friends of friends, and people thousands of miles away whom we'd never met. We taped personal stories of childbirth and parental transition. We asked a lot of personal questions, such as: How did parenthood affect your marriage? Your family? Your other adult relationships? Your self-image? Did you feel inadequate? Angry? Confused? Happy? At peace? Fulfilled? How do you cope with these feelings, and with whom do you share them?

We sent out 500 questionnaires to mothers and fathers across the country and received some 250 responses with candid insights from parents representing a wide spectrum of lifestyles and family arrangements. This questionnaire appears at the end of this book.

We interviewed experts in fields ranging from sex therapy to interior design, as they relate to the adult needs of parents. We visited parent support groups and taped candid discussions about work, family life, post-partum adjustments. And we did a lot of good, old-fashioned reading and research in the current literature on parents and children.

By the time we started writing the book, Roberta's son Nicky was one and a half, and Maria's son Jud was four. Their daily lessons in parental survival, heightened in June, 1981, with the birth of Roberta and Neil's second child, Allegra, continue to this day. People say, "Now that you've done all that research and written a book on the subject, surely you must have your own adult lives in perfect order!" Alas, we're still only human.

If, as we believe, the parental stage of life is characterized by interpersonal adjustment and readjustment, temporary balance and intermittent chaos, there is no perfect order, no "right" answer or technique or attitude that will snap life perfectly into place.

The two years we spent writing this book were, in retrospect, a typical parental comedy. Babysitters deserted at the crucial hour. Both husbands decided to leave their jobs and work at home. A surprise baby was conceived and born as we struggled against deadlines and bill collectors. Friends came and went, sometimes in a huff. Family learned to put up with us. Roberta and Neil encountered the Terrible Twos, and Maria and Jay, the separation pangs of first grade. Ear infections, self-doubts, marital squabbles, diminishing space, and an incredible mixture of fatigue and exhilaration constantly reminded us of the need for this book even as we were writing it.

We hope it fills many of *your* needs as parents.

Roberta Plutzik
Maria Laghi

BROOKLYN HEIGHTS, NEW YORK
JANUARY 1983

THE PRIVATE LIFE OF PARENTS

1

You

THERE'S MORE to parenthood than *parenting*. Parenting, the job of raising kids, is a new term that describes just one of the roles that make up the complex experience of *parenthood*. Parenthood is a state of being, a rite of passage—a life stage. It encompasses the spectrum of emotions and experiences you encounter as you take care of your children *and* yourself.

The challenge of parenthood, beyond the very real demands and rewards of taking care of the kids, is finding out what you're going to make of your own life. How does parenthood fit into your inner world? How does it shape who you are and who you will become? How do you, as a parent, fit into the outside world of work, family, friends, strangers? And, finally, how does parenthood redefine your intimate relationship with your partner?

For many of you, these concerns are very private—indeed, you may keep them secret from your partner, or avoid confronting them honestly yourselves. If you land that big job, for instance, what you decide to do about your preschooler's care is entirely up to you. Few outsiders want to hear about the trouble you had finding a housekeeper, or your running battles about which parent stays home when Mikey's fever spikes. In the workplace, *this* is your private life. And for parents there is also the private or personal life of career aspirations, leisure, dreams, and your very growth as human beings, for you do not abrogate the right to love and take care of yourselves when you marry or have children. Rather, you hurt the marriage and the parenthood by being less than what you could be.

Yet parents soon realize that, while others may show enthusiasm, compassion, and fascination with your new family, they can't answer your most urgent private questions or alleviate your many private doubts.

The Private Doubts of Parenthood

You May Feel Inadequate and Afraid to Admit It

As one mother wrote us, "Parenthood is so full of 'shouldisms'—you should (or shouldn't) express anger; you should (or shouldn't) want time to yourself; you should (or shouldn't) enjoy, feel, want. . . . No wonder we're shamed into secrecy when we don't act the way we *think we should.* If you let people know that, despite your love for your child, you have "bad" feelings such as anger, boredom, and frustration, will that make you a bad parent?"

The idealized parent of traditional child care books doesn't catch the flu, is never grumpy, and isn't male. But that's the old breed of super-parent. The new breed is even harder to emulate. The idealized parent of new-world child care books should not only be a perfect mom or dad, but a super-human adult as well. He or she "has it all," to quote one book—a great job, perfect marriage, wonderful kids, and a foolproof recipe for play dough. If we admit to private fears of inadequacy about our parental *and* adult performance, we risk losing esteem and support.

You May Feel That Sex and Parenthood Can't Compete

The first practical problems of fatigue, pain, and disorientation are gradually supplanted by more subtle changes in attitude. As new parents develop a working partnership, their sexual and emotional relationship may take a permanent back seat. But they're not going to tell anyone else—or even each other—how lonely and abandoned they feel.

You May Feel That the Life of a Parent Isn't "Normal"

Life with a new baby is not familiar, even if you come from a large family. You never experienced anything like parenthood before, and life will never be the same again. Better? Often. Worse? Sometimes. Unpredictable? Always.

Parenthood is not *typical.* As traditional role models vanish for parents—as they have for virtually everybody—we're set adrift in a world where almost any lifestyle goes. The trick is to make yours work for you. Creating a personal design for living is one of the monumental tasks facing every new parent.

Finally, parenthood is not *static.* It is a process of constant adjusting and readjusting. In the first chaotic months of family life, we look for reassurance from family, friends, experts—a promise that, if we play our cards right, everything will settle down and become "normal." "Just wait, it'll all fall into place as soon as the baby gets over colic . . . sleeps through the night . . . is one year old . . . starts to talk . . . goes to nursery school . . . enters first grade . . . survives adolescence . . . enters college . . . moves away. . . ."

Parenthood is plain hard work. Things *don't* simply fall into place, even if we devote ourselves singlemindedly to the care of our child. The traditional parental mystique—that a good parent is a self-sacrificing one—has led us to equate self-care with selfishness. The hardest thing to admit is that within our love for our child and our hopes for ourselves as parents there is also a growing anger that somehow we've been duped, that the parental commitment, no matter how strong, cannot by itself define and fulfill us as complete people. Parental commitment must coexist with a commitment to each other and to ourselves *as adults*.

You May Feel Overwhelmed by Seemingly Mundane Problems

When it comes to parenthood, every abstract theory eventually boils down to its lowest common denominator—the homely happenings of everyday life. Let's take as an example Irene and Ralph's innocently sabotaged dinner party.

After eight months of intense parenthood with few grown-up diversions, Irene and Ralph invited over their old friends, Ray and Sandy, a childless career couple thinking of starting a family. Eager to get back into a normal social life, Irene and Ralph pulled out all the stops —fine wine, gourmet menu complete with soufflé, considerable last-minute preparation, and, for Irene, that size-eight silk blouse that finally fit her again.

The guests insisted on spending time with little Benjie. They felt sure that a half-hour of hands-on experience would help them with their own important decision. What they got was three-and-a-half hours of Benjie, who never went to sleep. In fact, this usually good-natured baby spent the evening crying and spitting up. Everyone took turns trying to console him, while Irene and Ralph managed a truncated version of the planned menu—minus sauce, style, and conversation.

By the end of the evening, Irene and Ralph had had three harshly whispered arguments in the kitchen. They were angry at each other for not somehow salvaging the evening; with their baby for not being "good"; and with their guests' for not trying harder to conceal their annoyance and pity. And Irene was angry at herself for wearing her silk blouse, soon soiled by Benjie's tears and indigestion.

How Irene and Ralph handled the evening grew out of the state of their partnership. They hadn't talked beforehand about who would take responsibility for Benjie that night. In fact, they hadn't been doing much talking at all and saw the evening as a respite from the quiet tension of their nights alone. Also, knowing Sandy and Ray were "window shopping" made them feel on trial. They wanted to carry parenthood off with a flourish, and a well-behaved child was a necessary prop. Why, then, did they give him that late afternoon nap? (But how else would they have found time for their intricate dessert?) When it was finally over, they couldn't just laugh off their experience as a typical parental misadventure. It had cost them too much in energy, money, time, and disappointment.

What went wrong? Was this ruined evening an example of bad luck and the "parental lot," or did the superficial events of the dinner party camouflage deeper questions? We've learned that with planning, with an understanding of who you are as a parent, a partner, and a person, there are ways to roll with the punches, if not avoid them.

The modern parenting slogan is: "There's no one right way to parent." By extension, there's no one right way to *live* as a parent. Our aim is to offer you resources to find the answers right for you. Still, no amount of information and how-tos will spell the difference between truly coping with your new existence and just making do. Why do some parents, even in the most trying circumstances, maintain a sense of wellbeing and contentment, while others never get a grip on their lives? We've found, after talking to hundreds of parents and many experts, and after searching our own fallible souls, that the difference begins with *attitude*, not technique. Like faith, positive thinking in parenthood rests on a personal set of principles. It involves the willingness to see parenthood as a time of personal growth, as a testing ground for values and commitments, and as a re-evaluation of our spiritual direction.

The Search for Parental Wellbeing

For us, there are six basic principles of parental wellbeing.

Give Up the Illusion of Being a Perfect Parent

You can master all the techniques and recipes of success-in-parenting books, talk fluent "childrenese" according to Ginott, and live a totally child-centered life. Still, you won't feel perfect as a parent. Unless, of course, you're a perfect person. Does anybody out there fit that description? Except for the few parents who abuse or neglect their children and who desperately need professional help, we are all *imperfectly* good parents. We try our best and sincerely hope that the love, attention, and modern know-how we lavish on our kids will see them through. But there isn't a parental closet without skeletons—the lost tempers, the inconsistencies, the bad moods, the aversion to building blocks, the pervasive fear of "not enough."

The most common problem associated with striving to be a perfect parent is guilt. In a *Family Circle* article, advice columnist Ann Landers wrote a few years ago that "If I were asked to select the one word that best describes the majority of American parents, that word would be *guilt-ridden*." The tally sheet on guilt begins with birth. We fear that the mistakes we make will accumulate like lead poisoning and irrevocably damage our offspring. Neither the doubts of our competence nor those "mistakes" we see as proof of our fallibility are likely to make a substantial difference in the long run. Our children are shaped by us, yes, but it's not so much what we do every minute of every day, but who we are over the long run that counts.

Look for Information, Not Prescriptions

All the research, all the writing, all the admonitions and guarantees directed to new parents can overwhelm and undermine even the most sensible among us. One couple told us that by the time their child was born, their bookshelves were filled with child care books. "The trouble was, all this accumulated information did not reassure us," they said. "Instead, we were left with the subtle feeling that as mere laymen we weren't up to our new role."

Arlene Skolnick wrote in *Psychology Today* that "popular and professional knowledge does not seem to have made parenting any easier. On the contrary, the insights and guidelines provided by the experts seem to have made parents more anxious. Since modern child-rearing literature asserts that parents can do irreparable harm to their children's social and emotional development, modern parents must examine their words and actions for a significance that parents in the past had never imagined."

By definition, child care books focus on the needs and development of children. Even if the author has forgotten you exist, don't *you* forget you exist. Put your parenthood into context. Who are you and what are your limitations and capacities? Who is your child and what is her temperament? What community do you live in? Are you alone or have you a partner? All these factors must be taken into account in determining what particular style your parenthood will take, even if you follow the teachings of one parenting guru.

Success. Effective. No-Lose. Natural. Winning. These are words widely used in child care books. Their implied opposites are *failure, ineffectual, no-win, unnatural, losing.* When you consult the experts, look for the implicit message as well as the explicit one. Today, common sense is being re-emphasized as parents grow tired of empty promises and veiled threats. It's a good idea to remember that professionals in child care have dealt with the failures of parenting, the extreme cases that result from a spectrum of causes including child abuse. They care about children, and their understandable frustration often slips into their advice as hostility.

Learn the Art of Making Decisions and Setting Goals

Diaper service or disposables? House in the suburbs with a long commute to work or a smaller but convenient city apartment? Career acceleration or take it easy for a few years while the baby's small? Nurturing mother and providing father—or vice versa?

Since the sheer intensity of early parenthood tends to obscure and complicate daily decision making and, in many cases, completely obliterates long-range designs for living, a lot of us adopt the familiar parental shoulder shrug: What can we do?

We say you can do a lot. You *can* lose those extra twenty pounds. You *can* find time for that long-deferred project. You *can* take control of your present and your future. Yet it's so easy to put off adult decisions altogether and make do: The long commute goes on, the overtaxed living space frays nerves even further, the work load intensifies, and dreams of fifty-fifty parenting are deferred until the kids are grown.

There's nothing magical about the decision-making process. But with kids, each goal involves dozens of arrangements, compromises, and alternatives, and decision making is nothing short of a survival skill. As for goals, your big one until now may have been just to have a child and let the rest of life sort itself out.

Goal-setting is a way of taking the reins. Having and sharing goals reassures us that life isn't just a predictable routine. We all have dreams. The next step is to work toward making them come true.

Accept Parenthood as a Series of Tradeoffs

From the moment of the baby's birth, we've got to develop a new approach to problem solving. Suddenly there are three of us crammed into the same life, all with legitimate needs that can't be satisfied in equal degree at the same time. And it's the parental needs that are bound to be deferred. Our parents used to call this "sacrifice." We believe there's a much healthier approach to the natural give-and-take of parenthood. To feel good about being a parent, you must be conscious of the specific tradeoffs every decision entails. This kind of problem solving takes patience, flexibility, commitment, and self-awareness. There's no way anybody can tell you what your tradeoffs should be. They must be custom-made to suit your unique priorities.

Two teachers we know decided on tradeoffs that might seem unworkable to other parents but suited them fine. Herb and Kate wanted to continue their jobs, his at the university, hers at the high-school level. But they were also committed to maximizing time with their two small children. They enumerated their goals: to raise the kids without paid help, to make enough money to maintain their summer house, and to have the summer months free to work on personal projects—Herb's book and Kate's weaving. In order to realize these goals, Herb switched from day classes to night, though this move was not career-enhancing. Kate took a higher-paying job in a suburban high school, despite the long commute. The advantages were extra money, at least one parent at home almost always, and summers off for both parents. The major disadvantage was that for nine months of the year, Herb and Kate hardly saw each other on weekdays, though they paid special attention to family weekends and took on no outside work during the summer.

Herb and Kate's tradeoffs reflect their child-raising philosophy *and* their personal needs. Another couple might feel that time as a family every day takes priority over a summer house. The crucial point here is to know which is important to you and to make the necessary decisions with your eyes wide open.

Don't Try to Do It Alone

The plight of first-time parents who find themselves strangers in a strange land—isolated even in their familiar neighborhood—is all too common. Parenting literature, family, pediatricians, and trusted contemporaries can't fill that vital need new parents have for peer group sharing—a place to exchange ideas, test realities, provide reassurance, and find understanding in a non-judgmental form.

Beginning in the mid-1970s, the first of what now is a network of groups for parents came into being. They were independent of one another but charged with the common purpose of providing community support, discussion groups, shared services, counseling, and a meeting place. Post-Partum Education for Parents (PEP) in Santa Barbara, California, COPE in Boston, Massachusetts, the Mothers Center in Hicksville, Long Island, Parents Resources in New York City, the Family Enhancement Program in Wisconsin, and Family Focus in Chicago—these were just a few of the groups.

Bernice Weissbourd, founder and president of Family Focus, told us: "There is a sharp, growing awareness that the way parents feel about themselves has a significant effect on the way they relate to their child. It's not enough to know where the *child* is developmentally; it's becoming apparent that human development is a constant process. Parenthood is one important stage in an adult's life. Groups such as ours help parents look at themselves, not only as vehicles for their children's growth, but as people developing in their own right."

These new parent support groups have flourished and proliferated (a nationwide directory appears at the end of this book) because they are not rooted in the problems of today's families, but in their strengths. Parent support groups serve the vital function once met by the old extended family—support without stigma. There's nothing wrong with admitting you need help as a parent. In fact, reaching out for moral support, practical help, and peer companionship is essential to our survival as adults and as parents.

Look After Yourself

One friend of ours, reminiscing about his much loved parents, said they not only taught him the elements of a well-balanced life, but infused him with a sense of their own wellbeing. Wellbeing for contemporary parents means, more often than not, striking a balance between responsibility to one's child and responsibility to oneself and partner.

But many parents simply don't consider themselves important enough to warrant the nurturing that we all need to the end of our days. It's not always a question of walking a tightrope, of having to please everybody at once. The self-aware parent will begin to know, through practice, how much freedom of choice is available in each situation and will be able to deal accordingly with new problems and recurring ones. Parental wellbeing is feeling grown-up but still growing. It's the belief that parenthood makes us become more than we were before and that we gain a special wisdom and perspective offered in no other school of life.

2

Initiation

WHAT IS PARENTHOOD supposed to be like? In our search for answers during pregnancy, intensified during the weeks of preparation for childbirth, we put great stock in education, control, and awareness. Instinctively, we hoped that if we did everything "right," reality would come up to expectations. Yet when Roberta—who was pregnant herself at the time—asked new parents to tell about their childbirth experience for a magazine article, they invariably replied: "We'll talk about our experience, but it wasn't what we expected, and it certainly wasn't typical."

If "normal" childbirth encompasses a vast spectrum of possibilities, it follows that "typical" parenthood does too. Nevertheless, many of us expect our baby's behavior to match the precise descriptions offered in some child development books, and our own performance to meet their often impossible, Utopian baby care prescriptions: The ideal parent nurturing the typical child. Little wonder then that we look up bleary-eyed after the first weeks of colic, hemorrhoids, and ambivalence to exclaim, "Hey, this isn't what I expected at all!"

Cynical babywatchers have been heard to exclaim, as they observe harried new parents struggle, "You'd think they were the first parents on earth!" In one sense, this is true: each of us *is* "the first parent on earth," and our uniqueness should be respected. There are few, if any, valid generalizatons about the experience of parenthood today. Still, as we increase our diversity, we are learning to share our "secrets"— the ways in which we cope, or fail to cope, with the circumstances and emotions of our unique parenthood.

In this chapter we'll talk about some of the more common physical, emotional, and practical tests of the post-partum weeks. We call this chapter *Initiation* because many first-time parents compared the early weeks to a "trial by fire." They reaffirmed our belief that the post-partum period is as much a test of endurance as of judgment and skill. Also, like any initiation, the entry into parenthood presents an intense, distorted, and often frightening picture of what lies ahead. Most of us spend the first weeks alternating between thrilled acceptance of our new life and fear that it will remain as difficult forever—until some kind six-month veteran reassures us, as did one respondent to our questionnaire: "The newborn period is wonderful—and, thank God, *temporary.*"

Getting Through the First Six Weeks:
A Parent's Survival Manual

In our questionnaire we asked new parents to share their personal suggestions for coping with the demanding first weeks of parenthood. Here's what they said.

Support

There's no substitute for the physical and psychic support *partners* can give each other. "Your spouse is your greatest ally and friend during it all," one parent observed. But to help each other, you must make *time* for each other. "Even participating together in what seems like a contrived 'truth' session is good—so feelings, no matter how stupid they sound, can be shared and aired," another parent wrote to us.

The second most valuable support resource is *family.* Parents stressed time and again that relatives, even those living far away, can bolster us through phone calls and letters and talk to us when we need someone to talk to. Of course, being there is better. Most new parents were pleased to learn that babies do, indeed, bring you closer to your family emotionally, even when parental and in-law problems clouded pre-baby family ties.

Parents believe in the necessity for *friends.* Respondents to our questionnaire recommended that new parents seek out friends who already have a child, preferably not more than a few months older than one's own. They also talked of the rewards of reaching out to new people they'd met through their children and of the bonds that grew out of their new mutual interest.

Many parents formed their own or sought out existing *support groups* offering structured discussions, "warm line" telephone advice services for non-medical, non-crisis child care questions, and the opportunity to meet other parents to receive non-judgmental information and bolster self-confidence. "I started my first support group when my son was ten days old. Finding parents who solved similar problems in dissimilar ways, I learned that there is no one 'right' answer to any question," wrote one respondent.

New parents are so hungry for information, help, and guidance that they will often accept information without support, but that leaves them feeling less than adequate. "Disregard 50 percent of what you read in child care books, and most of the advice of visitors and people on the street," one parent wrote us. The purpose of support is to underscore the new parents' *strengths*—not highlight our weaknesses.

Practical Help

Aside from their partners, most parents cited the new grandparents as their prime source of help. Both mothers and mothers-in-law headed the list of early helpmates, and the practical help was often underscored by a new sense of closeness between the generations as both relived the previous cycle of parenthood and childhood. Our *Family* chapter deals in greater depth with the transition of family relationships, but here are some points to keep in mind specifically when asking a relative to help in the first weeks:

✓ Try to be as specific as possible when you discuss what *type* of help would be most valuable. Very often a new parent—especially a mother recovering from a Caesarean—requires more *adult* care than infant care. Help with cooking, housecleaning, and channeling visitors is frequently more useful than instructions on diapering or bathing the baby.

✓ If the relative is moving in with you, you'll be making a double post-partum adjustment unless you're used to spending a concentrated amount of time with that person under less than tranquil conditions. If at all possible, invite your volunteer for a weekend *before* the birth. Spend that time talking about the event to come and how you both feel about it. Even if you "beat around the bush," you'll get a general idea of how it will work out when the time comes, and you can decide accordingly whether to accept this offer of support.

✓ When parents come to help, don't expect them to suddenly treat you differently because you are now officially "grown-up." Grandparents have to work through their own conflicts and unexpected reactions to the birth—especially if it's a first grandchild. While many unpleasant parent-child patterns are eliminated by the birth of your baby, some are intensified. One mother told of having to comfort her own middle-aged mother who had moved in to help but had been overcome by memories of a long gone post-partum depression.

✓ Don't expect the help to work miracles, even if it's your mother, who has symbolically worked miracles since your own infancy. Colic doesn't disappear at a grandmother's touch any more than at a mother's or father's.

ꞏ Don't try to prove anything. Rejecting (politely) old wives' tales is understandable, but many grown children feel they have to score a point or prove themselves interminably to their own parents. Doing so adds an unnecessary burden to the very real tasks of new parenthood.

ꞏ If the arrangement isn't working out, find a gracious way to end it before it becomes any worse. New fathers frequently complain that live-in grandmothers and new mothers unconsciously conspire to make them feel unnecessary. If old hurts and unresolved conflicts can't be temporarily shelved, or if your living arrangements are too uncomfortable or unconventional for the visiting relative, the added stress isn't doing anyone any good. Call it quits and give everybody a break.

Ask a friend to take over care of your plants until things calm down, or to bake a double batch of macaroni and cheese. The generous question, "Can we do anything?", does *not* have to be answered automatically with, "Thanks, we're fine!" Friends can help with errands and birth announcements. They can help walk a colicky baby while you put your feet up, or listen for her cries while you take a languid bath. One extremely shy and self-sufficient woman we know was mortified when the birth of twins made her feel helpless and highly visible at the same time. She forced herself to ask small and large favors from friends, since simply getting around was such a challenge, and was surprised at how grateful most acquaintances were to take part in her exciting experience.

Paid help is a permissible luxury in the first weeks or months. Paid dog walkers, lawn mowers, and errand-runners, professional laundry services, housecleaning help, and, of course, babysitting, can all ease the pressure on overworked parents. If you simply can't cook or haven't had any food contributions, *don't* save money by bringing home a fast-food dinner. A wholesome, balanced take-out meal from a good restaurant is worth the investment.

What About Baby Nurses?

If you've already decided to hire a live-in baby nurse for the first days or weeks of parenthood, it's essential for your own wellbeing to understand her function. The baby nurse is there to help you gain practice and confidence in the skills of parenthood, and to ease the initial demands made by the infant. Her duties include all baby-related chores plus light housekeeping involving the baby only—

cleaning his room, changing his sheets, for instance. It's essential that a baby nurse be used by the parents to *learn*, and when she leaves the parents should feel stronger for having had the experience.

What the baby nurse should *not* be expected or permitted to do includes the following:

⚡ Convince you that *her procedures* for bathing, feeding, laundering are the only acceptable techniques for raising a healthy baby.

⚡ Foist upon you old wives' tales and antiquated nurturing techniques with which you are in instinctive disagreement, such as not picking up a crying baby.

⚡ Squeeze the father out of the picture by criticizing the way he holds the infant, hinting that his behavior is overstimulating, or implying that fathers belong at work, not in the nursery.

⚡ Criticize or undermine your independent efforts to adjust to your new role.

⚡ Undermine your efforts or otherwise make the nursing experience more difficult.

Looking Out for Yourself and Your Partner

Get as much sleep, food, and rest as you can. Don't compete for these natural resources with your partner; both of you are probably under stress and it's easy to think that *your* need is greatest. Begin now to share parental assignments, and remember, it's important to share responsibility as well as execution of baby-related tasks. (See our chapter *Marriage and Sex.*)

If the mother is at home with the new baby, it's important for her to have time out that she can count on, and not on a "catch as catch can" basis. Give each other guaranteed private time.

Be alert to one another's feelings, no matter how uncharacteristic and absurd they may seem. Indulge one another emotionally and physically—and talk, talk, talk. Get all your thoughts out in the open —good and bad—and explore each other's reactions to them. It's a time of sharing.

Comic Relief

Step out as a couple as soon as you can handle a brief separation from the baby. Meanwhile, it helps to import some recreation in whatever form suits your taste and pocketbook. Some new parents invest in cable TV, knowing their theater visits will be limited for years to come. Magazine subscriptions, book clubs, new records, periodic take-out banquets, imported beer and fine wines—whatever it takes to make an appealing change of pace for you should be part of your post-partum budget.

"No new job is ever a breeze," wrote one parent. "In an eight-hour-a-day job, you feel pressure so you go home and 'rebuild.' The job of parenthood affords no rest and relaxation time to speak of, so the stress builds and builds. Pictured that way, it's easier to see that we must try to get out of the house for release time."

Getting out of the house—with baby, alone, and as a couple—was a universal recommendation of parents who responded to our questionnaire, as well as the many, many others we spoke to. We agree.

Visitors

If you haven't talked this over with your partner before, *now* is the time to work out exactly how you wish to control the flow of visitors. Remember, this baby will be around for a long time and everyone outside the immediate family can simply wait until you feel strong enough to have them over. Naturally, you will be inundated with phone calls and requests for visits. Here are some visitor guidelines to help you organize the first weeks as hosts.

✔ Remember that most people are anxious to show you how pleased and excited they are *for you*. Once they've expressed this enthusiasm (after all, not to call might be interpreted as rudeness), most will accept your request for a grace period. Some will even be relieved to have their visits postponed until they find time to work you into *their* busy schedules.

✔ We recommend that someone other than the mother take on the social secretary responsibilities. The father, baby nurse, or whoever else is helping out should screen calls with statements such as: "She's resting right now. She'll call you back as soon as she can," or, "We're following doctor's orders. No visitors the first week. We'd love to have you over and we'll call you as soon as we can," or, "We're really glad you called and would love to see you. As soon as the dust clears from all the relatives, we'll give you a call so we can arrange a quiet visit together."

✔ A telephone answering machine (available from about $75 and up) is a benefit. Message machines are now considered a practical time-saving device for personal use as well as business. First, record a birth announcement message all callers will receive while mother and baby are still at the hospital. Here's a sample:

"Hi. This is Rick Jones. Our daughter, Amanda Louise, 7 lbs. 6 oz., was born Thursday morning, Jan. 6, at 6:45. Mother, father, and child are doing well. If you'd like us to call you back, please leave a message. . . ."

Later, when baby is home, the machine can be plugged in (with a revised message, of course) whenever you are busy, tired, sleeping, or simply need some uninterrupted time. You don't want to miss your calls, but at this pressurized time it's awfully nice to be able to return them when most convenient.

✓ If a visitor asks, "What can I bring?" be bold and say, "Bring dinner!" Accepting food gifts, like accepting help, actually makes friends and family feel more comfortable and useful when they visit. More important, they help free you of time-consuming kitchen activity.

✓ Politely stipulate the time of arrival *and departure* of guests with such phrases as: "We'd love to have you over on Sunday between 3:30 and 5 PM. That's the best time for us because it's between the baby's nap and bath." Or try this: "How about coming for coffee on Saturday night, *after* dinner? We usually fade out around 10 o'clock these days, but you'll have plenty of time to see us and the baby if you come around 8:30."

✓ An hour and a half to two hours is really plenty of time for all but your most cherished and intimate friends to see you and the baby. Fortunately, most people realize this and are happy to give tired new parents a break. But if your guests won't budge, you have every right to resume your normal routine and give them signs that it's time to depart. Don't be intimidated by lavish gifts, or try to award extra time to the most beneficent givers.

✓ Other than offering coffee and a biscuit, you are not really expected to play host and hostess. Also, this is not the time to be concerned about the appearance of your home.

✓ If you live in an apartment building or community where impromptu visiting goes on, attach a sign to your door with visiting hours or other requests, such as "Please don't ring the doorbell." One couple came up with a sign that included their baby's photograph and birth statistics and this note: "We're trying to get our act together. See you all in a week or two." It worked.

✓ If you are flooded with requests for visits, sit down with your partner and decide which people are truly top-priority. Bunching all visitors together regardless of who's closest to you is not only a strain, but fails to take into account that some family and friends are special and should have private time with you and the baby.

⟶ Don't hesitate to cancel planned visits if you're too tired, or if the baby is fretful. Visits at this time should be a pleasing experience for the parents and for their guests.

Coping with Post-Partum Emotions

When Roberta and Neil heard Nicholas had to stay in the hospital an additional thirty-six hours, the knowledge of his basic good health was reassuring on one level, but did little to dispel their underlying feeling of despair; the fantasy of bringing baby home to the nursery had been replaced by a reality for which they were painfully unprepared. Instead of coming home as a family, they returned alone and waited for what seemed a very long time.

Maria and Jay left the hospital with new baby Jud and the whole world suddenly seemed imperfect and inadequate. The taxi was filthy, the road bumpy and crowded, and their spacious apartment, taken for the purpose of starting a family, appeared drafty, shabby, and full of potential hazards. Looking up from Jud's bassinette, Maria noticed minor ceiling cracks for the first time and imagined imminent structural collapse. Never known for domesticity, Jay spent the first day home in a frenzy of housecleaning. Having decided at the onset of her pregnancy that she would breastfeed, Maria was dismayed when nursing did not come easily to her, and she began to grapple with more pervasive feelings of failure.

"*Nothing*—no past experience, no amount of training, reading, or preparation, or conversations with other parents—can prepare you beforehand for the rush of emotions that accompanies parenthood," one father told us. "And while no two people experience parenthood in the same way, it's comforting to know that we *all* have our ups and downs."

Do you feel overwhelmed by the unexpected, conflicting—and sometimes "forbidden"—emotions of new parenthood? The following chart, compiled by Julie Armstrong, Judy Edmundson, Jane Honikman, and Judy Mrstik of PEP (Post-Partum Education for Parents), a parents support group, reflects the commonly expressed reactions of both

MOTHER	COMMON FEELINGS	FATHER
physical demands are difficult to meet; sense of responsibility toward baby	OVER-WHELMED	more complicated lifestyle; mate more demanding
new dimension of feelings toward mate, baby	LOVING THANKFUL	new dimension of feelings toward mate, baby
inexperienced; fearful; lack of confidence toward new responsibility	PANIC	financial worries; inability to handle baby
baby's cries, short sleep schedule; no time for self; mate not helping	IRRITATION	demands by baby, mate; crying; interrupted routine
sense of accomplishment; new challenges	EXCITED SATISFACTION	new challenges; we did it
result of birth; increased work load; excitement	TIRED	change in lifestyle; new demands of family
complications from birth	PAIN	
hormonal changes; mate insensitive; birth discomforts	SEXUAL FRUSTRATION	result of birth; baby in the way; mate not sexy
inexperienced with baby; not appealing toward mate	INADEQUATE	afraid to handle baby; not sure of mate's feeling
societal pressure on motherhood role	INSECURE	societal pressure of being a father; increased financial burden
change in routine; no help in home; duty to be full-time mother	TRAPPED LONELY	sense of duty to help; no social life
attention focused on baby; mate not helping	RESENTMENT JEALOUSY	attention on baby; mate too demanding
natural result of birth; inability to cope; hormonal	DEPRESSED WEEPY	inability to deal with mate; can't cope with change

Reprinted by permission of Post-Partum Education for Parents

mothers and fathers in PEP's post-partum discussion groups. (The address of PEP and some fifty other parent support groups are listed in our *Help* chapter.)

Post-Partum Depression

Post-partum depression is a catch-all phrase describing a spectrum of negative reactions revolving around birth. It can be characterized by a few days of crying shortly after the initial birth elation, and, in rare cases, by clinical depression or other psychological disturbances doctors now feel *may* be linked to hormonal imbalance.

Most cases of post-partum depressions—89 percent of new mothers and 62 percent of new fathers, according to a 1981 study for the National Institute of Child Health and Human Development—are marked by mood changes ranging from inertia to hyperactivity, sleeplessness, withdrawal, over- or undereating, preoccupation with minor physical ills, and general malaise. All this adds up to an extended period of feeling bad and of searching for answers to questions we never imagined in our pre-birth fantasies.

There are many "good" reasons for post-partum depression—from fatigue and isolation to working through a negative birth experience—but many parents feel depressed without any legitimate excuse. Guilt ensues, and, as parents search fruitlessly for permissible causes, the doldrums intensify. They can hit anyone, including adoptive parents, grandparents, and, of course, fathers.

The depressed new father is in a double bind. Not only is he faced with the awesome responses and responsibilities of parenthood itself, but with the Catch-22 of contemporary fatherhood. He's *expected*—indeed, expects himself—to be a nurturing father, but still not *allowed* to feel the complex emotions that nurturing entails. Can you be a modern father and still "act like a man"? "A new mother who doesn't want to come right out and admit she's depressed at least has a few obvious and legitimate sources of discomfort," says Judith Glickstein, co-founder of the Yale University Health Services Parent Support Group. "The father doesn't have a protruding stomach, an episiotomy, or swollen breasts. He can't call the doctor and complain about concrete physical ailments as an excuse to talk about how he feels."

Many fathers carry an added sense of helplessness as they try to deal with the mother's depression, and that, in some cases, heightens their own despair. Those who had been involved in childbirth preparation, and were thrilled by the role they played in the delivery, may later feel like vestigial organs without the prescribed roles or recognition awarded to their partner.

Contrary to traditional belief, post-partum depression is not limited to the first weeks or months of parenthood. Mothers' and fathers' reactions can be delayed for as long as a year or two. One woman who had a particularly traumatic Caesarean birth successfully blocked the memory for more than a year, then was overcome by a rush of panic and a desperate need to talk through the experience. Spells of weeping and a profound sense of failure engulfed her as the memory returned.

DEPRESSION AND THE "FUN MORALITY"

In her study of the evolution of child care advice in the United States from 1914 to the early 1950s, published in her book, *Childhood in Contemporary Cultures*, co-authored by Margaret Mead, Martha Wolfenstein pointed out that while our grandparents were guided in their parental roles by an overriding sense of "duty," modern parents are more likely to anticipate parenthood as a source of unmitigated pleasure.. "Parents are promised that having children will keep them young and give them fun and happiness." Wolfenstein writes that "the characterization of parenthood in terms of fun and enjoyment may be intended as an inducement to parents in whose scheme of values these are presumed to be priorities. But it also may express a new imperative: You ought to enjoy your child. . . . [The mother's] self-evaluation can no longer be based entirely on whether she is doing the right and necessary things but becomes involved with nuances of feeling which are not under voluntary control."

We think that depression in parenthood can arise from the dichotomy between what we think we're *supposed to feel* and what we really *do feel*. If we persist in the belief that parenthood is always a matter of pleasure, we condemn ourselves for sometimes feeling pain. But, of course, how can we ever really experience parental "highs" unless we know and admit to having felt the "lows"?

THE SEARCH FOR "PREPARATION D"

Sonia was depressed for months after the birth of her first child. She read "up from depression" books and tried their techniques— walks, exercise, help with baby. She did everything except mingle with other parents in the neighborhood because "I just can't identify with them." Later she told us: "At this point you could have told me my depression could be cured by a trip to Lourdes. But I've found that what matters now is not what my *depression* needs, but what *I* need. The depression took on a life of its own, became more important than I was. What I'm learning to ask myself is not, 'Why am I depressed?' But 'What's bothering me? What makes me feel bad?' And to admit that it wasn't the other parents I couldn't identify with —it was myself. I couldn't see myself as a parent."

Turned off by words like *counseling* and *help*, Sonia felt more comfortable attending a neighborhood discussion group described as a research project on parental feelings. Many parent groups today understand the reluctance of new parents to seek outside support. Traditionally, we have applauded the self-sufficient, self-contained unit, and to seek support has been defined as admitting to failure. In fact, until recently the only services available to parents have been crisis-oriented. Today's support groups are designed to enhance the functioning of normal, healthy families. When further counseling is necessary it's available through referral.

Although many of us would wish that the magical "Preparation D" could be administered in the privacy of our own homes, contact with other parents is, in our opinion, essential to the cure.

Parent and Pediatrician

The parent-doctor relationship is a crucial and highly delicate one. You're not the patient—and, for most "well-baby" check-ups and consultations, neither is your thriving child. You are, instead, the doctor's *partner* in the continuing health care of your child, and, simultaneously, your child's *agent* who oversees all care. In the first tentative months of parenthood, parent and pediatrician have to literally stick together "in sickness and in health." If the new parent is feeling particularly vulnerable the doctor can become either a prime source of support and information or, as parents frequently report, an autocrat who merely heightens existing feelings of inadequacy, confusion, and isolation. Ultimately, explains New York pediatrician Rodney L. Hite in the November, 1978, issue of *Parents Resources Newsletter*: "If you and your pediatrician do not function well together, then the medical care provided to your child by your doctor—and by you—may not be the best it can be."

Finding a pediatrician is a simple matter. Your friends, obstetrician, family doctor, or local hospital can recommend qualified community doctors. But finding one who will turn out to be what Dr. Hite calls "a good fit" requires a little more insight, planning, and legwork. Here are some guidelines for the search.

╮ Jot down any personal preferences and characteristics that would make you feel more comfortable in your association with a doctor. Would you prefer a man or a woman? Older or younger? A doctor with children of his or her own? Someone to function as a surrogate parent to you? These subtle prejudices are perfectly valid, but they can stand in the way of a good working relationship unless acknowledged right from the start.

⚹ If you live in a large community, chances are you'll have several doctors to interview in your neighborhood. First, call the ones that have been recommended by friends and make appointments for personal interviews in the doctors' offices. Make sure to ask whether there will be a charge for these interviews. If a doctor can see you only after office hours, make sure to return another day to observe regular office routines.

⚹ Some points to note while you are awaiting your interview: Does the office seem overcrowded? Is the wait a long one? Is there a separate waiting area for sick children? Is the office cheerful, friendly, well-organized, clean? Is the staff pleasant and helpful? Is there a bulletin board listing community services such as parent support groups, babysitters, post-partum exercise classes, and other information that reflects the doctor's involvement in the neighborhood?

⚹ When you meet the doctor you should have not only a list of pertinent questions, but you'll also want to get a personal reading of manner, personality, and attitude. This will be impossible if the interview is carried out in the waiting room, or while the dotcor is conducting other business. Ideally, you should be taken to a consulting room for a private chat.

⚹ Don't be embarrassed or defensive about this interview. A good, self-confident pediatrician will welcome your questions as a sign of parental concern.

⚹ Don't feel you have to impress the doctor with a show of medical or educational knowledge. If all you want to do is quietly absorb the doctor's "vibes," that's okay.

⚹ Check out the doctor's diplomas, usually on display in the waiting or consultation rooms. Membership in the American Academy of Pediatrics means the doctor has passed, or is at the very least eligible to take, the pediatric boards. The American Medical Association publishes a book listing physicians' educations, experience, and hospital affiliations, if you want to do further research. But during your interview you can also ask specific questions such as: What are the doctor's qualifications, training, and personal philosophy? Is he or she hospital affiliated? Does this hospital allow parents to stay overnight with sick children, to be present during all tests and examinations, and to otherwise take part in the care of the sick child?

⚹ How available is the doctor in person or on the phone? Does he or she have a regular "advice hour" during which calls are accepted immediately? What about house calls? Who covers when the doctor is on vacation, during weekends, at night? What are the office hours? Are they the same year round? Observe (because the doctor probably won't volunteer this) whether "block" appointments (many patients clustered at the same time, taken on a first-come, first-served basis) or consecutive scheduling is a practice. If the office is run on a block system, you'll want to arrive as early as possible for each appointment. In any case, a wait of longer than an hour is absolutely unreasonable for any parent and child, regardless of the degree of illness.

✓ An important part of the initial interview is a discussion of fees, including any extra charges for immunization and other procedures. While in some cases a doctor may take on a patient at special rates, this is the time to discuss your financial situation, or to inquire about the doctor's receptivity to Medicaid reimbursement, not after a visit or when you receive the bill.

✓ Talk a little to the doctor about yourself and your partner. Better still, visit the prospective doctor together, so he knows who you are. He should know if you're the kind of parents who like to do everything "by the book," and therefore look for a certain kind of advice, or if you're looser, more intuitive, in your attitude. A little idle conversation on general beliefs can tell you a lot, too, about how you will all fare as a team.

Later, when you choose a pediatrician, you'll want to make your visits and phone conversations as productive as possible. Keep these points in mind:

✓ There's nothing wrong with asking the doctor to repeat or write down any medical terms or action you'll need to take when a child is sick. But you, too, must be professional in your approach to the doctor: Listen carefully to what he says.

✓ Find out which drugstores deliver and which are open all night, Sundays, and holidays. *Keep these numbers handy* in case the doctor needs to call the pharmacy with a prescription. It's your responsibility to supply the phone number, so don't rely on the doctor to do it.

✓ Learn to express your dissatisfaction with a doctor if it arises. Be polite but explicit.

✓ Understand that you are not bound to *any* physician. If you feel uneasy about the general quality of care, information, and support, or feel that a second opinion is warranted, or a specialist is needed, don't worry about hurting your pediatrician's feelings. He'll understand. Your child, after all, comes first.

✓ A pediatrician should be reasonably flexible and understanding and should not try to impose non-medical opinions on parents. Unless the parental lifestyle directly endangers the child's health, it's basically none of the doctor's business. You should not be made to feel guilty if you are a working parent, or a single parent, or have nontraditional ideas.

↗ Always list the subjects or questions you want to cover with the doctor *before* making the phone call or office visit. Sometimes it's even easier to hand over the list, especially if you're really flustered and the baby is inconsolable.

↗ If you're in the doctor's office for an immunization, it's wise to ask questions first. Shots not only make babies cry; they very often upset parents, too. When a simple examination prompts baby's tears, insist that any detailed explanation of how to deal with a particular illness, or new instruction involving diet, be carried out after the baby calms down and is comfortable. Some pediatricians leave parent and child alone during the recomposure period, then talk with the parent in the calm of the consulting room. A parent should not feel embarrassed to write down important points of discussion for future reference.

↗ Your doctor may have a telephone hour, an assigned time during which he is free and eager to answer your questions. Or else he accepts calls any time of day. Whatever his practice, inform the nurse clearly of the urgency of your call. Tell her, or the doctor if you've reached him directly, your child's name and age, then a specific description of the problem. Be brief and to the point, and write down any advice the doctor gives you. If you're waiting for call-back from the doctor, keep your line open. If he's trying to return your call after hours, appreciate the fact that he may be phoning you from a cold street corner. Don't tie up your line or engage him in longwinded conversation when he reaches you.

Colic: A Parent's Perspective

"Throughout my pregnancy I had the typical parental fantasy: my husband and I, arms around each other, smiling contentedly over our adorable, sleeping baby. Although prepared for hard work, I never anticipated having a 'difficult' child. I always skipped over the colic sections in books. Why would *we* have a child with colic? So when the incessant crying started only a few days after we came home, both Douglas and I were totally unprepared, not only to deal with Chris's misery, but to understand and handle our own reactions to the fantasy that didn't fit.

"We admit it now. There was *absolutely no pleasure* during the first three months with Chris. And that was a very difficult thing to live with, to feel so totally negative about somebody so helpless and obviously miserable. Nothing seemed to work for me as a mother. In the hospital I started breast-feeding and feeling that it would be a glorious experience. But after two weeks at home, I was ready to give up. It was such a battle. The baby wouldn't stay still long enough and would often begin to cry before nursing *began.* My husband, who had been involved in the Lamaze classes and labor, made an innocent remark that left me devastated: 'Breast-feeding seems so natural . . . like the easiest thing in the world.' Then why couldn't I do it? Why didn't my baby seem to like it?

"Douglas and I are both professionals who had led a very consistent and organized life before Chris. We felt we would be able to use all of our considerable talents to calm our infant. But there was nothing we could do. We thought, if he's tired, put him to sleep. If he's hungry, feed him. Right? Wrong. The pat solutions of child care books— swaddling, rocking, walking, medication, change in diet, clean diapers —added to our inadequacy: Chris kept right on crying.

"We also weren't prepared to face other people's reactions to our 'problem' child. With a colicky baby, people automatically focus on the colic and almost ignore the baby. They feel compelled to offer practical suggestions, even if they've never experiencd a colicky baby before. They assume you've mismanaged the situation, that you're burping him improperly, feeding him wrong, or that you're too tense. At the beginning I would find myself minimizing how much Chris actually did cry and how unhappy I was. The truth was that he cried, literally non-stop, from about 4 PM to 11 PM and between short catnaps during the night. He'd catch up with sleep mornings, then start looking unhappy by early afternoon and work up to high-pitched crying by 4 all over again. Douglas would go to work feeling like a wreck. I'd often be too agitated to sleep when the baby slept.

"We both felt a strong sense of shame when we explained to friends without kids just what our condition was. Talking to people who had 'good kids' was even worse. Jealousy crept in. In the end, our pediatrician gave us the kind of emotional support we really needed. Chris was about six weeks old, and by then everybody had concluded we were exaggerating, incompetent, and neurotic. One morning I called the doctor in desperation and cried. He asked me to come with Chris to spend the day in his office so he could see the crying pattern himself. Every time Chris started up, the doctor would examine him. In the end, he admitted Chris was definitely one of the most colicky babies he'd ever encountered, but healthy, nevertheless. The infant was thriving, as almost all colickly babies seem to do. It was the *parents* who were on the brink.

"Our marriage was definitely in trouble. Douglas, who had been so involved before the birth, seemed to disappear when the baby became difficult. And other pieces of our lives seemed just that—pieces. Sex? Forget it. I was too tired and resentful. Meanwhile, Douglas felt jealous, isolated, and angry. My concentration was totally on the baby and the 'problem.'

"For weeks we couldn't bridge the tension. Later, when we began to talk, we realized that we had both been depending on magical solutions to the very real problems we had with the baby and with our marriage. Douglas expected me, as the mother, to possess some mystical quality, to calm the baby with a single touch. And I wanted Douglas to have the magic to make *me* feel better. Neither of us had that magic, so inevitably we felt we'd failed one another and the baby.

"What advice would I give other parents going through the same experience?"

✔ Don't blame yourself for the colic. Reading and listening to advice that centers on the parents' nervousness, anxiety, and inexperience won't help the baby's problem, and it will add to yours. I've known tense parents who had "good" babies and relaxed ones whose *second* child has been a screamer. Similarly, nursing is no guarantee against colic, nor is the suppression of negative "vibes."

✔ Colic is *not* a disease. There is only one universal symptom of colic: crying. Colicky babies otherwise seem completely normal before and after bouts of crying. Some babies do have gas or abdominal pain, but colic can just as easily be experienced by perfectly well babies.

✔ A supportive pediatrician is a must. Your doctor should perform a thorough examination to rule out any problems, but it's just as important that he or she understand your parental plight.

✔ There are plenty of home remedies for colic, and it's worth trying all of the safe techniques under your doctor's supervision. Swaddling, walking, rocking, warm water bottles, peppermint and other herbal teas, soothing records, rolling the carriage back and forth over a bump, and pacifiers have all worked for some infants some of the time. Some parents "wear" colicky babies in a front pack as they go about their day. Don't worry about spoiling, and don't give up. What didn't work yesterday may work today.

✔ Try to find another new parent in the same boat, or locate a parent support group where you can share your feelings without censure. You may hesitate to join a post-partum group in which mothers are expected to have their infants present. If yours is disruptively crying, you'll find it impossible to relax and talk. You might prefer an adults-only group, or one in which baby care is provided in another room. In any case, you should not be made to feel like a nuisance, an oddity, or an inadequate parent, even if your baby does scream through the session.

 ⸍ Colic is often like insomnia—it can seem worse than it really is. Try timing your baby's crying spells and you might find the "hours" are really minutes, especially after a long day when time seems to drag anyway.

 ⸍ Get out as much as you can, but don't expect to leave your anxieties behind. Douglas and I used to imagine, as we bolted down a nervous dinner at the local spaghetti house, that we could hear Chris's sobs five blocks away!

 ⸍ Admit to yourself and to each other that your reactions to a constantly crying infant may be negative. False cheerfulness can be more wearing than the admission of temporary defeat.

 ⸍ It's important for you and your partner to talk about these feelings, but not to accuse each other of crimes of negligence or inadequacy.

 ⸍ Remember that colic *does* go away at about six weeks to three months. When it does, the grateful family is left to enjoy a peaceful togetherness that they, unlike "spoiled" parents of docile babies, never take for granted.

Good News for Parents of Colic Sufferers: It's Not Your Fault

Christopher and Dale Farran, in *Parents*, wrote that "All in all, the first victim of colic is parents' *confidence* in their ability to care for their child."

The Farrans, having experienced colic when their daughter was born, reassure concerned parents that recent research has exonerated us once and for all. "The studies indicate that colic bears no relation to a number of variables: the age of the mother; illnesses she may have had during her pregnancy; the number of children in the family; the infant's birth order, birth weight, or sex; fetal hiccups; prematurity; diarrhea in the infant; the number of times the baby is fed each day; and whether the baby is breast-fed or bottle-fed."

Although they report that "family tension has been universally discredited as a cause of colic by every recent responsible study," it's quite possible that Western familial *attitudes* play a large part in our perception of colic. It's not so much that other societies don't have colicky babies. They probably do. But the parental experience of colic is much less arduous when there are many hands to rock the cradle, and the incessantly crying baby is viewed as just one more fact of life.

Feeding Your Baby

The decision to breast- or bottle-feed is often made during pregnancy or in the first few days after birth. Like so many of our pre-birth theories and choices, the preferred feeding method is put to the test once the baby arrives. Because feeding an infant has become such an emotionally charged issue, it often serves as a focus for troublesome questions. Breast-feeding mothers may battle with early difficulties. Fathers must grapple with feelings of jealousy and exclusion. Then, too, breastfeeding simply doesn't work out for some families. The decision to change from breast to bottle is often complicated by feelings of failure and inadequacy.

Meanwhile, mothers who choose at the outset to bottle-feed may wonder whether they're doing right by the infant, especially if the child suffers from colic, allergies, or frequent illnesses.

Frances Wells Burck, in her supportive book, *Babysense*, writes that "There is little argument that mother's milk does have an edge over infant formulas. And if we were to make choices on a strictly rational, factual basis, breast-feeding probably would be the preferred method. . . . But people don't work this way, especially during one of the most vulnerable periods in their lives. . . . We make decisions based on all sorts of things—on feelings and attitudes that come from our unique histories, how we feel at the moment, how we think the baby is doing, how we plan to share the care of the baby, and how available we can be to feed him."

We believe that feeding choice has nothing to do with parental success or failure. More important than the choice itself is the *way* that choice is made. You will feel much better arriving at a decision—or altering it somehow down the line—if, as Ms. Burck suggests, you take into account the context of your parenthood.

Support for Parents of Premies

A 1977 study by the department of psychiatry at The Hospital for Sick Children in Toronto, Canada, found that parents of premature babies were much better able to confront their children's needs, and to organize a regular visiting schedule, once private fears were shared with parents of other premies.

In the Toronto experiment, 28 families met for more than two months with a nurse and a "veteran" mother. "Parents who had participated in the groups visited their infants more and rated themselves as more competent," the study revealed. These classes brought parents face to face with hospital routines, equipment, and procedures, and with "how to deal with a busy intensive care neonatal unit." Organizers of the study, and of similar ones at other hospitals, are in agreement that, once parents of premies begin to understand the methods by which their infants are nurtured to full health, they tend to treat them as healthy babies and not as fragile dolls needing special protection. Once confident that they would not hurt their babies in the first days home from the hospital, these parents were more willing to occasionally leave them with babysitters in order to resume some adult interests. Parents of premature babies, the Toronto study asserted, "need an occasional rest from their children."

"The Premature Infant," a handbook prepared for these parents by Nancy Shosenberg, RN, of the staff of Toronto Sick Children's Hospital, and other hospital personnel, says this about parents of premies:

"You are the most important person to your baby on the team that is fighting to help your baby get well. At first you may not feel very important because everyone else seems to be doing so much for the baby, but no one else will ever be your baby's mother or father."

Here are tips for parents of premies, adapted from this excellent handbook:

✓ Don't be afraid to phone the hospital day or night. The bustling atmosphere on a neonatal or newborn unit should not intimidate you. Jot your questions down on paper. At the beginning of your hospital visit, alert the staff to the fact that you have questions and ask them to confer with you when they have a spare moment.

✓ Do not expect to become knowledgeable about the intricacies of neonatal care instantly. You need time to learn terms and to become articulate about your child's condition. Don't hesitate to ask the same question more than once if you don't understand.

✓ Get to know your baby. While hospital staff constantly changes, your presence remains the baby's one constant. Just sitting beside the isolette, watching, talking to him, and observing his movements, patterns of breathing, and feeding schedule are important. Begin to help with his care: make sure his mouth is moist, the sheets don't bunch in the wrinkles of his skin, the tubes connected to him are in place and not causing irritation, his diaper is fresh, and he is receiving adequate body stimulation. Touching is important.

⤳ Do not hesitate to name your baby, even if his physical state remains precarious. Let the hospital staff know his name, so they can begin to use it when they talk to him.

⤳ Bring your baby a toy, such as a music box. As long as the staff can sterilize it, any small item is worthy.

⤳ Parents of newborns are apt to feel tired, worried, angry, guilty, upset with friends and relatives, unable to concentrate, optimistic while one's partner is pessimistic, not hungry, hostile to the hospital staff, left out if it's not logistically possible to spend time with the baby. Frequent visits to the baby go a long way to dispel these feelings, as does greater participation in his daily life. Sharing parental confusion with other parents of premies helps. Since the single parent is especially vulnerable and isolated, special permission can usually be obtained from the hospital to allow a friend to accompany the single parent on visits.

⤳ Write down your thoughts about the new baby in journal form and take pictures you can look at when you're not able to be with the baby.

⤳ Try to get lots of exercise during the stressful period.

⤳ In "The Premature Infant," Shosenberg also writes that "It is common for parents to blame themselves for prematurity. They think things like, 'I should have stopped working,' 'I shouldn't have gone on that trip or to that party,' 'I shouldn't have had sex.' *These are not reasons for prematurity.*" The sooner parents come to terms with this kind of self-destructive attitude, the easier it will be for them to respond to their new and quite special needs and the needs of their child.

Parents and Hospitals

"Like all eager first-time parents, we'd read everything about what pregnancy, birth, and living with the new baby would like. Or so we thought," said a long-time teacher discussing the agony of her 12-day-old son's sudden high fever and subsequent emergency hospitalization. "Completely knocked out" by a grueling birth experience, this mother later blamed herself for not being "rational enough to exercise my right as a parent to information" when the baby was subjected to X rays, spinal tap, and blood samples "from every part of his tiny little body."

"The doctor on duty did explain these procedures clearly, and when somebody tells me my baby might have meningitis, I'm not going to say, 'Don't do a spinal tap,' but even so I felt alone and frightened. Over that week, the hospital took undeniably good care of the baby, but whenever I posed a question to ease my mind they acted as if I was bothering them. I got information by being persistent and aggressive. The baby was on an intravenous, for instance. The doctors, however, kept saying 'Don't worry.' But I wanted more information, and had to call a doctor friend in another city for explanations. The problem was that I didn't know hospital routine and I wasn't used to the environment, which is a closed sub-culture. I didn't know which of my questions made sense."

This parent's tenacity paid off. She successfully carried out her plan to continue feeding her child with breast milk by using an electric pump rented for $2 a day. Her husband managed to see their baby evenings, despite strict hospital rules to the contrary.

Forced to leave a full-term baby behind, or to readmit the baby in an emergency during the first months, parents can find themselves unable to pose the "right" questions to hospital staff, questions that would help explain what ails the child and how she will be treated. Only with information can parents make some peace with themselves during the baby's absence. "You are forced to acknowledge that you can no longer take care of your child. You cannot protect her from pain; in fact, you often assume the role of assistant to those inflicting it," Kay Holmes reflected in a recent *Parents* magazine article on her 20-month-old daughter's hospitalization. "The depersonalized attitude inherent in hospital life only serves to underline parental agony. One's sense of helplessness is overwhelming," Holmes continued.

Hospitals, like other bureaucracies, are slow to change. Healing, the primary task of hospitals, after all, is often at cross-purposes with the need for patient closeness with family and family understanding of the patient's condition. But in the last few years, hospitals have begun to become more responsive to patient and family needs; witness the acceptance, however limited, of rooming in, Vaginal Birth After Caesarean Section (VBACS), and midwifery in some hospitals.

Many health professionals believe that these innovations are inextricably connected to other good medical procedure, but the impetus for change has to come from consumers. The persistent and aggressive questioning by the mother in our story contributed to this opening up, and so will your own requests for information when you need it most.

According to lawyer George Annas, in his book, *The Rights of Hos-*

pital Patients, though many hospitals still restrict patient visiting hours, "if the law or the hospital requires the parent's consent for treatment of the child, the hospital *cannot prevent or restrict* parents from being with their children while in the hospital . . . parents have the legal right to stay with their children during all tests, procedures, and administration of anesthesia, and to be present in the recovery room." Of course, parents must remember to temper their advocate's attitude with common sense and to ask, periodically, whether they're helping matters by monitoring every procedure with the same high level of concentration.

In a 1981 special report on pediatric hospitalization, New York's Parents Resources support group recommended parents consider these points when their children require hospitalization:

⌐ Have some prior knowledge of the hospital or hospitals nearest to you (and, later, their proximity to the daycare or nursery your child attends). Participate in visitor tours of these facilities, if possible, and direct questions to the admitting office. Be aware that if your pediatrician is not affiliated with the hospital to which you take your child in an emergency, you may be in for some hospital care complications in a crisis situation.

⌐ Low fever in a small baby may still mean infection, while high fever may not mean anything more ominous. Routinely, many hospitals admit babies younger than two months if their temperature exceeds 100°F. Some tests routinely performed on babies include urinalysis, chest X ray, and blood tests.

⌐ Request rooming-in privileges as soon as possible, as these are not universally available. If rooming-in is not offered, ask how you can maintain the closest relationship to your child while she is hospitalized. Special parent sleep rooms are sometimes available.

⌐ If a mother wants to nurse a hospitalized baby, as long as the baby is taking fluids orally this should not be considered out of the ordinary. Intravenous equipment does not have to interfere with nursing, and mothers are sometimes allowed to wear sterilized garments, especially if protective measures against infection are in effect. If a baby cannot take fluids by mouth, breast milk can be administered intravenously. Ask about electric breast pumps to facilitate this task.

⌐ Don't underestimate your importance to your baby. If you see that an intravenous tube is blocked, or if you become aware of any other discomfort, report it. Don't be afraid to speak up.

⌐ Carry appropriate insurance cards with you always, to facilitate your child's entry into the hospital and to enhance his chances of prompt high-level care.

⁊ Do not hesitate to disagree with hospital staff about the care of your child. Continue to be your child's chief advocate throughout the hospital stay. Remember that "pediatric hospitalization can be very much like good care at home, with the addition of necessary medication, treatment, or surgery. You can, and should," Parents Resources advises, "be involved in your child's daily routine—feeding, bathing, entertaining."

Although hospitals are becoming more responsive to family needs during a child's hospitalization, parents must realize that old stereotypes die hard. Mothers, especially, are vulnerable to hospital staff labeling as being over-protective, neglectful, pushy, aggressive. Fathers may still be viewed as distant breadwinners, outsiders too busy to become involved in hospital routine. Therefore, parents must continue to aggressively monitor and lobby for nothing but the best care for their child, despite the subtle or overt disparagement of some of those who treat the baby.

We add that one of the main problems in a parent's search for answers in the hospital is finding hospital personnel with enough time to sit down and talk. "You are going to have to find one person involved in the care of your child—a medical student, intern, for instance—who is on often enough and regularly enough that you can count on continuing communication," says Dr. Martin Finkelman, a Brooklyn Heights pediatrician. But he argues that many parents become so overwrought by the initial hospital experience that they lose perspective. "During the time your child is acutely ill," Dr. Finkelman told us, "parental worry is truly in inverse proportion to the seriousness of the ailment. The child is getting better but the parents often become even more worried than before because they fear the hospital staff is diverting their attention elsewhere. You have to understand that once your child's crisis is over, someone else's has to be attended to."

Dr. Finkelman also advises parents to understand the nature of hospital consent. Routine X rays, blood tests, and examinations by various health care professionals on the hospital staff are all part of the initial consent when you sign hospital admitting forms. Allowing the hospital staff to undertake non-traumatic, non-dangerous procedures can aid in your child's speedy recovery. Other medical procedures may need additional specific consent. Don't automatically assume that a procedure is dangerous because consent is required. In some instances, hospitals require this individual consent because a procedure looks on the surface—to the parent—to be risky. The hospital recognizes that parental consideration of options is a necessary part of the recovery program. Then, of course, there are the *really* dangerous procedures the parent is entitled to question if he or she sees fit.

If Your Baby Is Handicapped

A child with major mental or physical disabilities is born to one family in ten; the ratio of less severely impaired children is even greater. If your child is born handicapped, you will likely experience stages of emotional turmoil during the first months of parenthood and after. The stages, according to the National Easter Seal Society, may appear in no predictable order and may be encountered more than once. They include:

✓ *Denial*, or the inability to hear or cope with difficult-to-accept information about your baby. The results are isolation and unreality. One suggested remedy is to share these feelings with your partner, who is probably struggling with similar conflicts. "Denial temporarily protects you against a blow you aren't prepared for," writes Elliott Cleary in "Your Child Has a Future," a publication of the Easter Seal Society.

✓ *Questioning*, or "What did we do that impaired our child?" "Does the baby have a future?" "Are we, the parents, up to the task of providing special care for our baby?"

✓ *Depression*, or feelings of helplessness, guilt, self-deprecation.

✓ *Anger*, or "What did I (we) do to deserve this?" Anger is a legitimate means of pulling out of passive depression, but if it is aimed at your partner, your child, or health professionals, it can be destructive.

Getting Help

First-time parents, especially, need counseling to help adjust to their situation and to acknowledge and deal forthrightly with what may seem to be insurmountable problems. Accepting your child's disability is a grief experience that must be worked through before you are able to embark on a rational program of care and education for your child. The Easter Seal Society, local school psychologists, social workers, and speech pathologists in your school district are good sources of information on parent support groups that can help, even when your baby is small. Check your library or health department for listing of local health services. Local private and public agencies often supply overworked parents with homemaking and health respite (babysitting) care services. Parents of handicapped children need time alone, together. Make a point of going out and resuming some pre-baby activities you enjoy.

Keeping Records

The sheer amount of information and advice you'll receive once you begin seeking it, cannot always be retained by memory alone. Keep a record of recommendations and observations of health care professionals, plus important names and addresses. By law, your baby's hospital records are available to you. It's especially important to obtain them if you have any doubts about care and whether you've been told exactly what you need to know.

If a doctor interprets medical findings for you, write down what they are. Begin researching your child's handicap and any secondary problems on your own. Finally, don't be afraid to seek second or third or fourth opinions if you feel these are necessary. Health care professionals today *expect* that you will do so, and they will not be offended by your attempt to do the best for your child that you possibly can.

If You Adopt

The trend toward having children later in life carries with it the possibility that conception, most statistically probable for a woman in her twenties, may not be possible. Men, too, are finding that environmental and physiological obstacles prevent the siring of a child. Adoption remains a viable alternative. Though prospective adoptive parents learn the ins and outs of the convoluted process *leading up* to the awarding of a child, they are not always prepared for the flood of complex feelings that complicate their earliest days of parenthood. For them, and for friends and family who care to understand the emotional process of becoming adoptive parents, here are some guidelines.

✓ While natural parents have time to prepare emotionally for their baby's arrival, for adoptive parents "the whole idea of a baby in your house is actually quite theoretical," Louise Raymond and Colette

Taube Dywasuk point out in their book *Adoption and After*. Often, though the process of obtaining a child takes years, the baby arrives quite suddenly, and the parents must acquire appropriate space, furniture, clothes, and sundries on a few days' notice.

↗ Adoptive parents should expect to experience "sinking feelings" and "stage fright" not only at the impending reality of parenthood, but at the very sight of the baby. The moment you see his new face, "your deepest feeling may rise up to 'deny' him at the same instant you are reaching toward him in love and thankfulness and affection: at the same time that you are going out to him you are pulling away from him," Raymond and Dywasuk continue. But this so-called "involuntary" withdrawal will quickly pass as you adjust to your parental self-image.

↗ Adoptive parents tend to be more anxious, defensive, and conscientious about being parents in the beginning. They may worry about how they are doing and become even more guilt-ridden over imagined shortcomings. To combat these feelings, they resort to trying even harder. The cause may be an unconscious feeling of responsibility to the baby's natural parents. One remedy is to remind yourself that those natural parents gave up the baby to ensure his care; the true responsibility is to the child and to your own mental and physical health during parenthood, not to the shadowy spectre of those "real" parents you do not know.

↗ Just because adoptive parents did not endure the rigors of the labor and birth does not mean they'll be any more able to entertain friends and relatives in the days after baby comes home. You are still exhausted and preoccupied, and may have to contend with mood changes in a child who has become attached to other adults before coming into your house. He will need time to mourn his loss and begin to know you. Furthermore, the baby's arrival in a household where infertility has been a highly charged issue may set off intensified feelings of inadequacy, particularly in the husband. A man preoccupied with the belief that he has fallen short because he was not able to sire a child may be at least temporarily less participatory as a father.

↗ Support of adoptive parents is not always the same as that rendered to natural parents by friends and family. Adoptive parents may find that others are not as excited for them, and that "subtle, ambivalent attitudes toward the adoptive experience" persist, making the parents feel uneasily "different," say the committee of psychiatrists who authored *The Joys and Sorrows of Parenthood*.

↗ If the baby is not a newborn, employing a registered nurse or nursemaid specializing in newborns may be unwise. She may not wish to cope with the demands made by, say, an active crawler.

↗ By all means send a birth announcement. Special adoption announcements are available, or you can use regular birth announcements, filling in a date of birth and another date signifying the baby's arrival into your family.

↗ Think carefully about what you tell relatives and friends about your child's natural parents and the reasons she was given for adoption. Later on, poorly explained facts may come back to her, facts which you told others long before but never explained to your child.

↗ As much as you can, prepare for the time your child will ask about the natural parents. Some children get the rejection-connection early. One four-year-old listened to the familiar story up to a point, then, his face crumbling in pain, said to his mother, "Why did she give me up?" Before the mother could reply, he answered his own question. "Because I was little and sick and no good."

Another child might never ask the direct question, so you must find ways to comfort her. And never, never say anything negative about the natural parents. Your child's teenage identity crisis will be tough enough without any extra burden.

↗ Compile a baby and family picture album, starting with the day your child joined the family. This will encourage a sense of belonging in everyone.

↗ Tell your child he is adopted. The prevailing philosophy is that children who understand sentences are old enough to be told, gently: "We're so glad we *adopted* you." This should be done in relaxed, positive circumstances. "The earliest years are the easiest in many ways where telling is concerned, because as far as your baby knows, *everybody* is adopted," say Raymond and Dywasuk in *Adoption and After*. Search out children's books to help your child understand adoption. At 3 or 4, when your child asks where babies come from, your task is to tell him more about the process of birth common to all people and to follow up with the fact of his own adoption. Parents say that encouraging the child to adopt a pet at this juncture can help. However, if the child is encouraged to identify too closely with the pet as another adoptee, unhappiness can result if the animal dies prematurely, or must be given away for any reason.

3

Marriage and Sex

BETTER PARENTS make better partners, right? Wrong. Parenthood can be disastrous to a weak relationship and doesn't automatically strengthen a sound one. All the love and energy we rightfully pour into our parenthood does not necessarily fuel our couplehood. Postpartum relationships are fragile and complex, wavering as they do between the new intimacy and isolation imposed by parenthood.

Parenting, as a job, involves hard work. It forces a new kind of togetherness, a *working partnership* that calls for a whole new set of emotional and practical contracts. Who does what? Who nurtures whom? How do we plan for our child's and our own future?

And, of course, the experience of parenthood is complex, and different for each partner. There are, in effect, three new people in the family. So we struggle simultaneously to comprehend the baby's existence, come to terms with our own metamorphosis, and understand a partner who's also "not himself."

Still, within the fragmented and shifting threesome is a valued, vulnerable twosome. The task of rediscovering and adapting the couple relationship within the new family is not always an easy one, but well worth the effort. Marriage within parenthood does not thrive without special care.

Recapturing the Style of Your Relationship

After the initial frenzy of the post-partum months, new parents are often forced to piece together what they used to take for granted— the basic character of their relationship. The realization that "something's missing" may come when the child is six months, a year, or even older. The longer we wait, the more difficult it is to reconstruct consciously what used to be instinctive. Although marital style is as individual and complex as marriage itself, it does break down into some basic components.

Style encompasses *the ways in which you have fun and enjoy each other as a couple*—not necessarily the actual events (which are harder to duplicate now), but the mood and emotions they engender. What were the activities that sustained and recharged you? Dinner and a film? Long walks? Quiet talks at home over a glass of wine? An evening with close and comfortable friends? Sharing popcorn and beer over a televised ball game?

For some couples, going out was never a priority. Friends of ours were pushed by family into a fancy restaurant dinner as an escape from post-partum doldrums. They returned early after a dispirited and expensive meal, realizing that this just wasn't their style. When they reinstituted their favorite form of relaxation—card playing with best friends—the couple felt distinctly happier.

Another pair missed the spontanous "discovery" walks they used to take around the city, the shared adventure and time for talk. They decided to re-create the style, if not the substance, of those walks by taking their child to new playgrounds around their large city. The baby was as stimulated by new places as they were and was perfectly happy to play nearby while his parents enjoyed uninterrupted conversation and a sense of discovery once more.

Marital style can also mean the ways in which you make each other feel good. It's important to acknowledge exactly how you pooled your emotional resources as a twosome and to make some effort to do so now. "One of the reasons two people are together is that there are specific things each does to make the other feel good," says Judith Glickstein, co-founder and coordinator of the Yale University Health Services Parent Support Group.

What small and large things did you do for each other in the past? Did you exchange back rubs? Secrets? Gifts? Jokes? Favors? Compliments? Celebrations? There's a mistaken notion that the unique, sometimes un–grown-up accessories of our adult relationship have to be traded in for a new single style of life called parenthood.

Style is also determined, in part, by the couple's *social context*. Did you pride yourself in being thought of as a "great couple" by an admiring audience of peers? Did much of your private conversation revolve around the emotional sagas of friends? Was most, even all, of your leisure time spent in the company of others? New parents who have cut off their old friends may find themselves alone and adrift unless meaningful social contact, even abridged, is made a conscious priority in their new lives.

Family context is another important feature of marital style. For couples who prided themselves on independence, the forced and welcome closeness imposed by parenthood is liable to be confining. As new parents, we pay for help, support, security, and a sense of belonging with the coin of privacy, autonomy, and couple "space." Like newlyweds, we're forced to deal with in-laws, questions of loyalty, and the sheer weight of numbers—that is, which parent's team has more players.

Some couples see themselves as family people and others just don't. It's important to talk over how you're going to integrate your family needs and obligations without being over-dependent or overwhelmed on the one hand, and isolated and aloof on the other. (See our *Family* chapter.)

It's a literary truth that nobody wants to read about happy marriages or families. If we were to suggest talking over your marriage, your immediate thoughts might run to problem solving, or "telling it like it is." It's sad that few of us pay attention to the personality of our relationship until it sours, usually after long neglect. We're suggesting here that you and your partner try something new. Talk over, in detail, all the things that made your marriage work before. Then see if you can carry over that *essence,* if not the actual events, into your present context.

Parents as Partners: Evolving Contracts

Though marriage vows are often the only *formal* contract between husband and wife, evolving marriages embrace many more spoken and unspoken contracts: "She's going to work, I'm going to law school. . . We're saving one salary for a down payment on a house. . . We'll only have children when it's right for us. . .We share domestic chores and pool our income. . . Each of us goes out alone with friends once a week. . .We try not to go to sleep mad at each other. . . ."

No matter how well (or badly) these past agreements have held up, the birth of a child presents a whole new arena for contract-making and new criteria for judging the fairness, or mutuality, of past contracts. Many marriages today are based on a "you go your way, I'll go mine, and we'll meet and talk about it over a nice quiet dinner" philosophy. What happens to this freewheeling contract unless it's equitably renegotiated—that is, unless both partners sit down and talk about how they'll actually style their lives with a baby? You guessed it. The usual result is one free wheel and one stuck at home with baby, a sadly typical parental imbalance.

Forming Equitable Contracts

By equitable we mean fair, and not necessarily equal in that a tally sheet is maintained on household chores, money earned, diapers changed, etc. The equitable contract is one in which both partners are conscious of tradeoffs toward a mutual goal, even though the tradeoffs may be temporarily greater for one partner than the other.

One couple had developed a mutually productive relationship before the birth of their first child. The husband was an industrial film-maker, the wife an art teacher who collaborated with him on film scripts and accompanied him on location. Their combined salaries supported them comfortably.

The birth of their first child put a strain on their established life-style, but didn't change it significantly. Both continued to work, but she began to feel the pressure of driving a long distance to school, child care problems, and general fatigue. When they both decided that she would take a leave from her job, they explored together the necessity of a career change for the husband, realizing that it would mean less time for the family. Now he owns a thriving business which often takes him on the road. As a result, the couple is no longer able to spend as much time together as they would wish. With the birth of their second child, the new contract seemed even more realistic, although the tradeoffs were great for both.

"We've agreed to restructure our lives because we both want the same things—our own home, good schools for our kids, and the possibility sometime in the future of having enough money to write, produce, and direct our own films," admits the wife. "I may not like the immediate circumstances of our lives, but this was our five-year plan, so to speak, and we're sticking by it."

Translating Theory into Reality

In the planning stages of parenthood, we spend a lot of time talking about what kind of parents we'll be. It's in the nature of these fantasy contracts to generalize about how we'll live and reciprocate day to day. But if one parent has a date to play golf Saturday morning, after a week with a difficult project, and the other a date to play tennis after a week with a croupy toddler, they'll have to find some working arrangement about child care and personal time.

This contract should evolve from both their goals as parents—that is, those that have withstood the test of actual family life—as well as the demands of the moment. If this couple has agreed that weekend parenting chores should be shared equitably, that their child care philosophies preclude paid Saturday morning babysitters, and that each parent has the right to personal time, the Saturday morning dilemma is halfway solved. All that's needed is a little logistical shuffling: they postpone one engagement to the afternoon, take turns minding baby, and take pride in their mutual respect for each other's commitments.

If, on the other hand, they've never come to terms on the basic theoretical groundwork of their parenthood, the Saturday morning question takes on all sorts of symbolic meaning: Who had the hardest week and therefore "deserves" a Saturday morning off? Child care is *your* job. Why didn't *you* arrange for a sitter if you wanted the morning off? I'll make up for Saturday morning on Sunday. Who keeps tabs on parent-hours, anyway? I simply need more personal "space" than you do, so you've got to arrange your schedule around mine. . . .

Allowing one parent to act as chief theoretician of the family is unwise. Parents should talk over their ideas and philosophies *frequently*, and then put these ideas to the test of daily living. Despite the vagaries of work and personal demands, sound theories facilitate rather than complicate good parental contracts.

Maintaining Flexibility

"We don't need a rigid schedule. We like to be flexible about our life," boast a lot of parents who confuse being flexible with simply being haphazard. We define flexibility as meeting each partner's changing demands with a basically solid routine. Routine implies a conscientious attempt to fit the disparate elements of life into a cohesive pattern. Once both parents know what the pattern is, and feel comfortable within it, they're more able to allow each other (and the baby) leeway. With the haphazard approach, there is much bickering about who will do what in the coming week. The couple with a flexible routine, on the other hand, will have talked over increased work loads, tennis dates, doctor's appointments, and sitter needs at the beginning of the week.

We advise both parents to sit down every Sunday night with calendars in hand and review individual and joint commitments for the coming week. You'll probably find that what starts as a mundane planning session will give you an excuse, if you need one, to talk over goals, theories, feelings, doubts—whatever may not be otherwise opportune.

Here are some suggestions for the weekly planning session:

⚡ Write down both your own and your partner's appointments in your date book. Don't count on one person to record appointments.

⚡ Decide at once who will arrange for babysitters when you'll both be out.

⚡ Make sure to specify whether your partner or a babysitter will be filling in for you when you're out.

⚡ Try not to come to your partner with a rigid plan for the coming week. Some commitments will be unchangeable; others can be made more loosely. A doctor's appointment may be hard to reschedule, but not an after-work drink with a friend. Be realistic in weighing the relative importance of your commitments.

⚡ Speak up! If you're "just home with the baby," you may feel your schedule is less important than that of a working parent. Treat each other's plans with mutual respect. If a commitment is important to you, it's important, period.

⚡ Beware of overscheduling. If you must, make "appointments" to do nothing together at home several times a week. Treat these commitments as seriously as you would other dates.

Weekends present special challenges for parents. The blocks of time are much greater, and the very concept of what weekends *should* be motivates (and intimidates) us more than we'll admit. Even if our ideal is a totally unstructured Saturday and Sunday, some scheduling is necessary.

At your Sunday night planning session, ask yourselves the following questions for the coming weekend. What task (work or personal) does each want to accomplish, and on what day? If this will be a heavy work week, do I expect to bring home work on the weekend, or go into the office? How will this affect my family's plans? Is a group activity planned? If so, do we need to get tickets, or to check the car, or to make arrangements with relatives and friends? How will we balance structured and unstructured time without overtaxing our own or our family's strength? Have we set aside time for each other as a couple?

On the short term, establishing a flexible routine is healthy for the couple relationship. In a shared process of living, each parent knows that his/her tasks and obligations are equally important, and doesn't need to worry about being tagged "it" by an unthinking partner. Long-term weekly scheduling eases you into new roles and directions *as they evolve*. Decisions about major career changes, child development, and your own need for growth and space without guilt are much easier to make when you're in the habit of accommodating and respecting one another.

Coming to Terms with Conflict

During the first year of life with baby, many partners feel totally alone within the new intimacy of parenthood. Both mothers and fathers talked to us of feelings of abandonment, jealousy, and isolation within the relationship, which were doubly painful in those couples who approached childbirth as a team. How could they have been so united before the birth and so inexplicably divided afterward?

Marriage and family therapists note that the problems of shattered relationships are extreme examples of experiences we all share. "The crucial difference is that coping and communication mechanisms have broken down," Dr. Martin Cohen, a New York City family therapist, told us. Furthermore, the most threatened marriages are not necessarily those that erupt into frequent arguments, but, says Dr. Cohen, those that "fizzle out" in relative silence.

Many so-called primitive societies have traditional rituals for solving family conflicts, which they see as a normal part of human nature just as crying is a normal part of infancy. In our society, however, the instinctive desire is to achieve some boundless plateau of harmony— or at least the semblance of peace—often at great personal cost. Like the baby who's left to cry it out alone in his crib, we, as new parents suffering natural marital growth pains, are left to work it out in private. Since we equate conflict with failure, can we be blamed for avoiding confrontation for fear of admitting defeat?

The first step to resolving conflict is to admit that it exists, that it's OK for things not to be peachy all the time. After all, parenthood has been called a "life crisis" by some sociologists. Once we've granted ourselves permission to be angry and hurt with one another occasionally, we have to begin examining the roots of the problem at hand, not necessarily its outward manifestation. Repeated fights about money, for instance, may have less to do with dollars and cents than with how we share our resources, how we care for one another, and our interpretation of parental responsibility and the payment of emotional debts.

Dr. Gabriel Smilkstein of the University of Washington Department of Family Medicine has devised a brief questionnaire that has been administered to more than 2,000 couples and families. Called the Family APGAR, after the delivery room test for newborn health, Dr. Smilkstein's checklist is not designed to help you "rate" your marriage, but rather to help you recognize the fundamental strengths and weaknesses of your partnership. The family APGAR divides marriage and family behavior into the following components:

✓ *Adaptation* How resources are shared, or the degree to which a member is satisfied with the assistance received when family resources are needed.

✓ *Partnership* How decisions are shared, or the member's satisfaction with mutuality in family communication and problem solving.

✓ *Growth* How nurturing is shared, or the member's satisfaction with the freedom available within a family to change roles and attain physical and emotional growth or maturation.

✓ *Affection* How emotional experiences are shared, or the member's satisfaction with the intimacy and emotional interaction that exists in a family.

✓ *Resolve* How time (and space and money) is shared, or the member's satisfaction with the time commitment that has been made to the family by its members.

FOR EACH QUESTION,
CHECK ONLY ONE ANSWER

	Almost always	Some of the time	Hardly ever
I am satisfied that I can turn to my family for help when something is troubling me.			
I am satisfied with the way my family talks over things with me and shares problems with me.			
I am satisfied that my family accepts and supports my wishes to take on new activities or directions.			
I am satisfied with the way my family expresses affection and responds to my emotions, such as anger, sorrow, or love.			
I am satisfied with the way my family and I spend time together.			

"Problems can be addressed a little bit better if people can identify clearly what they are," Dr. Smilkstein told us. "Rather than accepting pain and avoiding conflict, couples should learn to view them as symptoms of something that's gone wrong. Then an attempt should be made to identify what's gone wrong and correct it."

The sharing of resources, power, affection, support, and room for growth—the five components of APGAR—is a special challenge for parents. As you answer the questions below, keep in mind how arrangements made *before* baby differ from those which have evolved since. It's tempting to think that a child strengthens certain marital bonds and weakens others. In truth, it does nothing of the sort. "Parenthood is the acid test of marriage," one father told us. "If you didn't know what kind of marriage you had before, you sure will now."

Communication: The Missing Link

What do you do with all those wonderful insights you've gained from the APGAR test? The final and most difficult step to confronting problems is to communicate them—to let your partner know how you feel without turning her away, and to encourage her to share views with the same candor and compassion you tried to exhibit. Here's how one couple tried to close the gap:

Joan and Barry hadn't really talked for weeks. The silence was deafening. So they looked for some simple prescriptions for reviving intimacy. They hired a sitter and went out on a "date" to a double feature. Then they came home exhausted and went to sleep immediately, too tired to share thoughts about what they'd seen or how they felt. Turning away from each other in bed, each keenly felt the absence of intimacy or even a clue about how to revive it.

A book they read said: Talk. They finally found time, after the baby was asleep, at their usual, early bedtime. They didn't feel very enthusiastic. They'd had a grueling day.

"So? Start talking. What's bugging you?"

"I don't know. What do you want me to say?"

What's so hard about communication? We're frequently told that communication is the great missing link in adult relationships. With the birth of a child the need for it becomes even more pronounced because we're in partnership—we're literally doing a job together. Imagine a business that can run without meetings, without memos, without planning sessions, and without problem solving. Impossible? Yes. And yet we expect to carry on the work of parenthood—with its implications for couplehood—without any rituals for communicating. We're not going to suggest writing memos (unless you find it easier to express yourself honestly on paper), but we offer suggestions for evolving regular and cooperative problem-solving techniques of your own.

Tips for Communication

✓ *Do* plan a mutually convenient, reliable time for your meetings. Dinner or special occasions are *not* good times. If one partner can't make it to a session heightened by candlelight and soft music, the disappointment goes beyond the missed opportunity to talk.

✓ *Do* present the problem, not the solution. *That* you have to work out together.

✓ *Do* give each partner equal time, even if you have to use a stopwatch. We all know how easy it is for the more talkative one to dominate a conversation.

✓ *Do* articulate the ways in which you want specific behavior to change, but expecting or demanding changes in personality are a bit much for starters.

✓ *Do* get promises in writing, if you feel that's what you need. If you find yourselves constantly disagreeing about what was resolved at your last meeting, it doesn't hurt to take minutes or to record your resolutions. You'd be surprised how easy it is to get the other person's point of view when you can hear yourself as he/she does!

✓ *Do* look at conversation as a valid way to spend time. If your initial meetings begin hesitantly, break the ice by talking about a movie you've both seen, or what's happening with friends. The important thing is to *get started*.

✓ *Do* attempt to sort out some of your feelings and beliefs before you talk so that you are able to express yourself as you would like. Confusion, frustration, vacillation and simply lack of "talking" skills often translate themselves into increased anger at the other person for your own tied tongue.

✓ *Don't* "communicate" as if it were some incomprehensible skill. What you're doing is talking. Attitude is essential. The more open you are to your own feelings and thoughts and the more receptive you are to what your partner has to say, the easier it will be to get started.

✓ *Don't* deliberately intimidate the more reserved or reticent person by dangling lofty goals, or a "work ethic" approach. "Let's figure out a way to stop fighting forever" and "We have eight problems to get through tonight" are not workable goals.

✓ Don't save your sessions for problem solving only. If you get into the habit of talking about ideas, good and bad, you've laid the groundwork for problem solving later on.

✓ Don't save conversation for late at night, or right before bed, when one or both partners are tired and the talk may be cut short by sex, which is certainly a fine close to a day but not a substitute for verbal exchange.

✓ Don't substitute accusations or generalizations about the other person's behavior for how you really feel. Instead of "You always make me feel . . . ," try "I feel disappointed and hurt when . . ." Try to talk more about yourself than the other person.

✓ Don't always talk about your child.

✓ Don't attempt a serious meeting when children are underfoot, or when family, neighbors, or friends might drop in. And don't compete with a blaring TV or radio.

✓ Don't expect immediate results when you sit down face to face. If you think only in terms of product and instant improvement, you may be blocking rather than furthering future communication. Remember that what you're trying to create is an *environment* in which conversation is valued.

Eight Questions That Can Save Your Marriage

1. *What were the traditions and milestones of your relationship before baby? Have you made an effort to celebrate the important ones, if only in spirit?*

Roberta and Neil have a New Year's Eve tradition: staying home, eating a quiet dinner for two, and reviewing their lives together over a glass of champagne. When Nicky was ten months old, their first parental New Year was ushered in smoothly: he slept through. But a year later, the champagne chat was interrupted by the wails of a sick toddler. It took effort to get through their ritual conversation, but they agreed it was worthwhile, even with champagne minus bubbles and the certainty of further interruptions.

Naturally, it's impossible to live life exactly as you always did. But traditions and milestones are a notion apart. We're talking about the events created by *you*, the couple, and nourished by your deepening relationship over the years. These rituals are distinctively different from the habitual ceremonies you, as a couple, are expected to attend. Birthdays, anniversaries, favorite restaurants, Scrabble games: if they had special significance to your relationship, they should be acknowledged and modified to fit your present lives. As parents you will discover joyful new occasions for celebration, yet these should not replace valued husband-wife connections.

2. *Is your baby your excuse for not nurturing your couple relationship?*

"Our child turned two and suddenly I realized I didn't know who I was anymore—or who my husband was," one mother wrote to us. Part of our pre-birth fantasies revolve around our visions of what mommies and daddies should be. Some of us become so wrapped up in playing what we think is the appropriate parental role that we lose sight of our other adult roles. The subtle encroachment of "Mommyism" and "Daddyism" begins with our appropriate feeling that the baby has all-consuming importance. Soon, we may begin to feel self-conscious when we touch each other; we may begin to deny our own needs for privacy; we may eliminate all traces of non-baby conversations. "Later on," we tell ourselves. "There's just not the time, energy, patience right now."

Some of us learn to play the waiting game better than others—the rationalizations come fully formed and convincing. "Let's wait until the baby goes to school . . . until I get that promotion . . . until our vacation . . . until we're less tense." The bottom line is, how long can a marriage remain in hibernation?

3. *Are you willing to change old patterns to make married life with baby more livable?*

She's sloppy, he's neat. She's frugal, he's totally irresponsible with money. He likes to bring people home for dinner unexpectedly, she functions much better with a more scheduled social life. She's a night person, he's an early bird. She's absent-minded, he used to think it was cute. . . .

Some of the idiosyncrasies you tolerated during courtship were no longer acceptable after marriage. It follows that after the birth of the baby some of your habits and proclivities will now strike your partner as intolerable. Parenthood forces so many compromises and accommodations of its own that we simply grow less patient with one another's foibles.

Changing old patterns requires frank self-appraisal, however. Start by being militant about your own bothersome idiosyncrasies. Acknowledging them without vowing to do something about them—"It's just the way I am"—is worse than doing nothing at all. Finding an empty explanation, such as your horoscope, isn't much help either. ("I'm a Gemini and Geminis are changeable. Nothing we can do about it.")

We know that while personality cannot be changed, behavior can, and often should, be overhauled. When you deal with your partner's idiosyncrasies, review the problem without supplying remedies. Don't dwell on the feelings engendered by your partner's annoying habits. Simply present the practical side: "It's no longer practical to have guests unexpectedly, or to spend as freely as we used to."

And don't unconsciously encourage unwanted behavior. For instance, if you hate dirty socks on the floor, don't always volunteer to pick them up (unless of course they're yours). Instead, you might put a dirty sock basket in the bedroom. Some partners encourage over-dependency ("He's my first baby . . ." "She's so cute and helpless . . .") while privately resenting the dependent partner now that there's a *real* baby in the house.

When destructive patterns become too complex and ingrained, how-ever, it's usually wise to seek professional counseling. But unless your grievances are major ones, be realistic in your demands and expectations for yourself and your partner. Neither of you should expect to become a quick-change artist, or the ultimate grown-up. Concentrate only on those habits that are in conflict with your daily *survival* as a couple.

4. *Can you forgive each other's mistakes and oversights and appreciate each other's achievements, differences, and need for growth?*

Stress and exhaustion sensitize us to our own needs, but can make us less compassionate at the same time. A familiar scene is the meet-ing of parents at the front door. One has worked all day, the other has been home with baby. Each is at the end of the proverbial rope. Each expects the other to take responsibility for the child immediately. Each wants sympathy and recognition when there's simply not enough to go around.

One couple, after being in this situation one time too many, hit on a clever solution: a "Who Had the Worst Day" chart. Instead of accus-ing each other of being hard-hearted, they sit down and list the grue-some events of each partner's day and usually wind up relaxed and laughing. The key to compassion is knowledge. Knowing in detail what the other person does all day helps. One father, responding to our questionnaire, was typical of many when he said: "I never knew how hard it was to be a mother until I filled in one day. My job suddenly didn't seem like the toughest way a person could spend 8 hours."

The work of parenting is fertile ground for arguing about the right and wrong way to do things—from taking the baby out without boots on a rainy day to judgments on candy, discipline, education, values. It's fine to present a united front on the most basic beliefs of child-raising, but you don't have to play Tweedle Dee and Tweedle Dum to be effective parents and effective partners. If, before you had a child, you perceived your differences in philosophy and attitude as complementary and enriching, then the child—and your marriage— should only benefit from a pooling of these diverse resources.

Finally, as a learning experience, parenthood embodies mistakes, major and minor victories, setbacks, and even profound turnabouts in personal philosophy. Babies are a catalyst for these changes in perception. As we know ourselves to be growing, so should we allow and welcome our partner to surprise us, too.

5. *Do you see the difference between sharing responsibility and merely helping out?*

Baby Sheila's 5:30 A.M. reveille put an enormous strain on Beth, her mother. Ron said, "Sure, I'd be glad to get up on Sunday to relieve you. Just remind me the night before, make sure to set out bottle, change of clothes, and whatever, and then give me a little nudge when you hear her crying. You know what a deep sleeper I am." Beth tried just that. But when Sheila began crying for her morning feeding, Ron wouldn't budge. "I'm just too tired, honey," he mumbled. "You know I've had a hard week. I promise to play with her all afternoon. Just remind me later. . . ."

Let's face it, many people simply cop out on child care responsibilities. In the final analysis, they do not accept the role of primary caretaker, responsible parent, without cajoling and accusation. Letting your partner switch off for a time to recharge his or her batteries is a *necessity*, no matter how busy and preoccupied you believe you are. Emotional and physical energy thus rekindled in your partner can be put back into the marriage, and, along with it, a fresh trust and confidence in the partnership.

Even the busiest parent should take part in the caregiving routine as a gesture of "being there." Empty promises and grudging help do not suffice.

6. *Do you talk over mutual short- and long-term goals?*

Dorothea and Roger always wanted a home of their own and purchased one in a distant suburb when Roger received a big promotion.

Their child was born shortly after. Though they loved the big old house dearly, they soon saw problems: no nursery schools were near-by; at-home child care was hard to find; their neighbors were older couples so they made few friends in the community; because of Rog-er's long commute and the added responsibilities of his new job, he rarely saw the baby and had no time for squash, his favorite pastime. Meanwhile, when she tried to get a part-time job as a graphics de-signer, Dorothea found none existed in her area. She would be forced to travel two hours a day to and from the city if she wished to pursue her career.

Though Dorothea and Roger had spoken extensively about the kind of house they wanted, it never occurred to them that there was more to moving than that. Most of us have made decisions without consider-ing all factors. With parenthood comes the need for periodic planning sessions where couples ask themselves candidly, "What's our blueprint for next month, next summer, next year, in five years? How do we really want to live? Just what are the tradeoffs and compromises necessary now and later in order to fulfill our dreams?" In the case of Dorothea and Roger, important personal needs were unwittingly traded for a house. Only later did they see the other options open to them. They might have compromised on another house nearer to work, schools, friends.

Declaring goals does not engrave them in stone, though. Repeated planning sessions allow you both to evolve and change directions. And having long- and short-term goals as a couple gives you a sense of your future together beyond your maternity leave, beyond the pre-school years, beyond, even, the child's leaving home.

7. *In juggling family, social, and career demands, do you take care not to schedule yourselves out of each other's lives?*

When their baby's three months of colic ended, Joan and Sid kept up the swing-shift system of child care out of habit. They ate in shifts, slept in shifts, and saw each other by appointment only. When they went out together, they had no strength to communicate. They were so tired at night that conversation between them dwindled to nothing. After a year, Joan and Sid wondered why they hardly talked at all—and saw their sex life as a casualty on the parenting battleground.

Scheduling is fine, and we suggest it as a means of couples getting together as well as accomplishing individual goals. But pure, unadul-terated swing-shift family organization should be carefully monitored and expanded to include regular and frequent time together as a cou-

ple, in addition to sexual time which is a necessity as well. In extreme
cases, overscheduled working parents divide time with their child so
completely that they begin to resemble a divorced couple sharing
custody, rather than a united family sharing family responsibilities.
Being parents together enriches marriages. Being adults together,
alone, when you still have the physical and psychic strength to communicate, is every bit as important.

8. *Are you able to see beyond specific and repeated conflicts to the
   riverbed of your relationship?*
   "Oh no, not *that* old complaint again! I thought you knew how I
felt about that."
   "Yes, but this time it's different. . . ."

There are positive and negative themes to every marriage. We welcome those that make us feel good, but we feel like complete failures
if we can't remove those nasty marital warts once and for all. Yet according to sociologist and marriage therapist Robert Blood, even the
best marriages are prey to recurring arguments and the same old problems in different guises
   One of the most common areas of parental conflict is the way you
want to bring up your kids. If one parent is more protective than the
other, for instance, their perennial disagreement matures beautifully
along with the child. Should babysitters be used generously, or spar-
ingly? Do we approve of nursery school? Is Johnny old enough at
eight to walk to school by himself? Can we go out on Saturday night
and not have someone stay with our eleven-year-old? Is our high
school daughter old enough to spend a weekend alone while we go to
the mountains? A basically sound marriage can bump along quite
nicely on a pebbly road of dissent and grow stronger in the process,
provided both partners are willing to renegotiate as needed.

Sex after Baby

At a general meeting of a parent support group where workshop
topics were being discussed, one father asked bluntly: "Doesn't anybody want to talk about sex?" His question hit a tender nerve. Everyone spoke at once, leaving no doubt that sex was a major concern of
new parents.
   In our questionnaire we asked, *"How long did it really take you and*

your partner to return to pre-baby sex?" Parents spoke frankly of their
surprise at the difficult physical and emotional readjustments. Many
felt they were alone as they grappled with their problems, especially
since the implicit message of most popular literature on pregnancy
and birth is that, despite doctors' warnings, most of us can't wait to
resume intercourse and often do so after two or three weeks. If we're
still not ready after the magic six-week deadline, we imagine we've
failed each other in one of the most fundamental contracts of our
marriage. Added to feelings of inadequacy, which lead parents to
question their ability to care for the baby, the lack of an active sex
life forces couples to question their ability to care for each other.

My wife didn't seem very interested in sex, which was fine with
me in the beginning. I was so gripped about being a father that I
wasn't at all turned on sexually. Suddenly I felt I had an immense
responsibility, and that I wasn't cut out for it. It was a long while
before each of us admitted our fears and hesitations, and even
longer before we did something about it.   *—Atlanta, Georgia*

After the birth I couldn't imagine resuming sex. I had no interest
and was still so uncomfortable physically. But after the "six weeks"
I felt it was important to try, especially to please my husband. He
was very patient and understanding of my reluctance. He never
forced me. We took our time together and worked on it and after
a few weeks I felt great. I enjoy our sexual relations now more
than ever.   *—White Plains, New York*

My interest in sex after the baby was born was nil. I've never felt
so unsexy in my life and I'm still getting over that almost a year
later. Yet I felt very close to my husband and incredibly grateful
to him for his support and love. Now, though the quantity of sex is
diminished, the quality of our sex life is starting to be better
than ever.   *—New Rochelle, New York*

I didn't fill out this questionnaire for weeks. The sex question
intimidated me too much. It really hit home. So I'll admit it: I didn't
find my wife attractive after she had the baby. She was so preoccupied with her own aches and baby chores that she didn't have
much time for me. It was a good 18 months before we began to pay
attention to each other again.   *—Buffalo, New York*

Our baby was a night waker and we almost never had an

uninterrupted session of lovemaking. I'm not sure we've ever
resumed our pre-baby sex life and our child is now three. I haven't
regained the desire I had before. It's not as good, somehow. . . .
            –Concord, New Hampshire

Some Physical Aspects of Sex after Childbirth

Before blaming your obstetrician or the hospital in general for post-
partum sexual discomforts, or assuming that the pain you feel is a
hypochondriacal reaction to emotional unreadiness and making dire
predictions about your future sex life, look over this list of normal—
and sometimes extremely annoying—after-effects. Sex after the baby
arrives is not always a case of mind over matter.

Episiotomy

An episiotomy (an incision made in the perineum to facilitate the
baby's passage into the world) is, in very plain terms, a wound. The
healing process should take a few days or several weeks, doctors predict. But they're not always right. Since upwards of 95 percent of the
women in this country have episiotomies, you'll do well to know the
side effects. The current medical consensus is that, aside from easing
the baby's passage, episiotomies shorten the time in which a woman's
tissues are stretched. Stretched too severely, tissues may never return
to former tautness, causing another kind of sexual difficulty. But in
those weeks following birth, episiotomies can hurt a lot, and the pain
does not always disappear like a charm. Dr. Robert Morris, chief of
obstetrics at New York University Hospital: "Although we talk about
a six- or eight-week period for a wound to heal, it may not heal completely for several months. In that period, disturbances in the nerve
endings in the cut continue, for the blood supply in that area has been
changed. It takes time. There will be pain in varying degrees. In some
patients it can be over in three weeks, while in others it may take
three months to be free of residual pain. In six weeks, the scar may
heal, but the sensitivity remains. There will be, sometimes, minor
changes in sensitivity over the long term, which are separate from the
wound pain. But it should be remembered that pain is part of the
healing process and at the beginning of sex, whenever that is, there
will be some pain and women should be patient with that."

Some women complain that their episiotomies are too tight, or too
loose. Dr. Morris believes that having intercourse will help tissues

return to normal. "If the opening is tighter in the beginning, in six months it should loosen up, though early sex will certainly be more difficult."

Regular Kegel exercises, designed to strengthen the pelvic floor muscles and, after birth, to nourish injured nerve connections, are a must. They're laughably easy. First, contract the pelvic floor muscles (those of the vagina, rectum, and urethra) for a few seconds, then relax. As you tighten, exhale. As you relax, inhale. Starting the Kegels during urination helps you pinpoint the exact area of importance. While only a few Kegels should be attempted the first time, up to one hundred are suggested each day while the healing continues. If the episiotomy feels tight and itchy, sitz baths, using either a portable bath available in many hospitals and pharmacies, or a tub filled with a few inches of warm water, are helpful. Cool compresses saturated with alcohol may help, but the incision should not be bandaged in any way. Dilators are available for those convinced that a tight episiotomy needs special stretching. Experts are divided about the need for dilators, saying that, while they can help, engaging in sexual activity with a sensitive partner is much more conducive to eventual resumption of intercourse.

Cervical and Vaginal Discomfort

Stretching, the pressure of the baby's head, and lacerations from forceps delivery can produce cervical and vaginal pain. The cervix and vagina are often swollen for several days following the birth, and it takes up to a month before the cervix closes again. During this period, infection is possible. Use of tampons is discouraged. Though uncommon, lacerations can be troublesome. "The entry into the vagina is the most sensitive in terms of nerve endings and stretchability and most vulnerable to lacerations. It's unusual to feel residual pain in the vagina, but it can happen," notes Dr. Morris.

Vaginismus

Some women describe spasms—shooting pains—in the vagina which virtually ruin sexual relations. No physiological basis for vaginismus has yet been discovered, but psychological ones do explain this disagreeable situation. Fear of becoming pregnant again immediately, tension related to the sudden mad pace of new parenthood, increased pressure to perform sexually when body and mind don't feel quite ready—these are all valid reasons for vaginismus.

Dryness

A woman's natural lubrication may seem to have disappeared. Surgical jelly, such as K-Y jelly, is helpful. When hormones are redistributed to pre-partum levels, dryness should become less of a problem. Petroleum jelly (Vaseline™) is not recommended because it is not water soluble.

Nursing

Whether nursing mothers feel more sexy or less sexy during the breast-feeding months is a subject of controversy. Masters and Johnson report in *The Pleasure Bond* that sexual desire is stronger "because now you have a greatly increased vascular supply to the pelvis." Some women occasionally experience orgasm while nursing, and, of course, constant stimulation of the breasts can be an erotic experience. Even so, other aspects of nursing discourage sex. Some women leak so much milk during the sexual act that romance disappears. Breasts may also be larger than normal, heavy with milk and sore from baby's sucking. A common complaint is an absence of sensitivity in the breast and nipples, as well as a failure of the nipples to grow erect when stimulated. Whether this is a physical or psychological problem is not known.

Vaginal Discharge

"Some women may have bleeding for upwards of six weeks, sometimes two or three weeks beyond. The physician may or may not feel the woman should begin intercourse because of the possibility of infection. Another question is how the couple feels about having intercourse when the woman is staining," says Dr. Morris. If it bothers you, just wait. The bleeding will pass.

Absence of Orgasm

Both psychological and physiological elements can eliminate orgasm for many months. Meanwhile, the body is returning to pre-pregnancy hormone levels. This, as well as the conscious and subconscious adaptation of the parents to new roles, affects resumption of orgasm.

Sex and Your Psyche: An Interview
with Dr. Shirley Zussman, President, American Society
of Sex Educators, Counselors, and Therapists

Q: How common is sexual dysfunction after the baby arrives?

A: If you're talking about intercourse, sex is reduced considerably. If you mean the many other activities that are possible, there doesn't have to be deprivation. It depends on your definition of sex. In all the fairy tales and story books, the baby brings happiness. A couple I saw recently had a common problem: the husband was jealous after the birth of the baby. Before, the wife paid attention to him. When he came home from work, she was available to him. I don't even mean sexually. They sat down to dinner together. He told her all his troubles. She told him about her work day. Now he comes home and what happens? They're both tired. There's less time together—less time for sex.

Q: When should a couple ask whether their sexual problems are more than transitory and seek outside help?

A: If, at three years, sex hasn't been worked out to the satisfaction of both parties, there's some problem there that should be looked at. It's no longer just the baby. The decision to seek outside help should rest not so much on the time, though, but on what the couple's sex differences are doing to the relationship. Let's say a year's gone by without much sex. The story could be reversed, but here the husband's very angry and upset. He's becoming irritable, angry. He's yelling at his wife. She's angry at him for not understanding her needs. They've got a problem. But if that doesn't happen for two years, that's fine, too. The problem is often most uncomfortable for the person who would like sex. Look, if you never had sex again and were satisfied with that, then it's not a problem. But in the context of a relationship, it usually *is* a problem.

Q: How important is it to talk about subjects other than baby right from the start of parenthood?

A: Extremely important. Sometimes, parents may believe they are relating to each other, but there's an artificiality about it. The baby not only becomes the focus of interest, but the element holding the couple together. On the other hand, babies are fascinating.

Q: What are some of the psychological reasons for a woman's lowered interest in sex after baby?

A: For new mothers, there is an undeniable emotional bond or tie to the baby that satisfies a lot of what sex tends to satisfy beyond the sexual element: the closeness, the feeling of being needed by another person. This can be very positive. The negatives related to caring for baby are the demands, the fatigue, and the presence of another person—the husband—also asking for something. The emotional attachment is so invested in the baby that there's very little available for other purposes, sex among them.

Q: So fatigue can play a major role in dulling a new mother's sexual interest?

A: Fatigue is an enormous factor and should not be underestimated. But it can also be a copout. Women who have not been interested in sex—and there are many people who don't have a strong sexual interest—now have an excuse. The baby is right there as a demonstration of your involvement. This can make the partner very guilty. If the mother is nursing, and she says she's tired—"Not tonight"— he feels like a bad person. She's so obviously occupied. He may not be doing much to help at this stage and feels guilty to even ask her for sex. There's rarely any other communication about it, unfortunately, such as direct questions like, "Is it really fatigue? If not, can we work this out?"

Q: What are some common masculine reactions to sex after childbirth?

A: Some men express the thought that the only reason the wife was interested in sex at all was to become pregnant, that she had no real interest. He says, "Now that she's turned off, I know what she's really like." This idea is expressed quite often. The husbands feel deceived. Then, there are men who, after the baby, lose interest in sex. As soon as the wife becomes a mother, she's in a different, taboo category. The man sees her as non-sexual, like his mother. This is called the Madonna/Prostitute Syndrome and is much more common than recognized. It doesn't even have to happen with a

baby. Marriage alone can produce it, and it's hard to overcome
since it's related to childhood feelings about the man's mother.

q: Are men more likely to have affairs during the post-partum
period?

a: Masters and Johnson make the point that in the post-childbirth
period, as in pregnancy, there is more marital infidelity.

q: Can a close father-infant bond help the sexual aspect of
marriage?

a: Babies are very sensual. There's a lot of touching you do to them
and they do to you. And they're not afraid. How many grown men
would like to be like that? In our society, men are very restricted
when it comes to touching or any direct physical expression separate
from sexuality. But hugging, touching, and kissing the baby encourages that behavior in men. A father's close contact with baby
breaks down some of that inhibition men have felt since childhood.
But fathers often feel less involved. When the mother breastfeeds,
he can't participate. He can give the baby a bath, but feeding is the
essential contact at the early stage of the baby's life.

q: Can the increased pressure some fathers feel as providers take
away from desired couple closeness?

a: Men are pushed at that point to take advantage of opportunities
to increase earning power, to alleviate all the expenses attached to
childbirth, to facilitate buying a house. Couples are definitely more
frightened by inflation now and they are trying to push as hard
as they can up the career ladder. In many cases, this detracts from
the very thing most young parents want today—to share the baby
care. But they can't have it both ways. They can't have it all. They
have to set priorities. If a man wants to father more completely,
to be part of this shared process, his career has to be looked at
differently. If a wife wants the father at home, helping, in most
careers that would mean some adjustment. The same holds true for
the woman's earning power.

q: One respondent to our questionnaire wrote, "I think I deserve
more out of life." She felt cheated materially, emotionally, sexually.

a: More of what? That's the big question. This is a common problem in sex therapy. For instance, the mother may want the father

home more to help. Or he may want to spend more time with the
baby but he's working to buy that new car. It's all a matter of
priorities. Each couple has to decide what's most important: to
share the baby care, to be together more, to have more time and
energy to make love, or to be doing other things.

Q: A common belief is that the togetherness engendered by
parenthood enriches marriage.

A: What often happens today is that a couple with a new baby is
together more than they've ever been—and more than the relationship might tolerate. Night after night you're there together, while
going to the ballet, for a walk, to a meeting used to be the norm.
Often you did things by yourself. Suddenly you're thrown together
all the time. That's a big strain. Couples have to learn how to do it.
All this togetherness can turn people off to some degree.

Q: Short of formal therapy, how can couples begin to work out their
sexual differences when they are new parents?

A: First, by thinking about that overused but necessary word:
communication. If tension exists between people, and it does
inevitably at some time during most relationships, confronting the
problem instead of burning up inside is important. Share the feelings with the purpose of trying to understand each other's reasons
for resentment, rather than accusing each other. After that, say,
"Well, what can we do about it?" To begin to be physical again,
a couple might just lie together naked, without any attempt in the
beginning to have intercourse. Just touching, caressing, stroking
each other. In sex therapy, we often leave out genital stimulation
in the beginning. Even if a woman doesn't want intercourse, she
wants to be held. She's giving a lot already. She wants something
in return. She's on call, so to speak, for that baby. So it is nice to
have somebody massage, caress, and stroke her and not ask anything
of her. In turn, she could offer that to him, and go on to some
manual or oral stimulation. Maybe that's all it can be at that point.
Gradually, a couple could move to more direct sexual relations.

Q: What are our responsibilities to our mate during this difficult
time?

A: The person most involved in the baby's care—usually, the
mother, still—has to recognize that the father has needs, too. It's

one thing to say that "the baby takes all my time," but, literally, it's not true. And wherever there is some help available—neighbor, sitter, relative—it should be accepted. Avoid the martyr complex.

Marriage as a Framework for Sex

"Nothing good is going to happen in bed between a husband and wife unless good things have been happening between them before they got into bed," according to William Masters and Virginia Johnson in *The Pleasure Bond*. In the early months of parenthood, when couples grapple with complex role transitions, sexual matters are apt to assume an almost adolescent importance. Think of the parallels with our earliest sexual experience: the absence of spontaneity, the danger of interruption by a third party, fear of pregnancy, and a self-consciousness about what we're doing. These very real concerns can't be treated as some sort of adolescent relapse, though. Too many people are honestly baffled by the rearranged perspectives of their couple relationship.

But sex and how able we are at it as new parents isn't a problem separate from the rest of our lives. The way we behave toward each other during the day—whether we keep promises, respect mutual needs for dependence and privacy—the general affirmation of ourselves and our other as parents and spouses surely carries over into the bedroom.

Sociologist Robert Blood reminds us that love isn't some transient, ineluctable thing, but "attachment over time." In the long run, knowing and feeling the specific nature of our attachment, and placing sex in a framework of love, companionship, cooperation, and compassion, we'll pull through.

Is Intercourse All There Is?

Sex researchers, therapists, and marital experts overwhelmingly urge new parents to discover the breadth of their physical relationship, to explore dimensions perhaps overlooked before. So conditioned are we to equate intercourse with ultimate sexual expression that we come to believe it is the *only* worthy sexual expression.

Counseling several young couples in *The Pleasure Bond*, Virginia Johnson insisted that rigid ideas about sex are destructive, that "sexual expression isn't necessarily a matter of yes and no, to bed or not to bed." Johnson and others believe it is much fuller: "It means reaching out just to touch, drawing close to share a mood, developing it or letting it drift. It means enjoying the sexual *feelings* of the moment without necessarily turning them into an invitation or a request or a command."

4

Single Parents, Stepparents

THROUGHOUT THIS BOOK, we've stressed the importance of parenthood as partnership. Yet each of us realistically faces the prospect that traditional father-mother-child relationships may take a different form. Statistics bear this out: half of the nation's marriages end in divorce. In the past ten years, more than nine million women have assumed head of household responsibilities—an increase of 90 percent. The number of single fathers with custody has increased by 70 percent. And consider the men and women who describe themselves as "single parents by choice" who have never married and may not reside full time with partners.

Social historian Christopher Lasch, in his book *The Culture of Narcissism*, observes these changes in the way we live: "Both men and women have come to approach personal relationships with a heightened appreciation of their emotional risks. . . . Although in some ways men and women have had to modify their demands on each other, especially in their inflexibility to exact commitments of lifelong sexual fidelity, in other ways they demand more than ever.

"For many reasons," Lasch contends, "personal relations have become increasingly risky—most obviously, because they no longer carry any assurance of permanence. Men and women make extravagant demands on each other and experience irrational rage and hatred when their demands are not met."

While we have come to accept the fact that some contracts, like marriage, can be broken, others, such as parenthood, are irrevocable. "There are two kinds of divorce: those with children and those without," writes lawyer Michael Wheeler in his book, *Divided Children*. The first major challenge facing a separating couple who are parents is how to reconcile their new separateness with their ongoing mutual commitment to their children. Our purpose here, as elsewhere in this book, is to help you, the separating couple, to evolve parental patterns with which you both can live.

Acknowledging the New You

At this vulnerable time, who are you, then? You're likely to think of yourself more in terms of what you're not: you're not married, yet you're not single; you're not part of a family, or so you believe; you're not a success at relationships; you're not approved of, nor accommodated; you're not part of the mainstream. Or are you? Statistics indicate you are, in fact, part of a growing social reality—one American child in every seven currently lives in a single-parent household; in New York City, the ratio is one in every five.

Sue Jones, executive director of New York's Single Parent Family Project, and the single mother of three, summed up the initial confusion of the recently separated: "While the numbers of single-parent families of all kinds are increasing, stereotypical images die hard. The dismantling of unfavorable images and the negative labeling of families—use of such terms as 'broken homes' or 'deviant'—is only a beginning. Attitudes must change if single-parent families are to be considered 'worthy' of support. *This change must first take place in single parents themselves.* Many single parents, and through them their children, accept a flawed image of themselves as families and often accept the guilt for problems which they encounter. They see the presence of problems in their lives as evidence of their own incompetence, inadequacy, and sometimes as a deserved consequence of having failed to construct the 'ideal' way of life."

Both custodial and non-custodial parents are prone to feelings of inadequacy, and parents who leave home *without* the child can feel special isolation. Simona Chazen, who directed a Rockland County, New York, post-divorce parent program, describes clients who, as non-custodial parents, "feel unnecessary and can't understand why they are important anymore" to the family. It's so dangerously easy to think of your ex-spouse as being the head of your ex-family, especially with preschoolers too young to make independent contact. So the parent who is alone feels "They're getting along without me," while the custodial parent works overtime to solidify that impression, often at great personal cost.

"Whenever one person attempts to perform any task intended for two, there will be some buildup of pressure, some shortcutting, some time constraints, and probably a feeling at some point that the task is impossible. For those parenting alone, carrying the roles of nurturer, breadwinner, manager, chauffeur, nurse, companion, guidance counselor, and playmate can create this same kind of pressure. 'Easy over-load' is the term which has been used to describe this state for single parents," Sue Jones of the Single Parent Family Project said in a re-cent speech. "Regardless of income level, racial or ethnic background, or gender, there is a delicate balance that exists in single-parent fami-lies—the breakdown of any carefully arranged support can cause a domino effect, collapsing other supports and jeopardizing a function-ing family unit. This breakdown is often cited as evidence of instabil-ity and indifference (if not pathology), unless one understands the precariousness of existence for single-parent families."

The trend toward joint custody arrangements, or at the very least a form of co-parenting in which both parents are involved in child-raising in meaningful ways, provides an answer for both overburdened custodial parents and those who feel disenfranchised. Before talking further of the ways of sharing parenthood, let's consider those funda-mental role patterns established long before the breakup but which contribute to overload and alienation later on.

Some parents, and, let's face it, many of these are fathers, have never learned to be active participants in their children's lives. Having practiced a passive parenthood in which they reap the benefits of fam-ily life—the sense of belonging, especially—without playing a direct nurturing role, they remain equally passive during the separation process and even welcome the absence of further child-related respon-sibilities. The truth is that many separated fathers have to do much more parental work than they ever did as married men. Because they just don't know how, they feel lost and disconnected. In order to re-main a part of the family, the father must do no less than create a new *home* (*not* a hotel room) where children's needs can be accom-modated, and must set aside regular time to see the kids.

Other parents—and the truth of the matter is that many of these are mothers—have gobbled up the entire parental pie, willingly or un-willingly. From the baby's birth they feel they have what it takes only to change diapers. In these cases, it's actually possible to gain a better balance *after* the separation, when subtle emotional contracts solidi-fied during marriage are open to renegotiation. Here again, both par-ents are going to find their own style of living and of childraising. While there must be some continuity for the children's sake, parents who insist on oneupsmanship are depriving themselves of vital support and the children of their birthright. It's important to clean the slate of nagging adult conflicts so that the job of raising the children can go on. For instance, if one parent says to the other, "Johnny needs to go to the doctor," and follows up with "Why don't *you* take him for a change? You never did before," past squabbles and inequities will be repeated. Instead, try, "Johnny needs to go to the doctor. Will you help me out by making the appointment and taking him?" By being specific, the other parent will understand that "helping out" means more than paying the bill. It also informs the ex-spouse that, whatever his/her parental style, "helping out" is welcome and needed. Admitting that can be hardest of all.

Agreement on how to help and when is particularly significant for single mothers who, after all, constitute the largest group of custodial parents. Many of the persons she must relate to only because of her children—pediatricians, teachers, Little League coaches, Scout leaders—often have strong stereotypical opinions about "broken families." Some even exhibit strong sexist feelings about the mother's perceived lack of competence. Having an ex-husband appear occasionally at school conferences, a visit to the doctor, or a ballgame can help a mother handle her "public relations" role and let the child know that there are two parents.

Divorce and Small Children

It is common for the parent who is leaving the household to believe that "dropping out," however temporarily, is best for everybody, that having to work out a new parental framework is more difficult than leaving altogether. This is a short-sighted view.

Psychologist Richard Gatley, divorced when his youngest child was still in diapers, told us that in a divorce involving the very young "the father is *expected* in many situations to stay out of the picture and can be reasonably worried about whether he will be able to do *any* fathering at all unless he claims his rights from the start."

Despite the promise of joint custody, legal and cultural supports and responsibility even today remain weighted on the side of the mother. It is she who will usually win custody of a preschooler. But even if your child is small—too small, you believe, to even remember a mother or a father—she will be much bigger soon, and parents must look to the future. Postponing involvement in the childraising process to some nebulous future time is dangerous for the father because he may not be able to win back confidence in his skills later on; for the mother because when she wishes for more independence, her status as custodial parent will already be solidified.

The critical realization facing newly divorced fathers is that "they have to get on with the *job* of raising their kids, rather than agonizing about the divorce," Richard Gatley continued. "All of the practical arrangements—finding a place to live, care of the children, career decisions, and time planning—will fall into place more readily when a father makes the decision to remain an active parent." This realization is most vital to those who haven't been partners during marriage, fathers who have to do an awful lot of catching up. Women, too, have catching up to do, especially those who have become out-of-touch with family finances and the job market. Custodial arrangements can have a far-reaching effect on dual-career couples. For instance, any parent holding a job with irregular hours may find it necessary to take stock of career objectives at this time. Parents are often surprised to learn that responsibilities that were not spelled out in the marriage contract, like shared child care, can work well as part of the divorce contract.

How to Break the News to Your Kids

Talk to your kids at their maturity level. While sparing them the cruel details of your separation, tell them the facts. Reassure them that both of you still love them and that they are in no way the cause of the breakup. Be prepared to repeat these facts many times. It's equally important to tell children all the details of their new life as clearly as possible: where you will be living, when you will see them and for how long, what you will do when you are together, where they will stay when they live with you—all those things that encompass their new reality. The smallest children have no trouble understanding that both parents are still their only mommy and daddy—even as they create other relationships with adults.

Telling Family

In a childless separation, couples can present their decision to their own parents as a *fait accompli* and can assume that as adults they have the right to make independent decisions. This is also true, to some extent, of parental divorce—except for one consideration: Your parents are also your children's grandparents and may have some legitimate demands to voice. If they've been involved grandparents, most likely they will want to remain that way. If you are the non-custodial parent, it's also possible your own parents will initially blame you, overtly or subtly, for being the weak link in the family chain.

For grandparents, just as for you, the greatest fear in the divorce process is the unknown. You'll be doing them a favor by revealing your separation plans *when you have some visitation specifics at least informally worked out*. Therapists find that not only do many grandparents have some inkling of the downhill course of their child's marriage, but that they also tend to side emotionally with their own offspring, even if it's hard for them to show it. If this is so, it can be a great support at a time when a grown child needs allies. But it can also backfire if grandparents criticize the other parent, especially in front of the children. Insist that your parents be aware of their negative remarks and when and to whom they make them.

Some grandparents assume that one adult will serve as the clearinghouse for all arrangements, information, and celebrations. If this is not the case—if both parents will be actively involved—it's advantageous to make that clear early on. If the father has weekend custody, for instance, it makes sense for grandparents to make weekend family connections—phone calls, cards, presents—through him. Channeling grandparental contact in this way also serves as tacit acknowledgment and support of the non-custodial parent's continuing role.

The parent who has been the clearinghouse will be happy to be off the hook. It's basically unfair for an in-law to turn to the divorced spouse of his/her child to learn about details of that child's life not related to grandchildren. After all, divorced parents have a lot to lose if they even *appear* to gossip about one another.

Finally, grandparents in more than twenty-five states now have the right to petition the court for visitation privileges with grandchildren. Arranging for grandparental access to the kids should, however, be more than an afterthought. The appropriate time to make these plans is during the divorce proceedings.

Telling Friends

Reactions of friends to your divorce may strike you as having ironic similarities to the way they accepted news of your impending parenthood. Some friends will be supportive and understanding, others will feel threatened and will identify almost too strongly as they struggle with their own unspoken relationship problems. More to the point, your upheaval is changing their lives, too.

One sobering thought: friends fall away as you pass through the stations of life. When you had your child, a natural realignment of relationships occurred, and that meant losing some people in the course of a *happy* event. So losing friends in the unhappy situation of divorce is hardly surprising. Barbara White, a single parent and family group leader living in Buffalo, New York, points out that you will see less of some married friends with children "because your divorce is a direct threat to their coupleness. It means that children are not a guarantee in the 1980s that a marriage will stay together. They may try to re-couple the single parent immediately, to 'make you back' to what you were before your divorce. Or they may just slip away. But some of them will eventually come back, and if you cherish their companion-ship, welcome them back. In the meantime," White says, "try invest-ing your energy in other single friends, with kids and without, either formally, through an organization, or by exploring your neighborhood. I've found these people more than willing to be supportive."

Therapists point out that while friends do serve as valuable allies, those who attack your former spouse are not always working in your best interests. Last, don't be ashamed to ask for help from friends who express their willingness to donate time and expertise in practical and emotional ways. If your separation occurs right before Thanksgiving, for instance, don't stoically turn down an invitation to spend the holi-day with them. (But don't be too disappointed if it doesn't happen, either.)

The Decision to Separate: Evolving Patterns

"Most people go through extended periods of preparation for the event, whether they are aware of doing so or not," write Richard Gatley and David Koulack in *The Single Father's Handbook.*

"The preparation may take weeks, months, or even years. . . ." The pre-separation period may be characterized by a subtle but growing distance, increased but unproductive fighting, or the construction of an independent other life outside the family. Underlying all this is a strong sense of denial. "For couples with children, the potential dan-gers of separation are likely to appear greater and may generate even stronger efforts to deny the seriousness of difficulties or to maintain the marriage in spite of them," they write.

Linda and Sam worked hard to share parenthood from the start, and even as emotional distance grew between them they were able to con-tinue their mutual attachment to their three-year-old son, Derek. But as the silence and tension increased at home, Sam found it less painful to spend longer hours at work and to cultivate friendships outside the family sphere. Although Linda was able to get paid help with her pa-rental responsibilities, Sam's withdrawal heightened her resentment.

She silently promised that he would pay for his absenteeism. As the months wore on, Linda made Derek more and more inaccessible on those occasions when Sam did want to see him. By the time they were ready to sit down with a lawyer to formalize their separation, the patterns were pretty well set. While Linda negotiated for full custody with vague visitation rights, Sam conceded on almost all points. In the chaos of reordering his life, he was relieved to be free of parental responsibilities *temporarily*.

Psychologists and single fathers Gatley and Koulack would recognize Linda and Sam's situation as a typical state of separation shock. "A sense of disbelief and a feeling of unreality separates each of them, not only from one another but from the rest of the world for a time," they write of this typically divisive period. "Perception is limited, with a sharp focus on personal needs for survival, especially for the one out in the cold. A preoccupation with the seemingly insurmountable emotional and practical problems may further numb or narrow thinking processes. And a sense of catastrophic loss may vie with a feeling of release from the long conflict. . . . With a narrowed perspective, you won't be able to foresee things that will matter to you later."

Divorcing parents who are willing from the start to settle differences either on their own or with the help of an arbitrator before the actual divorce are statistically less likely to need the court to untangle post-divorce custody differences. A Wisconsin study found that 52 percent of divorced parents in their sample returned to court within two years —more than half of them from two to ten times. In childless divorce cases, not surprisingly, only five percent of the couples returned to court. In California, a law mandating mediation in all divorce cases where custody is contested is also viewed as a symbol of good faith on the part of parents by the court. As one lawyer put it, "Courts like plans."

Here are some fundamental facts to help separating parents understand what they'll be getting into, and what they'll be getting out of, when they prepare to divorce.

⌐ So-called "temporary" custody arrangements, legally formulated or not, are very often translated into permanent decisions in court. In other words, the precedent is set early.

⌐ Parents are not required by law to hire legal counsel. Do-it-yourself divorce is a viable option. If a lawyer is retained, fee schedules start at about $100. Naturally, a complex, messy custody situation will cost much more than an arrangement worked out beforehand by the couple.

⸰ There are two distinct forms of what is known as joint custody. Child custody expert Dr. Doris Jonas Freed, interviewed in an article in *The New York Times*, calls joint legal custody "a sharing by both parents of the important decisions affecting the life of the child," while joint physical custody is "a sharing by both parents on an equitable but not necessarily equal basis of the residential care of the child." While joint physical custody, the "pure form" of the arrangement, is an impracticality for many parents, joint legal custody is desirable for parents who want very much to remain involved in the future of their child and, according to one Santa Monica, California, court study, one good way to reduce future custody-related parental squabbles that end up in court.

⸰ A term for joint custody that seems to go beyond the physical and legal custody issue is *co-parenting*. An attitude from which an arrangement is worked out, co-parenting is best described by Miriam Galper in her book *Joint Custody and Co-Parenting* as a tacit parental agreement that both parents "are intimately connected to one another through their children and that they respect the other's relationship with those children. . . . Some people feel that they co-parent even though the time they spend with their children is far from equal. For those people, a shared sense of responsibility may transcend time allotments."

⸰ In some states, mothers no longer can expect automatic custody just because they are mothers. Yet the notion of maternal superiority continues in many courtrooms, as do other traditional factors of custody consideration such as moral fitness, parental health, parent-child sex matching, homosexuality, unmarried living-together status, and unresolved custody battles. Other elements for discussion in court are the child's own family relationships and his school and community ties. A recent court ruling prevented one mother with custody from moving to a distant city where the father's access to his child would have been severely limited. The court found that the job offer the mother had received could be duplicated in her own community.

⸰ The clearer the terms of visitation at the start, the less likelihood of parental conflict and dissatisfaction later. Payment of child support during visitation periods is also an area that should be negotiated up front. That means that if a child spends the summer with his father, it's best to arrange beforehand whether the father will have to continue support payments to the mother, even when he has the child.

⸰ By law, parents are obligated to support a child financially, yet in most divorce situations the standard of living of both parents is apt to drop precipitously—as much as 30 percent for the non-custodial working parent, much more for the custodial parent. In cases of joint physical custody where two households have to be maintained, it's even harder to make ends meet. Obviously, the parent who continues to participate actively in a child's life is more likely to care where child support money is spent. Michael Wheeler suggests these financial support guidelines:

✓ Write cost of living adjustments into the agreement at the outset, based on possible escalations in the providing parent's income or on some other basis.

✓ If the parent providing financial support suspects the money is inefficiently or improperly spent, direct billing from schools, doctors, and the like is acceptable.

✓ If child support is irregular the court can arrange for payroll withholding at the providing parent's place of employment.

✓ While it's impossible to foresee all of the special financial requirements of a very small child, some early legal commitment to life-enhancing extras, from music lessons to braces on the teeth, is wise and humane.

Third-Party Mediation

A group of 20 single parents met for a panel discussion of alternatives to courtroom dispute settling. One of the panelists asked how many parents were still on speaking terms with their former partners. Fewer than one-quarter raised their hands. The results of the adversary system perpetuated by lawyers out to "win" cases for clients were painfully clear.

With increasing frequency, men and women who have experienced first-hand the combat of divorce see the adversary system as potentially cruel and destructive and ultimately counterproductive. The mother who wins sole custody along with alimony, the house, and the car too often ends up losing something more vital: her ex-spouse's care for their child over the long term. Indeed, divorces achieved through the adversary system are more often challenged in court later on by parents unable to live with harshly meted out dictums.

In 1981, California passed the country's first mandatory mediation law in cases where custody is contested. Where estranged couples would have gone directly to court, they now meet with counselors to draw up revised divorce plans in more benign surroundings.

Who are these mediators? They are people with relationship training and expertise in mental health, psychology, and law, whose job it is to work out agreements *cooperatively*, if not always amicably. They are as concerned with parental emotions as with the legal implications of divorce. More important, says Richard Gatley, "they know how to help families separate in ways they will be able to live with *indefinitely.*"

The Family Mediation Association, located in Bethesda, Maryland (see our *Help* chapter for address), serves as a clearinghouse, referral service, and training center for professionals in this new field.

The system works like this: the third-party mediator meets with both parents in a structured atmosphere. All points relative to the divorce are negotiated, not argued. The final document, either a separation, divorce agreement, or post-divorce renegotiation, is later checked for legal correctness by a lawyer and, when necessary, sent to the court for approval.

When Child Custody Disputes Escalate

Under the Parental Kidnapping Prevention Act, signed by President Jimmy Carter just before he left office, states conforming to the Uniform Child Custody Jurisdiction Act are compelled to enforce custody decrees that other states have imposed. Though the Child Custody Jurisdiction Act is currently a voluntary statute, 44 of the 50 states currently comply, and the American Bar Association is among those bodies lobbying for total state subscription. Additionally, the new law makes location of parents and children easier by requiring states subscribing to the Parent Locator Service, an arm of the Federal Office of Child Support Enforcement, to hook up to a national computerized information service. The service aids federal law enforcement authorities and the courts in search of wayward family members.

In the past, parents who abducted children during protracted custody disputes were frequently viewed by some courts as perpetrators of "custodial intereference" rather than of "child stealing." The Parental Kidnapping Prevention Act provides that the United States Attorney's office can be called on by one state to issue a federal fugitive felon warrant for a parent who has taken a child to another state.

Often, it's not custody that's the problem between former spouses, but custody *payments.* The Census Bureau recently found that one-third of all mothers with custody were not being paid child support. In the last few years, however, the Office of Child Support Enforcement (OCSE), 6110 Executive Blvd., Rm. 900, Rockville, Maryland 20852, has been working with the individual states to improve the situation. Laws are on the books that allow authorities to take possession of property and garnishee wages of parents from whom support payments are not forthcoming. The Internal Revenue Service helps by supplying records to trace parents who have disappeared. Cost of the OCSE service is about $20 if a case is undertaken.

Tips for New Single Parents from Veteran Singles

1. *Treat yourself to lots of babysitters.* "Single parents, even more than couples, need time to go out by themselves *without* their children. Otherwise they become overloaded with constant care duties. In order to give 'good time' to their kids, they must be relaxed. You can't be relaxed if you're on call 24 hours a day."

2. *Don't try to be both mother and father.* "Little things, like putting on the pajamas at night, something your spouse used to do, you're going to have to do yourself. You're going to have to do *everything* yourself, but trying to copy your ex-spouse's style is awfully hard. It's better to develop your own way of doing things, even if it takes time."

3. *Don't be bashful about accepting help when it's offered and going out and hiring help when you have to.* "Having people coming in and doing even little things is a relief. I remember when my son was an infant, if someone would volunteer to do something as simple as putting him in his car seat, it was an unexpected and welcome gesture. If you are a single parent with an infant, doing everything yourself can be a real burden. I also suggest not trying to act the part of martyr to friends, ex-spouse, etc. You'll just tire yourself out."

4. *Don't denigrate the other parent in front of your child.* "An old friend of mine who was a single father would continually badmouth his former wife in front of his kids. He referred to her as 'she' and used only the most disparaging language. The kids wanted to be on his good side, and they'd nod approvingly and laugh nervously, and I used to wonder if they felt it was wrong to love that other 'awful' parent. So when I was divorced, I vowed not to hog my kids' affection. When my wife and I had cooled down enough to speak, we agreed to try not to talk behind each other's back."

5. *Be choosy about which adult sexual companions you want your kids to meet and to befriend.* "How my new male friends relate to me is one matter; how they relate to my children is another and just as important. I personally don't like my guests to try to play out instant parental roles either by being overly affectionate or by being the disciplinarian. I'm especially careful if I know the person is someone I don't plan to know for any length of time. When the children become

attached, and the new friend suddenly disappears, they can begin to think, 'It must be me. *I'm* making him go away.'"

6. *Remember that Daddies (or Mommies, Uncles, and Aunts) are not interchangeable.* "I was seeing a fellow for a long time and the relationship was serious, but not to the point of marriage, when my three-year-old asked, 'Is this my new daddy?' I explained to him that his own daddy, whom our child saw every weekend, would always be his daddy, and that my present partner, even if he were to marry me, would be 'Mark,' his friend."

7. *Set consistent, specified visitation rights.* "The general phrase used in law is 'reasonable visitation.' When I heard that phrase, my hackles went up. My lawyer and my wife's lawyer assured me I'd be able to modify the hours as soon as I got back on my feet emotionally. But that seemed risky to me. I'd heard of too many parents who used visitation as a weapon against the other parent. I didn't relish using my child as a pawn. Today, knowing I have Allison every weekend and on Wednesday nights means I don't have to continually renegotiate my rights every week."

8. *Maintain communication about parenting issues with your former spouse.* "Even if you really hate that person, you should know what he or she is thinking and doing about the task of raising your child. When my daughter told me that her father let her watch TV until 10:30 P.M., and why was I so strict, I realized my former husband and I hadn't really talked about synchronizing our points of view. Bedtimes, basic discipline—it's all worth talking about. I think of it as basic information sharing, and even though I don't like to have the man in my living room, it seems to work just by talking on the front steps. I tell him what's bothering me about Doreen, and he tells me of the progress of his fatherhood. If she's been unhappy all week at my house, he should be prepared, and so should I if things haven't gone so well at his house."

9. *Don't rob your children of grandparents and other important relatives just because your marriage is over.* "It seems that the person who has custody most of the time gets to choose how much to relate to the in-law grandparents. At first I felt a responsibility to do so and took the children to see them in another city. Then I realized that my ex-spouse could help out here. I very clearly spelled out that the kids liked his parents and that he should take on the responsibility of keeping that relationship alive. This also served to let my ex-spouse's parents know that he was still very much the father of their grandchildren. They had been worried about that, but when they saw him in action they changed their minds."

10. *Be prepared for subtle condemnation in your community, from your family, and from your child's school. Don't accept these put-downs as your due. Be assertive, and never apologize for your situation.* "After my divorce, I felt bashful about sharing my situation with anybody new. And I was meeting new parents through my four-year-old's expanding circle of friends. The few parents I did mention divorce to seemed uncomfortable, so I became progressively more paranoid. I even considered moving to another neighborhood where I heard there were more single people. But that would have meant sacrificing the services of my present community, which were definitely more family-oriented. I realized my daughter and I comprised a family ourselves, however small. We needed a good nursery school close by, a playground, and, yes, even other families around us. When I accepted our situation for what it was, I knew I would be accepted for what I was—a single mother. This was an insight I gained when I joined a single parent support group."

Romance and Remarriage

More than two-thirds of divorced parents become sexually active again within a year after separation from a spouse. This is not to say that "the majority usher a parade of lovers through their bedrooms," wrote Susan Muenchow, a research associate at Yale University's Bush Center in Child Development and Social Policy, in *Parents*. On the contrary, Muenchow cites research that casual sexual encounters rather quickly disappoint women and in the long run fail to satisfy men. What most single parents are really after, it seems, is intimacy.

Still, Muenchow, herself a former single parent now remarried, does not belittle the problems single parents have reconciling new romances with responsibilities to their children. "On the road to intimacy there may be some one-night stands," she writes, "and intimacy itself is hardly a guarantee of a long-term commitment." Furthermore, while single parents are usually counseled to exercise discretion in their sex lives, Muenchow adds that, in some cases, "single parents are not facetious when they say that the only way they can make time for both children and a lover is for all involved to live under the same roof." Even the most cautious single parent, she observes, may find the "well-entrenched image of [herself] as the poor, abandoned—but still responsible—single parent" in need of renovation.

We talked further to Susan Muenchow about the sometimes painful, sometimes joyful, process of reaching out again after divorce to discover meaningful relationships with other adults and children.

Q: Describe the isolation you must have felt as a new single parent.

A: What I remember most was not the isolation of living alone so much as feeling alone while still married. Even before I was a single parent, I felt like one. When I was finally alone, there was a sense of relief. I was able to set the pace of my own life, to find friends I needed, to talk about my circumstances openly. When we were still living as a couple there was the possibility that we might get back together and I didn't feel free to talk with friends about my life.

Q: Being alone can serve to clear your head, so to speak?

A: Yes. It can be a way of treating yourself to new experiences, such as doing things for yourself, taking time once a week to spend with other adults, time apart from romance or children. It can mean meditating on your crisis, if you perceive it as such. When I was first separated, I decided it wasn't the time to put a lot of effort into my work. Instead, I used the time to read and think and be with my daughter and to keep track of my dreams. I nurtured myself more than I had before—or ever have since. If I had remained a single parent, my rhythms and priorities naturally would have changed with time. I would have felt the need eventually to put more emphasis on my career. I was lucky to have a support group built into the cooperative daycare arrangement I used. These people are still my best friends and my daughter's best friends.

Q: When marital upheaval occurs and a very young child is involved, can parents become so caught up in marital discord that they miss part of the parent-child process?

A: Yes. I think many parents find it difficult to delight in the love of a demanding infant when they are so acutely aware of the loss of a spouse's love. It is hard to give when you are caught up in your own loss.

Q: The spectre of losing custody of children hangs over many living-together situations between divorced people. Is this fear justified today?

A: If a father were trying to get custody of the children in certain areas of the country where living together was still considered less than ideal, that information might be used against a woman—the mother—in particular. But today, I think, most parents in urban areas are more worried about what's going to happen to their children emotionally if they live with somebody. For instance, one parent was worried because her 12-year-old son was in the same class as her lover's son. She found that potentially embarrassing. If she and her lover started living together openly and it did not turn out to be a long-term relationship, it would be even harder to explain to her child, especially since he was in the throes of adolescence.

Q: Can single parents establish an adult social life without hurting the child?

A: The first step is to admit that it's okay for parents—single or married—to have a life of their own. We know about the isolation faced even by married parents and it is much more intense in single parents. So it's doubly important to insist on some sort of adult life apart from the children, whether it involves sex or not. Sometimes single parents immediately expect the person they're dating to be a very good friend if not an instant parent substitute to their children—almost as a condition for any further friendship, much less romantic attachment, on the adult level. I don't believe that's a very good way to approach it. You first have to have something going between the two of you. Even if you are a child's biological parent, part of being a good parent is to love the other parent. Children may be jealous, but they also benefit from the security that their parents have some life of their own. A child should not have veto power over his parents' love life. That's too much power for a child.

What discreet romance really does is protect you from questions you're unprepared to answer. Discretion may become more important when there is an older child. Older children are more aware of the possibility of remarriage, and, in some instances, are more apt to try to disrupt it. Discretion is not just to protect your child, but to protect yourself and the potential of your new relationship.

Q: Can children become the scapegoat for the lack of romance or sex in the life of a single parent—or of stepparents?

A: Yes, in the same way that many people are told that having
children will ruin their marriages. Certainly everybody has to work
to protect his or her relationship with a partner, but it's usually
unfair to blame children for its failure.

Becoming a Stepparent

Stepfamily living presents challenges unknown and unsupported
by much of society. And unfortunately, too many remarrieds . . .
embark upon stepfamily life as thought it were a *fait accompli*
or a replacement for first families. Whether the stepfamily looks
like, is mistaken for, or pretends to be like the traditional nuclear
family, its differences are vast. Its dowry includes children and a
web of extra relationships from the past, pulling and tugging at the
family's emotions and security as it struggles to establish its own
identity.   —Elizabeth Einstein in *The Stepfamily Bulletin*

Stepparenthood encompasses many human situations—singles who
marry into a ready-made family; divorced or widowed people who
have their own children when they enter into a new adult relationship;
those who marry a parent with only part-time custody; and growing
numbers of adults whose households merge without a marriage contract. Unofficial statistics put the number of "step" arrangements in the
United States as high as 50 million.

Undaunted by past experience, some 80 percent of divorced Americans remarry within three to five years of the final decree, many of
them into instant stepparental roles. Time and energy to devote purely
to adult matters is reduced from the start, so it is hardly surprising
that nearly half of these new blended family unions fail within five
years. Stated simply, complex parent-child and adult-adult relationships break down under the strain of "divided loyalties, unfamiliar
expectations, and an overriding urge not to rock the boat in a second
marriage," say June and William Noble in *How to Live With Other
People's Children*.

The complexities of stepparenting will vary according to individual
situations, but these guidelines can help newly blended families work
together better.

↗ If you feel the adult relationship is serious and permanent, don't
hide that fact from the children. Give everyone enough time to get to
know one another *before* the knot is tied. If there are two sets of chil-

dren, an adjustment period is crucial if you're all going to live in one house peacefully.

↗ When remarriage is planned, tell the children, and not at the last minute. Sometimes people are so wrapped up in the adult relationship that they gloss over the child's adjustment, especially if parent and child live in a joint custody situation. Still other people feel embarrassed or guilty or ill-at-ease with their own impending remarriage, and hesitate to tell their offspring. The results of evasions affecting parent-child understanding may be not only initial hostility on the part of the children, but a later attempt to undermine the adult relationship, either by refusing to acknowledge it or by trying to break it up.

↗ Don't rush to formalize the union at the expense of the child's wellbeing and hope to sort out feelings later. If the marriage is a sudden one, talk straightforwardly to the child, on a level he or she can understand, about what day-to-day life will be like in this blended family. June and William Noble suggest a "pledge to the child, in whatever way seems most natural and most comfortable, that the attachments and the involvements the young person has already formed will not be threatened."

↗ There's no substitute for candid adult conversations about your perceptions of family life, parent-child responsibilities, discipline, lifestyle, schooling, division of housework, and the place of the couple relationship within the blended family. Don't assume these elements will fall into place naturally without being directly addressed. "If you don't work out some of the problems you had in your first relationship, you better believe they're going to come up again the second time around," counsels Jeanette Lofas, president of the Stepfamily Foundation in New York.

↗ Some single parents embarking on a new union are torn between wanting to share their child with the new stepparent and protecting her when the stepparent tries to exercise authority. Stepparents should be given the chance to exercise discipline as it has been formulated by the couple, together. "First there must be agreement on how discipline will be meted out," Jeanette Lofas suggests.

↗ Resentment and testing of the stepparent by the child is common, as are the child's persistent efforts to reunite his natural parents, even when they have married others. The stepparent who is afraid to act like a parent simply encourages the child's fantasy that his natural mother and father will soon be together again. But Jeanette Lofas and other stepparents agree that trying to be a "real" parent when you are in a step situation is unwise. "You don't ever get a new father. You have only one father and one mother," Lofas told us. "There are no ex-parents, and children need to understand this."

⌐ When two families merge, it's not uncommon for there to be sub-divisions along blood or loyalty lines in a competitive situation. A couple may be torn between a cherished adult relationship and allegiance to children. Do you discipline all the children in the same way? Follow one family's rituals over another? Divide household space in an equitable manner? Choose vacations democratically? Large blended families don't always co-exist as harmoniously as "The Brady Bunch," but neither do nuclear families. You must pay attention to, and be honest about, coalitions.

⌐ Just as in natural parenthood, stepparenthood embodies many "illegal" feelings, including jealousy at the living proof—the child's presence—that your spouse has had another important relationship. Without wanting to, the stepparent may act out these unacknowledged hostilities on the child. On the other hand, it's also quite possible to dislike the child on personal grounds and the stepparent has a right to feel this way. In any case, the fantasy of parenthood for step as well as natural parents is frequently shattered by reality. Very often, sharing these illegal emotions, in a support group or through individual or family counseling, is necessary.

Stepparents fall prey to two common misconceptions: that the only "real family" is a nuclear one, and, that by working overtime, they can replace the natural parent. Parents are not alone in these fantasies. Until recently, many therapists treated stepfamily problems no differently from those of their nuclear counterparts. In addition, stepparents often engage in a painful struggle to earn a child's love, not realizing that zeal alone isn't enough. The Nobles, stepparents themselves, are particularly outspoken about this misguided love quest. "Perhaps the word *love* should be stricken from a stepfamily's lexicon. Since the family situation is artificial, even at best, we might do better to lay aside the emotion-fraught words *love* and *devotion* and substitute *like* and *respect*."

The New Adult Relationship

In a marriage that includes stepparenthood, of course the kids are important, but so are you. The *primary* reason for a long-term adult relationship should not be to provide a parent for your child. Those couples who work out step-related problems share "concerns for the other's children, each offering what they can and feeling grateful for the help of the other," write Jeanette Lofas and Ruth Roosevelt in their book, *Living in Step.* "There seems to be a common secret to their success. The couple has put themselves first. This means that, when there's a question of priorities, each spouse understands that the needs of the couple come first. The couple also understands their obligations toward the children and can meet them more successfully because of their commitment to each other. Husband and wife have put their ex-spouses behind them. They're a team, and they gear up together to cope. They're open with each other; they trust each other."

Observing several stepfamily situations, Michael Norman, reporting in *The New York Times Magazine,* said this: "The new extended families that survive, and more of them do than do not, are held together by people who have created their own rules and models and who have reexamined their ideas on love, marriage, and parenthood. Many remarried couples say that with the passing of their first romance, their first marriage, and birth of their first child, they also lose their innocence and their illusions about family life. They go into their new families with psyches that are often bruised and marked . . . aware that their new family groups are much more complex than the ones they left. . . . The roles change and shift and tangle, and the family that survives is one in which the members are able to sort things out."

Communication is the key. When the couple hasn't got it, when the children are unsure how to use it, the new blended family is in trouble. "One's ability to function as a stepparent is very much dependent on how one feels one is doing in the eyes of one's spouse and stepchildren," the panel of psychiatrists who wrote *The Joys and Sorrows of Parenthood* argue. "The growth of confidence in one's new role as stepparent is highly influenced by the feedback from the family."

What Stepparents of Pre-School Children Should Know

✓ Adults acutely experience the trauma of divorce. So do children, but they are not always able to express their confusion. "For this reason, little kids are often not especially likeable," Jeanette Lofas told us. "The more they begin to like the stepparent, the more they feel the conflict of loyalty: if I love you, my stepparent, it means I don't like my mom. The stepparent needs to allow the child to understand that you will never be his mother, that your relationship to him is different, and special."

✓ Guidelines for discipline in the new family must be formulated between the couple, with the biological parent taking the forceful frontline approach at first. What Jeanette Lofas calls a "whole rule," rather than dribs and drabs of a half-baked philosophy, should be presented to a child. "These children need adult authority and adults often don't want to take the responsibility for administering it. The aim should be *loving* authority, *loving* guidance, *loving* expectations. Structure equals love. At what age can a child start to assimilate this information? Authority is understood at birth."

✓ A supersensitive stepparent who has been trying hard to make connection with a child can be devastated when the child says, "I hate you." Jeanette Lofas: "The stepparent should respond that you don't like me probably because you're missing your mommy or daddy. He should stay right there with the child, trying to establish a rapport on some level, and saying, 'Okay, so you hate me . . .' Pretty soon the reason for the hate will come out. But a stepparent should never tell a child what or how to think or feel."

✓ Many new stepparents today have never before been parents and are pressed into service utterly without practice. If you are one of these brave people, give yourself time to become acclimated to a new life. Though younger children are often more adaptable to family change, they're also much more dependent on parental help and less able to give you the recognition you need to make you feel accepted. Sharing feelings of inadequacy and ambivalence with your partner is a big help.

✓ If you are a weekend stepparent and do not care to see the children every weekend, don't be afraid to take off by yourself, for a few hours, a day, or more. Not only will you reduce the pressure you feel to be a gung-ho instant parent, but you will clear the way for your spouse and the children to reunite without tension.

What the Kids Should Call You

✓ Don't force a child to call you "Mom" or "Dad."

✓ Don't force the use of "Stepmother" or "Stepfather," terms with historically negative connotations.

✓ Allow the child to use your first name, if he wishes, and later on combine your name with "Daddy," as in "Daddy Fred." This will distinguish you from the child's natural father, who remains just "Daddy."

✓ Rather than trying to convince a child that you are a replacement parent, and as such, imbued with the same powers, describe yourself as the "male or female head of this household."

5

Lifestyle

PREPARING FOR parenthood, most of us ponder the big questions: Am I up to the responsibility? How will we manage our finances? What is my theory of childraising? How do I feel about role sharing . . . surrogate caretakers . . . dual-career parenthood? While these questions are all pivotal to the way we shape our lives and the lives of our children, the day-to-day concerns of early parenthood bring us down to earth with a thud: rushing out for groceries . . . rearranging furniture . . . having company . . . finding sittters—coupled with major practical decisions, such as moving or taking a vacation. In this chapter we'll cover topics that may seem obvious or mundane, but they oil the wheels of everyday life so that coping goes a lot more smoothly.

Getting Out of the House

Seventy-five families joined a community "winter playground," an indoor drop-in center for housebound infants and toddlers and their parents. Each family paid $50 for a five-month membership covering the coldest winter months, and the majority agreed that morning hours would be optimal, since spirits, energy level, and predictability seemed to decline as the day wore on. Although centrally located, and open five mornings a week through the lunch hour, the indoor playground drew fewer than twenty regular customers, often no more than four or five parents and children on a given day. When asked why they hadn't been seen for months, absentee parents would almost invariably reply, "Much as I'd like to, I just can't seem to get out of the house before two!"

Nancy always does her housework in the morning . . . Peggy just can't get her act together before eleven, and by then the baby's ready for lunch and nap . . . Mark gets caught up with phone calls . . . Phyllis schedules all her must-do errands for the morning . . . and Martha is simply too depressed about her isolation to counteract it.

Getting out of the house in the first months of parenthood is both a blessing and an ordeal. There is a tangible need to change surroundings, to meet other parents, to touch base with the world, and, of course, to mail letters, buy groceries, fill a prescription. Going out is a prime antidote to post-partum depression and one of the minimum daily requirements of parenthood.

While there's no rule about morning outings, we've found that parents who *start* their days in a confining, oppressively duty-bound, or, conversely, depressingly disorganized manner, usually *end* their days feeling more tired, martyred, and isolated.

We recommend starting your day with an outing, even if it means you'll be more tired when your child naps—which she'll be more likely to do predictably after a little fresh air.

Next to simple inertia and disorganization, the biggest obstacle to going out in the first weeks is *fear.* Maria was terrified of the steep steps in front of her building and wondered how she would maneuver that huge carriage without spilling its contents. She also had a dozen nameless and unidentified fears: that she would be vulnerable as she pushed the baby carriage across the street; that a child on a bike would cause an accident; that the street noises would frighten the baby—you name it. Recognizing her own terror, she realized that she needed to feel the baby closer to her on outings, more protected. Carrying the baby in a front pack was the answer until she felt more at ease with the carriage.

Parents whose infants are colicky have admitted to being ashamed of sharing their eternally screaming youngsters with the outside world, and parents of twins resent the side-show quality of the attention they attract, not to mention the practical aspects of readying two babies. New fathers also have to wrestle with the public face of parenthood. Going out alone with an infant is, even in this liberated day, a statement of parental, marital, and sexual philosophy. Finally, many of us simply feel strange—surreal, disoriented, and disembodied—as we walk through familiar streets, run into neighbors, drive the car.

Looking back wryly over the first few months with each of her two children, one mother admitted, "My first baby was made of glass, or at least that's the way I treated her. If it was drizzling outside, or too cold or hot, or too close to her nap, or too soon after a feeding, I'd stay home rather than go out. Molly was on a terrific schedule, but I was a self-righteous wreck. When Jeffrey was born three years later, I had no choice but to loosen up. Molly went to nursery school rain or shine, and that often meant waking Jeffrey up from a nap, bundling him into a front pack, and braving the storm. I learned with Jeffrey how resilient glass can be. Now the one piece of advice I have for new-parent friends is this: just pretend you have *two* instead of one. Your decisions will be a lot more balanced."

The Peripatetic Parent

How to Make a Quick Getaway

A well-stocked *diaper bag* is essential equipment for getting out of the house. If you have it packed and replenished at all times, you can usually make it through the door without that frenzied last-minute search for the missing link to freedom. For infants, here's what you will need:

diaper changes
baby wipes
plastic bag for dirty diaper
change of clothes, sweater, and hat
tissues
bottle of ready-to-feed formula if you're bottle-feeding
clean nipple (wrapped to remain clean)
cloth diaper or washcloth for burping, etc.
pacifier, if baby uses one
rattle, diverting toy

Always restock your diaper bag immediately upon returning from your outing, and change the inventory as the baby grows.

For an older baby or toddler you might want to keep on hand a sealed can of juice, straws or cup, diapers and baby wipes, non-perishable snack such as pretzels or teething biscuits, and possibly a change of pants and socks. A sweater, sun hat, tissues, Band-Aids, and traveling animal "friend" or blanket are also helpful.

Here are some tips for a fast exit:

✓ Keep keys, everyday coats, hats, and mittens on hooks near the point of exit. Don't keep gear in the front hall closet if you and baby leave through the kitchen. Hang coats, stow boots, and deposit keys in the same place when you get home. If the snow suit goes into the laundry, put a substitute by the door *before* your next outing, or return the original as soon as it's laundered and dry.

⸱ If the ordeal of dressing, undressing, and re-dressing your child is what's keeping you housebound during the winter, streamline the operation as much as possible. For short jaunts, a hat, mittens, warm jacket, and, in very cold weather, a lap robe are enough. Snow pants and boots are unnecessary when your child won't be in direct contact with the elements. Buy a jacket or snowsuit with a *good* zipper—one that slides easily, does not catch on fabric, works from the bottom up and vice versa, and has a sturdy zipper-pull. Snowsuit zippers should open all the way down to the ankle. Snow pants should have ankle zippers to avoid shoe removal. If you do a lot of baby carrying, look for winter wear made of non-slippery material, especially if you're wearing a nylon jacket yourself. Avoid buttons at all costs. If you buy a jacket or snowsuit with a hood, make sure the hood is large enough to cover the head and closes securely under the chin. Have mittens attached to jacket with clips, or strung through sleeves on a cord. If boots are necessary, plastic baggies in the boots help slip shoes in more easily.

⸱ If your child must take a lovey or favorite toy on every trip, encourage the use of a special "outside friend" rather than looking for the one-and-only blanket before each outing. Leave this in the stroller or diaper bag on your return.

⸱ Prepare clothes for an after-nap outing before child wakes up. Set out next day's clothes the night before. Periodically weed out unwearable clothes in dresser and closet so that what you see is what you can use.

⸱ If you use your car for most outings, keep an extra supply of diapers, baby wipes, and other essentials in the trunk.

Getting Out by Yourself

As you and your baby settle into routines, you'll need some dependable outside time alone. Don't feel compelled to fill this time with "worthy" activities to assuage your guilt at having left the child. Doctor's appointments, professional commitments, washing laundry, and running errands are not what we have in mind.

Try this exercise: Take a couple of hours off to just walk. Be aware of your posture and how good it feels to be walking at your own pace. You will probably feel lighter on your feet. You're probably walking faster than you have all week, unencumbered by a bulky carriage or dawdling toddler. Take time to notice everything around you, perhaps in a new neighborhood or street. Savor a daydream, or several long, uninterrupted thoughts. Make sure to notice things you normally overlook during "on duty" walks. Enjoy yourself. You've done something worthwhile.

If you belong to a health club or the Y, use your free time to take an exercise course or to learn a craft. Join a parents support group . . . go shopping for yourself . . . visit the library, or browse through used book stores. . . . If you've always wanted to start jogging, this is the time. Meet your partner or a friend for lunch, but don't feel guilty that you're wasting time or being a self-indulgent parent.

If you can't afford a weekly babysitter, this is the time to join a babysitting coop or start exchanging daytime sitting with another parent. Many Y's have excellent nurseries that accept small babies and toddlers for a nominal fee while parents enjoy Y activities. If you can't arrange personal free time during the day, schedule it into your parental calendar with your partner. Your attitudes are all-important here: last-minute golf dates or overtime should not interfere with the at-home parent's weekly time alone. You will *all* benefit from it.

Babysitters

Probably the most common mistakes parents make about babysitters are waiting too long to find and use them and having too few. We've known parents who say, "When Jenny is old enough to understand, we'll leave her with a sitter." Unfortunately for parents—and for children—sitter awareness does not develop spontaneously, like rolling over or sitting up. A child who has never been cared for by anyone but his parents is less likely to welcome surrogate care at three or four, and less likely to understand why he's suddenly being left behind. Is it some form of punishment?

Other parents who tie themselves in with one sitter usually end up scheduling their adult social lives around her term papers and dating schedule. Even willing grandmas often resent the pressure of being, in effect, responsible for their grown children's leisure. Ideally, new parents should develop a network of babysitters. What kind and how many? That depends on the parents' lifestyle, personality, and pocketbook, as well as the child's age and temperament—and, of course, neighborhood resources. Here are some general guidelines to consider:

↗ Is your child an infant, or one who's never had a babysitter before? Consider an experienced and mature woman or another parent with whom you'll exchange babysitting hours.

✓ Do you go out regularly, occasionally, spontaneously? Do you go out on weeknights or weekends? Do you have many business social commitments that require reliable free time? Do you have subscriptions to theatrical or sports events? Do you stay out late or leave early? Think carefully about the nature of your babysitting needs, keeping in mind that younger sitters have curfews and weeknight limitations, and that some older sitters can't keep up with a very active child.

✓ Do you dislike the hassle of arranging for sitters? Think about getting a regular sitter once a week or once a month, or however often you want to go out. Many young or mature sitters are happy to form such a contract with you. Just make sure you work out terms of payment in case of cancellation.

✓ Can't afford a sitter? Try exchanging with other parents, or joining a babysitting coop.

✓ Are you a single parent? Do you and your partner plan to go out and come home separately? You'll need a sitter who can go home alone.

✓ It's best to have a *variety* of sitters to meet your special needs. Don't limit yourself, or allow your child to become too attached to one person, no matter how likable and qualified. One person just can't meet all your sitting needs.

FINDING A SITTER

A good place to start is your pediatrician's office. Ask the doctor or one of the assistants if he/she can recommend a sitter or a source of local babysitter information. If the doctor has a bulletin board in the office, chances are some of her teenage patients advertise their services there. Parent support groups are an excellent source of babysitter and other community information (as well as offering a springboard for babysitting exchange and coop arrangements). Supermarket, laundromat, church, synagogue, and other community bulletin boards are also excellent sources, as are senior citizens groups, high school and college placement services, and, of course, your friends.

While grandparents are a prime babysitting resource for new parents, other relatives are often equally happy to spend time with your child, although not all of them are comfortable with the term "babysitter." The bachelor brother of a friend of ours was only too happy to spend an occasional free evening with his infant niece as long as the parents didn't use the word "babysitting" for what the young man rightfully regarded as mutual entertainment!

For parents who are just beginning to leave their infant with other adults, peer babysitting exchanges provide the most peace of mind. Leaving your tiny baby with another new parent offers many advantages besides the obvious security of knowing that the sitter is reliable. First of all, it's free. In addition, exchanged sitting arrangements give new parents perspective on their own infants as they temporarily care for another. For many parents, it's the most palatable option at first.

WHEN THE SITTER COMES

If you don't know the sitter personally, have her visit a few days before you go out. Leave the room for a while and let baby and sitter get to know one another. If the child is an infant, you may want to get a more experienced sitter or a mature woman. Ask the sitter about his or her background. Any younger brothers or sisters? What sitting experience has she had? Is the sitter's schedule flexible, and how much notice is usually required? Does she have any regular sitting jobs, such as every Saturday night? Any curfew? If you have pets, make sure to find out whether the sitter is allergic to them. One couple left their son and dog with an extremely capable sitter who had an asthma attack halfway through the evening. Both the baby's and the sitter's parents had to rush to the rescue.

Either at this preliminary interview, or on the sitter's first official sitting job, clearly explain your requirements and taboos. These might include bedtime rituals, phone use regulations, information about your child's habits and personality, safety and emergency measures, and even a glossary of the child's special names for things he might require during the evening. Leave a list of important numbers: fire department, pediatrician, relative or neighbor who would help in an emergency, poison control center, superintendent of the apartment building. Make sure your sitter can work the locks on your front door, and be explicit about fire escape directions and any home hazards to be avoided.

Always leave a number where you can be reached. If you don't know the number before you go out, call in later in the evening. Unless you have more than one phone, you should discourage extended phone use by the sitter in case *you* have to get through and can't. The sitter is supposed to be *working*, and must give the child her full attention.

Let the babysitter know if anyone will be stopping by for any reason. Give her the name of the person, the reason for his or her visit, and any instructions. It's a much better idea not to accept any deliv-

eries or neighborly errands during the sitter's stay and to instruct her
not to open the door to *anyone*.

Discuss the sitter's fees in advance. Is there an extra charge after a
certain hour? Are the rates different if the baby is awake, or if she has
to be fed? If there are two babies?

Leave an adequate snack for the sitter and let her know what food
is off limits, if any. Be very clear about what activities you consider
taboo, such as baking cookies, going out, having friends over, playing
roughhouse, spanking, or smoking.

Finally, it's your responsibility to see that the sitter gets home safely,
especially if it is a young person and the hour is late. Have an adult
take the sitter home. Don't just rely on the youngster's word that
someone will pick her up. If you come home from your outing much
later than you had expected, don't worry about waking the sitter up
to let her know you'll be late. Chances are she'll have a parent worrying about her at home.

It's unwise to put the child to sleep before a new sitter comes. Waking up to a stranger is a frightening experience and one that lessens
trust in both parents and surrogates. Always let your child know when
a sitter is coming, who it will be, and what is in store for the evening.
When the sitter does arrive, it's best not to linger over tearful partings
or show hesitation about going out. Children have a sixth sense about
parental ambivalence, especially when they feel it's their duty to make
you feel wanted at home. Most children who cry before their parents
go out cheer up considerably after the fact. If you are concerned over
your child's crying, call from a nearby phone. Most likely your child
will be playing happily. On the other hand, it's important to watch
for serious clues to a child's unhappiness with a particular sitter.

BABYSITTING COOPS

A babysitting coop consists of parents who exchange babysitting
services free of charge. The advantages of joining a coop are many: a
wide selection of sitters and availablity; the assurance of having your
child cared for by a mature, experienced surrogate; an opportunity to
make new friends and feel a part of the community; the chance for
fathers to meet other children and gain perspective on their own; and
a *free* source of child care.

Still, babysitting coops are not for everybody. Potential disadvan-
tages include the time you must devote to sitting for other families in
order to earn babysitting hours for yourself. This can be a problem for
dual-career parents who already feel overscheduled. Single parents can

run into coop scheduling problems unless they accept babysitting assignments only in their homes. Finally, because a babysitting coop is a collaborative venture, organizational and social problems do occur.

Nevertheless, coops with well thought out (and recorded) ground rules provide one of the best babysitting resources available to parents. Here are some guidelines for organizing a successful coop.

Membership. There are several types of coops, beginning with spontaneous or unstructured exchange agreements between two or three parents. These arrangements work on a "You sit this Saturday, I'll sit next" basis, and usually don't require formal rules or payment system. For those who aren't joiners, and who are lucky enough to know other willing parents, this mini-coop can work well. Watch out for problems such as the tit-for-tat syndrome, in which one family accuses the other of staying out later or being less available. Even without written rules, it's best to articulate preferences and expectations at the start and to keep an informal record or calendar notation of who sat for whom and for how long.

When more than three families want to exchange services, you've got the beginnings of a formal coop. The first thing you'll need is a *membership list* indicating members' names, addresses, and phone numbers, and names, ages, and number of children. Some coops are organized with a secretary, whose job includes keeping and distributing membership lists. This job is often assigned on a rotating basis and sometimes includes other duties such as arranging membership meetings or recruiting new members.

Payment System. Each coop uses its own form of "currency" to keep tabs on babysitting hours earned and spent. A new member is given a specified number of these tokens: painted pennies, paper chits, poker chips, tickets, or whatever the group is using. Each token is worth a specified amount of time, such as half an hour. When the new member needs a sitter, he or she "pays" with the designated currency and earns it back by sitting in return.

Parents do not have to sit for the same family who took care of their child, nor does a parent have to sit at night to pay for nighttime care of his own child. A parent who has ten tokens might spend five on Saturday night, make three on Monday afternoon, spend another four on Thursday afternoon, and so on.

The advantage of this system is that you can go down your list of coop members until you find someone who can sit for you when you need it. This eliminates that desperate fear of not getting the sitter for Saturday night, and makes last-minute plans a parental possibility once again.

Who and Where. Some coop parents like to exchange with a small number of member families they know well and save others for emergencies. Also, if your child is slow to warm up to new people, you might want to introduce her to potential member/sitters during the day. Take your child to the new sitter's house to get acquainted. Stay with your child if you feel that's necessary, and offer to pay the coop member in tokens as a matter of courtesy.

As a rule, evening babysitting takes place in the child's home, while daytime sitting can be arranged either way. If you're a single parent who can sit only during the day or on weekends, you can still use your tokens to go out at night. Some large coops note time availabilities on membership lists as a service to single, working, or joint-custody parents.

When accepting a babysitting assignment, parents should specify whether the mother or father will sit and whether a ride or walk home is expected. Naturally, all coops have their own by-laws and features that evolve within the group, but even the most complex ultimately relies on a *spirit of cooperation* as its driving force.

Having People Over

"I thought getting out of the house was tough," one new mother wrote to us, "but it was nothing compared to having people in. Since I had always entertained lavishly for both business and pleasure, I was dismayed at how exhausting and *un*entertaining my first attempts were. Then came the revelation: I was used to thinking about staging events more than about seeing people. And this just wouldn't do in our new lifestyle, which had a bit more life than style! Now we just think about who we want to see and give them what we have to offer. Our good friends don't care if, as overspent parents, we can't meet former standards or seem ready to doze off at eleven."

Even informal entertaining takes *time, money,* and *energy.* Since these are invariably in short supply through the early months (or years) of parenthood, it's important to think carefully about the who, when, and why of having people over. The early post-partum period is not, for instance, the time to repay social debts. But it is a time when isolation can be a problem. One couple solved theirs with unaccustomed boldness. When their friends called to ask what they could bring on their first visit to the new family, the hosts replied: "Bring dinner."

Neil and Roberta resorted to invitations for finite visits, usually 5 to 7 on Sunday evenings, when they would serve cheese, crackers, sherry, and coffee. As Nicholas's bedtime approached, the evening was drawn to its comfortable conclusion and the guests left to eat dinner elsewhere. Subtle and not-so-subtle hints are in order if your guests don't take the cue. We feel that overtired new parents can be forgiven for making their condition known to overstaying guests. If it's eleven o'clock and you know the two- and six-o'clock infant feedings loom ahead, bring the evening politely to an end.

As your child grows older and your family routine and energies stabilize, you should think carefully about the kind of entertaining that fits into your new lifestyle. Here are some questions you might want to ask yourself:

✓ How much time can we reasonably devote to shopping, cleaning, food preparation, table setting, and other work? Is this time available?

✓ Can we take extra time away from other necessary activities, such as rest, without feeling unduly harried on the day of the party?

✓ Do we have help we can count on before and during the occasion —from partner, babysitter, friends, relatives?

✓ Have we worked out a definite and realistic budget for the occasion? Can we afford it?

✓ What are our reasons for entertaining? To impress guests with gourmet food, flawless presentation, and unruffled hospitality? The emotional aspect of entertaining can be far more exhausting than its physical demands.

✓ Have we reevaluated our previous entertaining style in the light of our new circumstances? Have we thought clearly about what kind of entertaining is right for us at this new stage in our lives?

✓ Do the people we're inviting understand our new situation? How terrible would it be if the evening were suddenly cancelled, interrupted, or cut short?

✓ Do we have a cooperative plan worked out for recuperating from a late and demanding evening, including cleaning up, sharing next-day child care, and helping each other to get added rest?

✓ Are our guests looking forward to spending time with our child or will this be an adults-only occasion? If the latter, have we prepared a careful game plan for last-minute child care and bedtime or do we just hope for the best?

Hospitality and the Parental Lifestyle

It's true even among your closest friends: You can expect some guests to want your kid around some of the time, but you can't expect all guests to want him around all (or even part) of the time. There are many wonderful mixed-age events in which children are a welcome and warming addition. Brunches, picnics, pot-luck suppers, and other all-family parties come quickly to mind. But if you are inviting adults to an *adults-only* occasion, such as a late-evening supper, one of your hostly duties is to have your child well taken care of but out of the way. Here are some suggestions for entertaining grown-ups. (See our *Friends* chapter for additional guidelines.)

⟡ Let your guests know whether your child will be present (as far as you can predict) for the early part of the evening.

⟡ If you keep your child up until guests arrive, remember that the number of hazards increase substantially in adult-oriented situations. Watch out for toothpicks, alcoholic drinks, hot dishes, knives, etc. *Don't* assume your guests will keep an eye on your toddler while you and your partner are in the kitchen.

⟡ Assume that people arriving from a full day's work would rather relax with a cocktail than a kid. If your guests are parents themselves, don't automatically think that they'll prefer spending their evening with someone else's child (especially since they're probably paying someone to take care of their own).

⟡ Even if the guests specifically ask to see the child, it's unwise to keep her up past her bedtime. Chances are they'll see her at her worst. Let them come earlier for the special treat, or schedule a daytime visit.

⟡ Decide *ahead of time* who will put the child to bed, answer crib-side calls, and handle other complaints and crises. Some people hire a babysitter to tend baby while they attend to their guests. This is especially helpful if you're worried that any cries for help won't be heard above the company's din.

⟡ If you can't serve dinner until the child is asleep, make sure to provide plenty of snacks for your guests.

⟡ Don't be surprised if your child has an unusually hard time falling asleep when you have company, or if she wakes up on hearing the added noise and excitement. Try using a noise-masking device such as a fan, humidifier, air conditioner, or softly playing music.

✓ Stay *flexible*. Remember that no parental endeavor is entirely predictable. If an adults-only evening does come to include an impromptu surprise, roll out the highchair and pass him a drumstick.

The Gourmet Toddler:
Or, How to Eat Out Successfully with a Small Child

After the first serene blush of infancy, during which the baby sleeps or gazes quietly as you enjoy restaurant meals, museum outings, and even movies, comes the Rude Awakening. Those of us with colicky infants may already be familiar with the precariousness of early family outings, but even so-called "good" babies usually give their parents a grace period of only a few months to a year.

The active baby who sits up and looks around can still be distracted and, of course, kept seated. But in the break-away stage—when baby wants to move, grab everything off the table, crawl between patrons' legs, or walk into the kitchen for a personal inspection tour—that's when parents begin to segregate adult and leisure activities and usually settle for a burger joint as the only family eating option. This is an unnecessary copout. For parents who want an occasional *good* restaurant meal, a little planning, scouting, and insight into your child's developmental stage and personality is essential.

On the surface, the effort and expense of dining out in a regular (as opposed to fast-food) restaurant with a toddler may seem extreme. We believe, though, that every child can be taught basic rules of social eating at a pretty early age. Obviously, you wouldn't take a one-year-old to a French restaurant, but even a child this small can enjoy finger food at an informal Chinese restaurant, and at the same time be instructed not to throw food or empty the sugar bowl.

The benefits of early exposure to social eating include not only more enjoyable outings for the family, but preparation for visiting friends for dinner, going on vacations, and family holiday dinners, and also the experience of eating as a shared pleasure. Add the special privilege of sharing an adult pastime, especially if both parents work, and time together is otherwise hurried and efficient.

But these savored pleasures come slowly, and most new parents can cite at least one occasion on which they expected too much from a

child too young, too tired, or too hungry. A fast getaway and a cry of
"Put our food in doggie bags, please!" is the only option available in
this situation.

Scouting Restaurants for the Family

Unless your child is an old hand at eating out, it's wise not to pop
into a restaurant that simply looks promising, or even an old favorite
that you visited often without baby. Food quality is only one consideration when dining out with a small child: equally important are atti-
ude (pro-family); atmosphere (moderately high noise level, informal);
service (the faster, the better) and space (adequate space between
tables so your spills and fidgets won't bother neighbors).

There are several ways to effectively scout family restaurant possibilities:

  ⚊ Have a meal there without your kids and imagine how the experience would be as a family.

  ⚊ Ask friends for suggestions.

  ⚊ Call ahead and ask about: highchairs, booster seats, children's
menus, milk and juice, busiest serving times (plan to avoid them), location of rest rooms, reservations and waiting time for tables, salad
bar, whether children are welcome—in short, whatever you feel is important for a successful family meal. Note the restaurant's response to
your questions. It's a good indication of the treatment you will receive
in person.

  ⚊ Rely on family restaurants. These don't necessarily mean fast-food
restaurants or pizza parlors. Many adult-oriented restaurants are run
by and welcome families. These include Chinese and other ethnic restaurants such as Italian, Pennsylvania Dutch, Greek, Mexican, Hun-
garian, and bourgeois French. Many chain steak houses offer salad
bars, which are a blessing for the restless. Smorgasbord and "all you
can eat" restaurants and cafeterias are also a good choice because they
eliminate the food wait and offer a fast retreat if necessary. Don't forget those restaurants you might have shunned as too noisy before
parenthood. You'll now welcome the din as your own family's hubbub
is anonymously absorbed. Finally, many restaurants that don't normally cater to children have a family night, and many more welcome
youngsters with parents during off-hours.

Tips for When You Do Take Your Child Along

  ⚊ When making reservations, let the maitre d' know you will have a child with you. Ask the restaurant to reserve a highchair or booster seat and an appropriate table, perhaps with a little more room and fewer touchables. Often the restaurant will assign you to a waiter or waitress who is especially good with children, or seat you in an area where your noise will be less intrusive.

╭ Remember not to purposely schedule your dining hour with everybody else's. Peak hours often mean decreased patience.

╭ If your child is an infant, take along an infant seat, but don't put it on the table where the child is vulnerable to accidents. Booths are best for this early age, especially for nursing families requiring some privacy.

╭ To facilitate diaper changes and nursing, select restaurants with clean and spacious rest rooms. Changing diapers at the table is taboo.

╭ For babies: take along bottle, juice, small toys, teething biscuits, baby wipes, and a bib. For older children: a few quiet, uncomplicated toys, paper and crayons, a washable toy pet or doll. No windup, electronic, musical, battery-run toys. If your child's favorite truck is enjoyed only with accompanying horn and screeching sounds, give everybody a break and leave it at home. Take a few crackers if your child simply *can't* wait for food. Also, familiar, child-sized utensils, such as a spoon or small unbreakable bowl or weaning cup, may ease the mechanics of the meal.

╭ With all children, timing is all-important. Ideally, the child should be hungry but not starving; rested but not restless. Late dinners or pre-nap lunches are not a good idea.

╭ Clear the table of lit candles, open bowls of condiments, hot-pepper sauces, toothpicks, and sharp knives. Keep hot soup, tea, and coffee at a safe distance. If food is served on super-hot plates or casseroles, ask for an extra, cool plate for your child and transfer his serving in child-sized portions.

╭ When ordering, dispense with cocktails, appetizers your child can't share, and custom-made entrees that prolong sitting beyond any child's endurance. It's more important to be able to finish a meal—no matter how simple—than to rush through an elaborate banquet.

╭ Let the server know which is the child's order and request that it be brought in first. There's nothing worse than seeing your escargots come steaming down the aisle while the child's chicken is still on the grill.

╭ Don't expect *any* child to blossom into a restaurant-goer without adequate preparation and practice. Make it a habit at home to eat as a family frequently. Encourage dinner table conversation and avoid watching TV or reading during family meals. Broaden your child's tolerance for "weird" foods and new tastes by serving a variety of foods at home (this is better nutrition, as well; see our *Nutrition* chapter). Expose your child to the pleasures of social eating by occasionally including her in dinner parties and inviting young friends for special meals. Stress age-appropriate manners at all times.

↗ When you go out to a restaurant, your family's behavior affects the mood and meals of all the other patrons. Firm and *subdued* discipline is an eating-out must. If the child has a tantrum, one parent should accompany him outside or to a rest room for a cooling-off period. Let the *child* tell you when he's ready to make a comeback and then go back to your meal without glowering or holding grudges. If the child continues to be disruptive, however, it's doggie-bag time. The only thing worse than a misbehaving child in a restaurant is a misbehaving child with loud, angry parents who spank or scold in public.

↗ Behavior we consider unacceptable in restaurants: peeking over the back of the booth to stare at, touch, or otherwise annoy other patrons; grabbing or throwing food; running in the aisles, standing on chairs, or crawling under tables; excessive noise; and demanding or rude behavior toward the waiter or other employees.

↗ Don't make restaurant going a test of hair-shirt discipline, however. If you make eating out an enjoyable experience, your child will usually live up to the occasion. Try not to spoil the expectation of what author Corrine Streich, in her New York eating-out guide, *Let's Lunch*, calls "the ceremonies and excitement of restaurants." She adds, "Children also know that in a restaurant . . . the pressure is off about finishing their soup. . . . And they can enjoy their dessert even if they don't touch their spinach."

↗ Going out to dinner with your unmarried college roommate? Don't take the kids. Family dining is an intimate public affair, and unless the friends are very old and very understanding, or very related to you, it can be a disaster.

↗ Fast getaway or not, don't forget to give the waiter or waitress a *generous* tip, especially if there was extra service involved. Also, try not to leave a mess. Clean the strands of spaghetti off the chair, and tell the management about any dangerous spills before someone slips. Your child learns a lot from the courtesy you exhibit in a public situation.

Traveling with Kids

Humorist Robert Benchley wrote: "In America, there are two classes of travel—first class, and with children." Indeed, there are those of us who wonder whether the term "vacation" can be rightfully applied to the process of transporting children to a new place and keeping them amused and healthy once there. Perhaps "change of scene" would be a more accurate term, at least in those first exploratory family holidays. Paul Rosenblatt, a University of Minnesota social psychologist, found in his study of family vacations that marital tension caused by a combination of high expectations and too much togetherness is all too common. And in a 1980 *Psychology Today* survey of 10,000 vacationers, the "family nurturers" were the group "most glad to be home after a vacation," proving, perhaps, that family vacations may be fun, but they aren't necessarily what we're used to!

Yet, as in every aspect of family life, we can survive the ardors of vacationing through a combination of experience, instinct, education, and luck. Add to this, of course, a revision of *expectations*. In the following sections we offer guidelines for getting away from it all, even when you're taking most of it with you.

Planning a Family Vacation

We're conditioned to believe that vacations are either for relaxing totally or devouring new experiences. We certainly wouldn't consider taking sales receipts along to the Bahamas, but as parents we do in a very real sense take the job along. And often the job becomes even more difficult as children respond to new surroundings, tiring journeys, and the general high-key "let's have fun or else" mentality. One couple we know went to a remote Maine outpost with a toddler for a four-week holiday. They came home a week early to get some rest. "We hadn't been there before," they confessed as they stretched languidly on the playground bench. "The terrain was rocky and hilly, there was a dangerous deck on the cabin, no children to divert our daughter's attention, and the beach was inconveniently located. Between the hazards and the hassles, we decided we'd be better off at home. Even so, we had a hard time wrestling with the feeling that Suzie had 'ruined' our vacation. In reality, we had ruined it for ourselves, by forgetting Suzie's needs."

One of the most attractive features of any potential vacation spot, in terms of minimizing parental stress, is *safety*. It's right to be wary of ravines located next to cabin decks, of lakes and streams in the back yard, of unsafe living accommodations. The beauty of a wild environment can soon turn ominous when you have a self-propelled child with you. We're not warning you against a lakeside summer—just reminding you that constant vigilance can be exhausting.

When Roberta and Neil were invited for a yearly weekend at a friend's rural cabin, they declined because the mere thought of policing 16-month-old Nicholas as he most certainly tried to investigate the farm machinery stashed under the porch was enough to make them choose a home-based weekend.

Getting away from it all may not be quite as desirable when you're leaving parental support and routines. In addition to minimizing parental stress, you'll want to think carefully about minimizing parental work. While you may have enjoyed isolation on your honeymoon, and look forward to holidays without much social contact, your child may think differently. Children who can't seem to get enough parental attention at home may quickly tire of Mom and Dad on holiday. And Mom and Dad may eventually yearn for the company of that brat next door to relieve them of some of the responsibility of amusing their own youngster.

Finally, it's wisest to contemplate family vacations with a spirit of adventure, tolerance, optimism, and flexibility. Planning is a must, but overplanning can be a disaster because it presupposes a degree of control no family with a young child can achieve. Also, if certain vacation spots hold a special nostalgia for you, it's best to avoid them. The only thing worse than unreal expectations is a family's attempt to duplicate childless vacations.

Very young children don't know very much about vacations. They will enjoy life or not enjoy it depending on how they really feel at the moment—not because they've been conditioned to regard vacations as somehow better than real life. With the above thoughts in mind, let's turn to a few practical suggestions:

✓ If you plan nothing else, be thorough in your search and choice of accommodations. A quaint country inn with small rooms, thin walls, and childless guests is an uncomfortable vacation spot. At the same time, that tacky motel with the pool, breakfast room, and separate bungalows that you shunned the last time around may be just the thing for your young family. Look for family-oriented lodgings, with some cooking facilities. Even if you don't plan to cook, your child plans to eat, and not always at convenient times. Among the many advantages of a kitchen is the fact that one of you can feed the child breakfast while your partner sleeps, and a fresh supply of milk and snacks can be kept on hand.

✓ If you don't plan to take a crib (or other child equipment) with you, make sure to reserve one way in advance. Even so, you can't always be sure of the quality and safety of hotel-provided cribs. A portable crib is a good investment, minimizing parental stress and providing a familiar, safe place for baby to sleep in.

⟋ Always take along your own crib bedding: sheets, pads, blankets, bumpers. Most places provide larger bedding, which becomes tangled and uncomfortable.

⟋ Inquire in advance about child care facilities. Many family-oriented summer vacation spots, such as dude ranches, farms, resorts, and bungalow colonies, offer daycare, especially if adult activities are on the agenda.

⟋ Consider going away with another family you know well, even if it's not ordinarily your style. You can rent a larger place and alternate child care responsibilities even if you don't spend that much adult time together. A playmate for your child is a special boon, especially in the country. Two couples we know evolved this plan for combining time alone and time together: They rented a large house for one month. Family A went up the first three weeks of the month, while Family B went up the last three. Both families shared the house during the middle two weeks of the month when their vacations coincided. But Family A had the house to themselves the first week, and Family B enjoyed solitude the last week.

⟋ If you plan to vacation with another family, articulate *in advance* just how the vacation expenses, child care, and other cooperative aspects of the trip will be divided. It isn't always wise to divide expenses at the end, especially if eating habits and leisure styles are different. Two cars are also a must.

⟋ Consider taking along a babysitter whose primary purpose will be to watch your baby while you do other things. Let your sitter know exactly when she will be on duty and when on her own, so she also can plan vacation activities.

⟋ Think about swapping a house or apartment with other families who have children. Professional services (see our *Help* chapter) can link you up to families around the world who want to experience life in your home environment.

⟋ Plan your days around the child's schedule as much as possible. Try to keep meals, snacks, naps, and bedtime to familiar routines for the child's sake as well as yours. Even if you previously enjoyed hotel hopping and cramming your days with activities, reconsider your usual vacation pace. Young children usually need a few days to adjust to a new environment, and many become cranky when overstimulated. It's wisest to choose one "home base" lodging and make day trips to surrounding attractions. Try not to fit more than one major activity into each day.

⟋ Next to *pace, balance* of holiday activities is the most important element in family vacation planning. Each day should contain some physical activity, for the child to let off steam, and some quiet time as well—in addition to naps, if called for. Alternate strenuous days with laid-back ones. If you go to an amusement park in the morning, plan a back-yard afternoon. If you are planning a long car trip, consider whether your destination will offer your child some physical release and enjoyment. A two-hour journey to a country auction may be fun for you but torture to a young child who has to remain seated and "good" until the grueling trip home. One family, whose first child was virtually born on their sailboat, spends all their weekends and vacations in the tight quarters of their boat. But they make sure to dock at least once or twice a day, preferably near a park or playground, where their children can stretch, jump, and run around.

✓ The success of your family vacation will depend in part on your child's adaptability to new experiences. If you've sheltered your baby against change, leaving him behind with a sitter while you took weekends off alone, or totally separating adult and family leisure, don't expect an easy transition on your first family vacation. Preparing for family vacations does not merely entail making reservations and packing a suitcase and baby gear. It's a good idea to get your baby used to sleeping in new environments as early as possible, to enjoy eating new foods in different places, to welcome the experience of meeting new people and doing new things. This kind of resilience doesn't develop overnight; it must be nurtured by parents from day one.

✓ *Don't* plan for vacations to be the only form of togetherness your family enjoys. If you go in separate directions all year long, the forced intimacy of holidays will not make up for year-long alienation. Most vacations with a "purpose" tend to backfire, or to be so fraught with meaning and intentions that they become a source of stress rather than relaxation. Do things and go places as a family all year long. You'll reap the vacation benefits after you've had practice enjoying family leisure.

Vacations Alone, and Alone Together

Let's not forget that sometimes it's very nice to get away from the domestic scene altogether. If you need a personal break, consider getting away by yourself and leaving your partner at home with the child. When Nicholas was 4½ months old, Roberta was invited to Wyoming for four days to do a story on the production of a feature film. Neil stayed behind and took care of Nicky with the help of their regular sitter. Roberta got her story and managed to squeeze in some leisure activities—whitewater rafting and swimming—while Neil had special time with Nicky. A few months later, Neil took a similar trip to visit friends on Cape Cod. The next year, Roberta was off to California, then Neil went to Martha's Vineyard. Such vacations don't replace family trips, but they do complement them, especially when trips away as a couple are not practical.

If you are lucky enough to have a relative, friend, or sitter willing to take your child for a weekend or a week, consider a vacation together alone. You're the best judge of when—and whether—your child is ready to be left overnight, but it helps to prepare her gradually for a longer separation. Start small by swapping sleep-overs with a friend. Or, instead of asking a grandparent to babysit at your house, take your child over there, armed with pajamas, lovey, and other sleep-over paraphernalia. Pick her up first thing the next morning to reassure her that Mommy and Daddy do reappear. Next time, come for the child a little later. *Don't* let her sense your guilt and ambivalence about this first long separation. Chances are your child will enjoy the special time as much as you will, provided she's not cued to think otherwise.

Getting from Here to There

BY CAR

✓ Crash-tested car seats, especially those that allow children to look out the window, are essential. What if your child won't stay put for eight hours? The only safe answer is to stop regularly, say, once every ninety minutes, let everyone stretch, let the child run around, if possible, and then resume the journey.

✓ A pillow, blanket, and favorite stuffed animal will help your child get to sleep, but here again the car seat is a must. Use the pillow to help your child's head rest at a comfortable angle. Never put any heavy objects in the space under the rear window, as a sudden stop can send them hurtling forward with dangerous force. Also avoid all sharp objects, such as pens or pencils, lollipops, scissors, or pinwheels. These can cause injury in case of a sudden stop.

✓ In a separate bag which you keep with you, carry lots of toys— palm-sized figures, cars, trucks, crayons, coloring books, paperback picture books. For older children, sticker books are fun and safe, as are follow-the-dots books. Parcel these goodies out slowly. Change the pace when spirits flag. Try not to let your child see exactly what you've got stored away for later, and don't let her curiosity rush you through your supply before you're halfway there. Save the really good stuff for last.

✓ Pack foods that are fun to eat—raisins, small sandwiches cut in amusing shapes, clean fruits such as apples, bananas, and grapes (avoid very juicy or stain-making fruit). Chicken, cheese, and other finger foods are also ideal for car travel, but watch out for nuts, hard candies, and other chokeables. Have plenty of water and juice on hand, preferably with spill-resistant cups available. Thermoses with a special spout for a straw are virtually spillproof and can be refilled from a larger container as needed. Cans, cups, and straws *can* cause injury in case of stops, so it's best to pull over to drink.

↗ If you stop for food, remember that a child who has been sitting in a car restraint for hours can not be expected to weather an elaborate roadside meal as well. Snack bars and cafeterias are not as confining as traditional restaurants.

↗ Take along a small tape recorder with a tape on which you have recorded songs, stories your child enjoys, riddles, whatever he finds amusing. Have the child prepare his own tape a few weeks before the trip. Children love to hear themselves on tape. If you are going to visit grandma, ask her to prepare a special tape describing all the good things you will do and eat on your visit. Your personal entertainment center can provide you with a few hours of fun and make the trip seem that much shorter.

↗ If your child likes to sleep in the car, leave right before naptime, or in the evening. Plan plenty of physical activity in the hours before leaving, even if it means delaying your departure an hour or two.

↗ Car travel games are usually geared for older children, but simple "I Spy" games, peek-a-boo, puppet shows, naming colors of passing cars, and singing songs are all enjoyed by preschoolers.

BY TRAIN

The primary advantage of train travel is that a child can walk around, doesn't have to remain in a car seat, can use the bathroom at will, visit with new people, and possibly find a playmate for the journey. It's also exciting for children to observe the comings and goings of passengers and conductors. Since parents aren't driving, they can take turns playing with the child. There's also much more to look at in the surrounding scenery than on most superhighways.

Be sure to choose a nonsmoking car, even if you yourself smoke (you can take personal cigarette breaks as needed). Many of the suggestions offered in the car travel section can be adapted to extended train rides, including our tips on travel food. The restaurant car is certainly an attraction, and some offer excellent food. But train menus can be costly and you may not want to make more than one or two visits to the restaurant car.

Some long-distance trains will transport your car as well as your family, and, of course, sleeping accommodations are available as well, although often at considerable cost.

BUSES

Buses have some of the advantages of trains, but they are often chilly, more confining, and noise always seems to carry more annoyingly. One big advantage to bus travel is that it's inexpensive and will take you to the heart of just about anywhere you want to go.

BY AIR

Heather Brenzel, a former flight attendant and currently a sales executive with British Caledonian Airways, is the mother of a preschooler. Like all of us, she dreaded her first long flight with baby, remembering other babies' transatlantic tantrums. But she was able to put her inside knowledge of babies and airlines to use and has rarely had an unpleasant experience in her many family trips to visit London grandparents. Here are some of her suggestions:

✔ When you make your reservation, specify that you're traveling with a child. Let the airline booking clerk know the age of your child and ask what services are offered. Available extras often include: bassinets, baby food, baby pack consisting of diapers and other infant needs, and, of course, priority seating. For toddlers and older children there are coloring books, small toys, and membership in the "junior club," which includes a flight badge and an official log of miles the child has flown, complete with the captain's signature. Some airlines even have a special children's entertainment channel available when you purchase the stereo headsets.

✔ Children over the age of two are entitled to a meal, but it's a good idea to take along the kind of food your child prefers. Beverages are usually available free of charge.

✔ Opt for a jumbo aircraft if possible, since there's more space between the seats, less noise, and generally more comfort.

✔ Ask for the bulkhead seats. You get more leg room and the child gets more body room. If you require a bassinet, you will automatically be assigned the bulkhead seat.

✔ Flight attendants will warm bottles, supply extra milk and juice, and help you with other needs. Just ask. One flight attendant is usually assigned to handle the needs of families with small children. He or she will help you with your bags, tend to you during the flight, and see you off the plane safely. Don't always expect this service automatically, however. You must ask for it.

✔ Flight attendants cannot help you once you leave the aircraft, but ground personnel will be only too happy to carry bags and belongings. No airline personnel are permitted to carry your child or assume any sort of surrogate caretaker function.

✓ Choose an airline with a reputation for welcoming children. Two such airlines are Swissair and Air India, and there are many, many more. Ask friends who have traveled.

✓ Flying during peak business hours is unwise. You'll find yourself surrounded by tense, preoccupied business executives and you'll be much more self-conscious. Night flights may be more tiring for parents, but a small child can sleep comfortably on an airline seat.

✓ Some airports have provisions in the rest rooms for changing and nursing babies comfortably. Ask airport personnel if these facilities exist and where they are located.

✓ Airplane bathrooms are not the greatest places for changing diapers. It's safer to do it at your seat, or on the floor if you have a bulkhead seat. Take along a good supply of baby wipes, something to put under baby while changing him, and enough disposable diapers to see you through possible landing delays.

✓ Carry your child's essentials on the plane with you. That way, if your luggage is temporarily lost, it will be merely an adult crisis. However, if you'll be traveling alone with the child, *do* try out your luggage a few days before the trip. In your trial run, carry your purse and on-board luggage, along with your coat, the teddy bear, and whatever else you'll be carting, while pushing your child in his stroller. Don't wait until the eleventh hour to discover you just won't make the grade as a pack mule.

✓ Children often cry on airplane trips because they are frightened or uncomfortable. If your child has never seen an airport before, try making a pre-flight visit to introduce her to the excitement of airports and travel. Watch planes take off and land, and point out other children who are obviously going places. Ask your librarian for picture books about airplanes and travel. Get a toy plane and play airport, acting out exactly what you and your child will be doing from the time you get to the airport to the time you arrive at your destination. Once you're on the plane, take time to explain exactly what's happening. Why is everyone asked to buckle up? What are all those lights dinging on and off? Where is that strange man's voice coming from? When the plane takes off, offer your child some gum or other chewy food, explaining that his ears might feel full for a while but will clear with chewing. Nurse or bottle-feed your infant during landing and takeoff for the same reason. Most of us have never conquered the fear of flying, and some resort to martinis. You can hardly blame your two-year-old for resorting to tears.

Going Abroad with Small Children

Susan and Richard Goldstein had their first child in Turkey, while Richard, an orthopedic surgeon, completed his Air Force tour of duty. Twelve weeks after his birth the Goldsteins and their son Daniel toured the Syrian desert. At nine months, Daniel accompanied his parents through Western Europe and the Mediterranean, staying in inexpensive hotels and campsites.

From Susan's diary of her experiences as a mother/traveler, we culled the following suggestions:

If you've been abroad before, expect a totally different experience on a trip with a child. You'll probably have to forego nightlife, but you will have more daytime hours to enjoy. As in any family travel, try to maintain the baby's schedule as much as possible. If you can't get back to the hotel for a nap, rest at a park or quiet plaza. Getting enough rest is essential for parents as well as children. Rest when your child rests. Don't fall into the trap of "getting your money's worth" through perpetual motion.

FOOD

Your child needs breakfast first thing in the morning, but you don't have to leave the hotel immediately as long as you have the necessary food. Keep dried cereals, bananas, and milk on hand, plus utensils to feed your child before you set out. European milk is now ultra-sterilized and sold in cartons which, unopened and unrefrigerated, keep indefinitely. Bananas are not only sterile, but can be mashed right in the skin and fed to baby without the use of a dish.

"You can eat wonderfully well in Europe without ever going to a restaurant," Susan told us. Each country boasts its own charcuteries and groceries where you can purchase supplies for park bench or hotel room picnics. Familiar brands of baby food in jars are available throughout Europe, as are disposable diapers, dried cereal, and formulas. The nursing mother is at a special advantage, since her milk is consistent, readily available, and free. Europeans have always had a more relaxed attitude toward public nursing, and many European pharmacies are equipped with baby scales—just in case you want to check whether your baby is thriving on his Grand Tour.

EQUIPMENT

For an infant, a sling or other baby carrier is as important as an "umbrella" stroller for getting around. Many parents swear by those metal-framed backpacks, but others find them inconvenient for public transportation. Strollers are great for getting around in general, but many museums won't allow them. If you'll be renting a car, make sure to take your car seat. They're just as important abroad as they are here! Traveling Europe by car has other advantages. You can take a light portable crib and other equipment that otherwise would be impossible to lug around.

Smaller essentials include bottles and nipples, a can and bottle opener, spoon and dish for baby feedings, and a special drinking cup if your baby uses one. A roll of plastic bags fills many uses, not the least of which is soiled diaper disposal. You'll need a clothes line and clothes pins, baby wipes, and adult eating utensils. Take along whatever special blanket or toys help your child to feel secure.

Your first aid kit should include such basics as acetamenophen or baby aspirin, adhesive bandages, larger dressings with tape, antiseptic cream, tweezers, scissors, a thermometer (with centigrade readings), sunscreen, diaper cream, insect repellent, allergy medicine, and diarrhea medicine. Take along cough medicine, decongestant, and any prescription drug your baby uses regularly. A mosquito net, sun hat, and itch potion are also important.

ACCOMMODATIONS

Some European hotels now provide cribs, but usually the small, family-run establishments offer only the bare essentials. Try to remain three or four days in each hotel, making day excursions to surrounding sights. There will be less upheaval for your baby that way. Very tiny babies can sleep in a padded dresser drawer placed on the floor near their parents' bed. The Goldsteins devised an ingenious system for bedding down their active nine-month-old son during their second European tour. If they had a room with twin beds, they placed some padding on the floor between the beds. Then they would take a blanket and tuck in securely under each of the twin bed mattresses, forming a sling that rested on the padded surface between their beds. The baby is not supported by this hammock. His weight rests fully on the mattress you've made up on the floor. But the tucked-in blanket keeps him from rolling under the beds and protects him from drafts. There's no worry about the baby rolling off the high adult bed or keeping you awake with his kicking. And, since he sleeps between the two of you, you can check on him easily during the night.

Always insist on a room with running water, even if you don't have a private bathroom. Use tap water to wash out everything except baby bottles and utensils. You'll want to use purified water for those. Ask your pediatrician for other hygiene recommendations.

EMERGENCIES

The American Embassy is always ready to help countrymen in distress, but it's vital to prepare yourself against the more common crises. Take a first-aid course before your family excursion. If you don't speak the language at all, keep a phrase book on hand, so at least you'll be able to describe your baby's symptoms to a foreign doctor, should the need arise.

Learn how to read maps, and take time to study the public transportation system of the city you are visiting. If you are driving, study road maps carefully *before* you set out. Study the layout of your host city and carefully plot each excursion. There's nothing worse than being lost, harried, and unable to communicate, especially when you've got a baby to worry about.

Plan your spending carefully and stick to your budget throughout your trip. Preoccupied and overburdened parents toting infant and equipment are especially vulnerable to pickpockets and purse snatchers.

Above all, stay loose. It takes a special attitude to travel abroad with small children. You'll probably find a warm welcome in many countries, but you will get the cold shoulder sometimes. Your own resiliency is probably the most important factor in the success of your family's first trip abroad.

The Home Front

Remember that cozy third-floor walk-up that set the romantic tone of your first years together? Of course you do. It's the same cluttered dungeon in which you've just spent a catatonic weekend nursing your croupy one-year-old. The neighborhood nightlife which you used to find so exciting is now the unsettling din that wakes your baby nightly. Your study has been transformed into a cramped nursery, and your closets, never adequate, are now bulging with outgrown layette, carriage parts, portable crib, and a growing assortment of baby paraphernalia. You realize you never spent that much time at home, and now, when you're most in need of light, space, and convenience, you're least able to afford it.

Very few people we know have ideal situations, and those few usually complain about the cost. Parenthood intensifies existing problems and brings to light new hazards and shortcomings, as well as the realization that the experience of parenthood is directly affected by living space. For instance, if your child's bedroom shares a thin wall with the living room, adult entertaining is liable to be a self-conscious affair. If it's overlooking a busy street, baby might wake up earlier than if the nursery opened onto a quiet garden. Rooms facing east get the morning sun. And the noisy preschooler in the uncarpeted apartment above may have more to do with your child's waking and bedtime schedule than all your well-laid plans. We, like most of the parents we know, have learned to make do with shortcomings. There is no way to turn a cramped, two-bedroom apartment into a spacious suburban home, but there are general guidelines for making family space more livable. Here are some that our friends have shared with us.

Familyspace, Privatespace, Kidspace

Before the baby is born we've already established our territorial rights: which side of the bed each of us prefers, favorite chairs, closets, mugs, and desks. A strict division of work, leisure, storage, and display space is important to some, while others allow home space to assign itself more loosely.

When the baby comes, it's amazing how both the loosely and more strictly designated adult space is shaken up. Here again we encounter different styles: some of us like to have an all-pervasive sense of parenthood, while others prefer a separation of adult, family, and child space from the start.

But even those of us who glow at the sight of dried-out baby wipes drifting like tumbleweed across the living room floor are inclined to one day reconsider our need for privacy and personal sanctuary, usually when the child becomes mobile. Is it remotely possible to have a private space in tiny living quarters? Anyone who has ever worked in a newsroom, secretarial pool, or other shared environment will tell you that it's quite possible to be alone in a crowd.

PRIVATESPACE

You don't need your own room, only a well-defined pocket in an area that serves other uses as well—a rolltop or other closeable desk in the living room; an easy chair next to a bookcase filled with your own reading matter; a personal shelf in the kitchen holding paperwork, course material, or other projects to pursue while the roast cooks. Your side of the bed can be expanded to include a lap desk and a night table containing more than just manicure equipment. If you entertain much less than you used to, convert the dining table into a work area, and use the buffet to store crafts materials.

The objects don't make the space private—attitudes do. If your partner respects your need for privacy, your children will learn to follow suit. Furthermore, don't sabotage your private space by situating it in a high-traffic area. Don't put your desk near the TV. Don't keep the Band-Aids or quarters for the laundry machine in your worktable, forcing others to interrupt you with their needs. If your desk is the only place your partner is likely to find envelopes, expect to see her rummaging around unless you provide an alternative source. Finally, children will more fully understand the meaning and value of privacy if they're allowed some themselves. Maria and Jay's son Jud has had his own desk, with appropriate (and frequently replenished) supplies, since he was two. His desk is as inviolable as theirs, and both Maria and Jay make sure to ask before borrowing such items as paper clips and Magic Markers.

Search out unused or underused space—an attic, basement, walk-in closet, or even a corner of a larger room that can be screened off. If you have high ceilings, consider creating a loft-sleeping area with desk space underneath. These are becoming increasingly popular in children's rooms, but they work equally well for adults.

FAMILYSPACE

As your children grow, so do the number and variety of things you'll do together at home. Where will you build that scale model of the Chrysler Building from the kit that Santa brought? Is there room enough to eat as a family in the kitchen, or will it accommodate only one lonely high chair? You wish you did more reading together as a watching TV. Baby's spitups leave souvenirs on the crushed velour, so now you all pile into the nursery because the living room is obviously taboo.

What do you like to do *together* as a family? The specific activities will change from year to year and month to month, but the general uses of family space will remain the same. The easy chair you and your toddler sat in last year to read Richard Scarry will be the same one you'll probably use to go over homework. The formal dining room that was off limits to the toddler will probably remain a never-never

land to the growing child. It's no accident that family rooms are frequently the most appealing areas of those houses lucky enough to have
them. They radiate warmth, comfort, and flexibility. They can often
tell you more about the family—what its members like to do together
and think of one another—than any other room in the house. A family
room that boasts a massive color TV surrounded by big and little
chairs and big and little snack tables offers quite a different portrait
from one decorated with books, toys, half-finished block towers, and
other evidence of doing things together.

For those of us who haven't the space to set aside a family room, the
problems of merging family and adult activties in one room, usually
the living room, become more apparent as our child's energies and possessions grow. Here are some suggestions for modifying existing living
space to suit the new togetherness:

✓ Try not to make family time an unnecessary hardship for either
you or your child. Your family room should be safe enough to prevent
accidents, but it should also be fairly safe against accidents to itself.
For instance, that silk-covered couch and white rug will put an awful
crimp on family time with the best-intentioned drooler. One young
couple thought ahead wisely and returned their priceless Chinese antiques to the grandparents for temporary storage.

✓ This doesn't mean that your former living room has to become
Romper Room. If you prefer not to see toys, children's books, or toddler crafts after hours, devise a storage system right in the room so
you don't have to cart things back to the nursery every night. Do you
like to read together in the living room? Set aside some adult shelf
space for picture books. Are there special toys, such as blocks, that
need the extra floor space of the living room? Store them in a wicker
trunk, or close off the lower shelves of a bookcase with doors and use
this for storage.

✓ Although you will want to clear all surfaces of valuable, fragile,
or dangerous family treasures, keep some appropriate items around for
exploration. A sturdy cigarette box can contain interesting shells and
other discoveries. A lower drawer of a desk can be stocked with all
kinds of safe surprises. Maria filled the bottom drawer of a small living
room dresser with old scarves and hats for dress-up play. Now, at 6½,
Jud still enjoys putting on musical productions in which he performs
with top hat and cane to tap dancing records of the thirties.

✓ Be kind to yourselves. Don't reupholster your furniture in old
sheets or slap down plastic runners marking the "safe" footpaths on
ivory rugs. If family time means constant discipline or uncomfortable

sacrifice of aesthetic standards, you will ultimately resent the tense time together. Find a more suitable spot in your house to be together.

CHILDSPACE

Not all children are fortunate enough to have their own rooms. Many first children, especially those born to city dwellers, are squeezed into the parents' bedroom, into an alcove, or even the living room. Special problems exist for families in these cramped circumstances. Yet, just as adults require personal space, so do kids—a place to put toys, clothing, collections. A place to feel easy in. If your child has only a corner of a room, that corner can be defined as hers. Bookcases, drawings, a small rug, and beloved objects will define the territory. But no matter what the size of the room or the opulence of its furnishings, one of its primary functions is simply to be *hers*. Childspace that works encourages independence, creativity, comfort, and adventure. It allows the child to feel private and safe at the same time.

Mary Stanton, an early childhood educator with a special interest in creating flexible children's space, gave us the following ideas:

↗ Many parents are taken in by the bright, multi-colored children's rooms of magazines. In the long run, over-decorated rooms add to clutter and confusion. Consider limiting yourself to one or two colors at most for all major elements such as walls, furniture, shelves, and toy chest. Then let the toys, changeable posters, and child's artwork provide color, design, and personality.

↗ Stress flexibility and clarity of presentation. In other words, don't spent $100 on a poster that you then consider too expensive to replace with the requested Darth Vader portrait. Hang pictures, including, of course, your child's art work, with adhesive mounting clay rather than hooks, so you won't worry about marring walls as you redecorate them periodically.

↗ If your child has a lot of toys, put them out on a rotating basis, storing the rest on high shelves or in a closet. This not only reduces clutter but heightens the desirability of toys whose attraction stales wih familiarity. Some parents keep a special "sick day" supply of puzzles and quiet toys, or a "cabin fever" supply for the housebound winter months.

↗ Try to create a quiet reading nook with a soft rug and books on an accessible shelf.

↗ Many children love a place to hide—not an area completely out of sight, but one where they can go to be separate, if not isolated. For instance, Jud's reading area is between the foot of his bed and the bookcase, a narrow space he can squeeze into and be alone with his books. When a friend comes over, they both cram themselves into Jud's secret spot.

↗ If you can manage it, provide a clear area for block building or other construction and fantasy games. If the child's room is too small, see if there's another space in the house that can be used for more active play.

↗ A quiet work space with a table or desk, chair, and paper supplies is also desirable when the child is old enough. This area is right for puzzles, drawing, playing office, and glueing. If you don't have a child-sized table, use a tray on the floor or even a large piece of fabric. When the child is finished, you can pick up the results effortlessly. Also, by having a clearly defined area for messy work, a child can learn to stay within bounds and avoid making an enormous mess or losing valuable game pieces and supplies.

↗ Most people underuse upper wall space. Rather than cut down on available floor space by adding still another bookcase, cabinet, or chest, build shelves. You can do this inexpensively with metal brackets and plywood, but make sure they're out of reach, to discourage climbing.

↗ Children hate to look for things and get easily frustrated when sought-for items don't call out "Here I am!" Organize small toys such as doll furniture, small figures, tops, and other odds and ends in see-through containers, such as sturdy plastic shoe or sweater boxes. Hang helmets and play hats on hooks where small children can easily find and return them. Opt for shelves rather than the traditional toy chest jumble.

↗ Make the child's room the safest room in the house. Double the usual precautions of plugging outlets by installing an outlet shield. Avoid metal lamps (which become hot), floor lamps (which tip over), space heaters, electric fans, and the like. Make sure all shelves are secure, all bookcases anchored. Never buy broken or dangerous toys, and discard all toys when they are damaged. Eventually you will encourage your child to play in her room alone. Her independence and your peace of mind go hand in hand.

Children's Furniture. Nobody says a child's room has to have children's furniture—except the manufacturers of children's furniture, of course. David Stiles, an architect, father, and author of *Easy-to-Make Children's Furniture*, believes that you can combine aesthetics, practicality, thrift, and longevity in furnishing your child's room. "I sensed, after going through the marketplace, that children's furniture manufacturers wanted you to buy a cradle, then throw that out; a crib, then throw that out; youth bed, regular bed, and so on. They love the idea of forcing change, and they know that they have a sucker in every parent. There *are* a few things on the market that transform with the child's needs, such as a crib that turns into a dresser. The idea is called retrofitting, from an architectural term for adapting an old space to a new use. So a cradle should become a crib, then a youth bed or couch. That's the ideal example, which unfortunately doesn't exist yet." Stiles supplies designs and instructions for making nursery items inexpensively. All of his furniture is convertible.

Moving

Maybe You Shouldn't

Why, as new parents, do we move so readily? Well, most of us need more space once the baby's born. If we've lost the income of one parent, the other may feel pressured to take an out-of-town job or transfer for a higher salary. The inevitable stresses of new parenthood may heighten existing dissatisfaction with present neighborhood, living quarters, and the behavior of family and friends. Also, the very natural tensions that arise between parents in the months following the birth of the first child have to be blamed on *something*. For couples who haven't learned to be honest with themselves, and with each other, about the "private" emotions of parenthood, being fed up with one's home is an obvious and acceptable scapegoat.

Still, finding a new home, transferring belongings, and settling in is an enormous source of stress, especially when added to the existing rigors and transitions of new parenthood. We've had friends who, already struggling with the added financial burdens of parenthood, took on an impossible mortgage "for a better life." This "better life" is sometimes one in which money for vacations and babysitters, contact with friends and family, and other personal needs are sacrificed, at least in the short term, for bigger and better living accommodations.

Whether you need to move for work, space, or itchy feet, it's important to make a *balanced* decision. When you ask yourself, where do we want to live, also ask yourself, *how* do we want to live—as adults, as parents, as a family?

When considering your main reason for moving, also enumerate the specific tradeoffs you'll be making. Did your partner just get a better job offer 300 miles away? (How does this affect your own career plans?) Are you a dual-career couple planning a move to the suburbs?

(How will the double commute affect your family time?) Thinking about that gorgeous and expensive cooperative next to the park? (Will you still have enough money for such parental "luxuries" as babysitters?) Always dreamed of owning a house in that lovely, manicured community down the road? (Are you willing to give up the friendship and support of other new and struggling parents in your own disheveled neighborhood?)

And, of course, never resort to that supreme copout, "We're moving just for the baby." Children thrive in every sort of community, provided that a few simple requirements are met.

Choosing a New Community: In the City

⟋ Even if you know your city well, don't rely on your pre-baby impressions of desirable neighborhoods. Visit potential areas more than once, and explore them on foot. Is there a park or playground nearby? Is it clean and is it *used*? Who uses the park? Uniformed nannies or parents with their children? Does the neighborhood seem to be family-oriented? Check out the local stores and read the signs on community bulletin boards. Is there a community newspaper? Buy it and read it. Stop at a luncheonette, laundromat, supermarket, candy store. Ask questions, and observe. If you're visiting on a weekday, make sure to come back on a weekend, and vice versa.

⟋ Are vital *services* within walking distance? Is there a competent pediatrician? A public library with a good children's room? How's the public transportation? Parking? Nursery schools? Daycare, if you need it? Parent support groups and family-oriented services such as a Y? Is the public school acceptable or will you have to consider the added expense of private school?

⟋ Is the neighborhood relatively safe, stable, and convenient? If you're afraid to go out at night, at least you don't have to worry about finding babysitters, but it will get you down eventually. Also, if you're staying in the city for museums, movies, theater, and so on, make sure you can get to them easily. Some suburbs are closer to the cultural heart of a city than its outlying urban communities. Finally, urban pioneering takes triple courage and work with a small baby. One couple we know moved to an unrenovated loft in a commercial-turned-artists' neighborhood. The radical chic appeal of their new home quickly wore off when they learned they couldn't buy aspirin or milk on Sunday, were surrounded by childless couples and singles, and were the only tenants on the block who didn't move out within six months! Chic isolation still means being lonely.

In the Suburbs or Country

Drive around potential communities, but get out of your car. Go to a few yard sales and start to chat. Ask about schools, services, and general community spirit. While city dwellers can be especially nomadic, suburbanites are apt to buy houses in which to raise families. In general, houses seem to pass through 15- to 20- year cycles, as children grow up and move away. Are you entering a neighborhood predominantly peopled by middleaged parents with teenage children? Even younger parents with school-age children won't always meet your personal needs for a peer group. Try to find communities where there is a mix of very new families and more seasoned ones.

Commuting is a rightfully hot topic in suburbia. Spell out exactly what the prospective commute will mean for you and your family. Will the working parent have to rise at five-thirty and arrive home after seven? Do buses and trains run frequently, or, if you will be commuting by car, are the roads direct and well maintained? Calculate the cost of commuting, and think ahead. Do both parents plan to work in the future? Will the choice of a home distant from the job market stymie your career plans? Studies have shown that women's work options are often considerably reduced when they become suburban homemakers.

Think about your marital contracts. Will a long commute shortchange your family in terms of time together and the sharing of responsibilties?

Find out what direction your new community is taking. Buy the community newspaper, visit shopping centers, churches, and community centers. Contact the local Chamber of Commerce. Is this a stable, family-oriented community? Is a shopping center slated for that lush meadow down the road? Are taxes climbing sharply? Is the school well attended and acceptable? Is there a country club or other facility your family might enjoy? Are they likely to enjoy you?

If you've never owned a house before, are you ready to start now, when your responsibilities are already enormous? Are you aware of the work and costs of taking care of a house and grounds? Some people have compared owning their first house to having their first baby. You love it dearly, but it can be pretty stressful!

Planning Your Move

If you can time your move, try to avoid the summer months. Many families move during vacation, but if your child is a preschooler, try to find a less crowded season. It's easier to locate a suitable mover and have your belongings arrive on schedule when you're not competing with hordes of summertime place-changers. When Maria and Jay moved across town one summer, the movers were six hours late; their earlier job had taken twice as long as expected. Exhausted and embarrassed, the Laghis were still clattering their belongings into their new building at three in the morning. (Beware: some buildings have strict rules about the use of the elevators for moving. Find out the moving hours and insist that the movers comply.) When relocating with a baby, it's especially important to find a dependable mover. The Interstate Commerce Commission requires all interstate movers to file an Annual Performance Report, which is available to the public. From your potential mover's report you can learn the following:

✓ The percentage of shipments delivered on or before the date specified in the bill of lading contract.
✓ The percentage of on-target non-binding estimates of moving costs.
✓ The percentage of shipments delivered without resulting claims of damage or property loss, and how quickly claims were settled.

The Interstate Commerce Commission is your best resource for moving information. The ICC offers several excellent and informative booklets free of charge.

Once you've decided on a general moving date, get estimates from at least three moving companies. Try to get the ball rolling about six weeks before your planned move—especially if you must move during the summer—and take stock of what extra services you will require:

✓ Do you intend to pack yourself, or have the movers do it?
✓ Do you own antiques, artwork, special hobby equipment, musical instruments, or anything else that needs special handling?
✓ Will you require warehousing of some of your possessions?
✓ Will you need special moving supplies, such as wardrobes and packing boxes?
✓ Will you be moving out of state? If so, you might prefer a moving company with an office near your new home, should any question or problem arise.

Carriers are now allowed to offer both *binding* as well as *non-binding* estimates for your move. The mover will usually charge extra for a binding estimate, but the advantage is that you know exactly what you will be paying at the other end. The binding estimate must include all services you've contracted for, and, to be effective, it must be in writing, with a copy given to you before your move. A copy of the binding estimate must also be attached to the *bill of lading*, which is the official contract between you and your mover.

A non-binding estimate will give you an approximate cost of the move, as calculated by the experienced moving company representative. There is no guarantee that the final cost will match the estimate, which must also appear in writing on the bill of lading and include all the services contracted for. This is for your protection, because when the carrier delivers your belongings, you are required to pay in cash, bank check, travelers checks, or charge card, only the amount of the non-binding estimate plus 10 percent. You will then have at least 30 days after the date of delivery to pay the difference.

The accuracy of estimates depends in large part on you. Make sure to point out *all* your possessions, including lawn furniture, attic contents, and your son's rock collection. Short distance movers most often charge by the man/hour, while interstate movers charge by distance and weight. Make sure you tell the potential mover of any special considerations—such as stairs—that would add to moving time. If charges are determined by the weight of your shipment, the figure is reached by weighing the loaded truck and subtracting the weight of the vehicle.

Movers can be held liable for only some of the damage that may occur to your property. However, there are different levels of liability, which are explained in the booklet, "Your Rights and Responsibilities When You Move," available free from the ICC. You can also purchase additional insurance through your mover or through a private insurance agency.

Be wary of very low estimates. They may sound good up front, but you'll probably end up paying the difference somewhere down the line in the form of unreliable service, failure to deliver your goods on schedule, or damage to your property.

Countdown to the Actual Move

If you've given the mover six weeks notice, then you've still got enough time to prepare your moving game plan. Some people are deadline movers—they will procrastinate for two months, then have a packing blitz 24 hours before M day. Others live with boxes and take-out coffee for six weeks. With a child, neither of these methods is practical. Here are some special pointers for moving with a preschooler.

⟡ Having the mover pack and unpack for you can be well worth the money, especially if both parents work. When the movers pack, they are liable for property lost or damaged in the packing process.

⟡ If you decide to pack, you will want to maintain some semblance of your normal routine as long as possible. A houseful of boxes and "don't touch" clutter is disorienting and dangerous.

⟡ Find one place in your house for the increasing pile of boxes, preferably a room the child does not use.

⟡ Start with items that are not essential to everyday life. Books, for instance, can be the first to go, along with out-of-season clothes, extra pots and pans, and outgrown baby things. If you listen to records every night, packing them six weeks ahead will prepare you nicely for depression. Similarly, don't add to the child's inevitable stress by denuding his room weeks in advance. Leave the child's belongings intact as long as possible.

⟡ Let the child know what's happening and why. Be prepared to repeat these explanations again and again. Explain that everything that belongs to your family will be taken along to your new home, and talk in specifics about what life will be like for your child in the new surroundings. It's quite possible that a very small child may worry about whether he'll be taken along as well. Get a toy moving truck and play "moving." Get an empty carton and show how things that are packed, such as blocks, come out again and look just the same. Ask your librarian for reassuring picture books about children and moving. One such book is *Goodbye, House*, by Ann Banks and Nancy Evans. If possible, take your child to visit the new home, or show him photographs.

⟡ Older children often enjoy maps. If you are driving to your new home, post a map of your route, showing where you live now, where you will live, and how you will get there. Subscribe to a local newspaper, and contact your new Chamber of Commerce for literature and pictures of your future community.

⟡ Sit down with your partner and compile a list of To Dos—a systematic, shared packing schedule that will cut down on last-minute panic. Don't forget to notify magazine publishers, your local post office, your insurance company, creditors, motor vehicle bureau, milkman, diaper service, and utility companies.

⟡ Accept any and all help. A neighbor or friend can keep you company while you pack, so that you have someone watching the child while you concentrate on the boxes. Don't try to pack and supervise a small child. You're asking for trouble, especially since hazards increase as moving day approaches.

⟡ Don't let your preoccupation with the move allow you to relax safety standards at home. Household chemicals have to be stored on a high shelf, and so does a *box* of household chemicals. Don't leave heavy items piled precariously. They can topple and hurt a small child. Empty things are fun to crawl into and climb. Nails and other small hazards are also tempting. If you pack at night, make a safety check before you go to bed. Accident rates rise dramatically during any family upheaval such as moving.

⚊ Be merciless in disposing of your unwanted possessions, but be generous about keeping your child's belongings, even if they seem dispensable to you. Being greeted by familiar things at the other end of a move helps a child's transition to new surroundings. It's a good idea for the child not to associate the move with a sense of personal loss.

⚊ So that you're not overcome at the other end with masses of indistinguishable boxes, implement a color-coding system. Assign one color to each room or person, pasting identically colored labels to the door of each room for easy identification. This is especially important for the child's belongings, which you will want to locate immediately. It's also wise to write more specific content descriptions on nursery boxes. That way you can locate bedding, toys, clothes, and other equipment readily.

⚊ Make sure baby's things are loaded onto the moving van last so they come out first.

⚊ Reserve a closet or corner of a room for all those things that you *don't* want to go into the van. Mark these clearly so that no mistake will be made. Include necessities for the child: crib bedding, favorite toy, change of clothes, diaper supply and accessories, necessary medicine, first-aid kit, baby food and utensils, potty, stroller, and whatever she can't live without. Don't count on memory or instinct when setting aside this family moving survival kit. Make a list of child and adult needs, including road maps, important phone numbers, and your moving papers.

Moving Day

⚊ Moving day is a prime time for accidents. Stacked boxes, sharp tools, open front doors, heavy moving equipment, and busy adults add up to danger. Find a sitter or devise a schedule for child supervision *at all times.*

⚊ Very often movers arrive later than expected, and the process takes longer than predicted. This might mean you'll be at home for two meals instead of one, or that the afternoon nap you thought would be taken en route to your new house will now have to be accommodated minus crib. Arrange with a friend or relative to have your child sleep there if necessary; keep snacks and beverages on hand if your child is staying with you.

Moving In

⚹ Set up the child's room first, making it as familiar and inviting as possible. Although it's wise to get child care help at the moving-in end, so that you can direct the move without distraction, it might help the child to see that those boxes going into his new room really contain the old beloved possessions. Let the child take some toys and belongings out of the boxes if you can, and if he needs reassurance.

⚹ You may be used to moving quickly and unpacking as soon as the boxes are deposited. But with a child, such an efficient schedule, which probably also includes some cleaning and decorating, may be overwhelming. Pace your unpacking so that you can give extra attention to the child, who needs it more than the knickknacks at this point.

⚹ As soon as possible—if the move is local, and it's practical to do so—invite one of your child's old friends to visit. Even a child who is ambivalent about the change is likely to feel proud of his new room, yard, and neighborhood, and happy to see that old friends have not disappeared.

Settling Into a New Community

⚹ Establish credit immediately with local merchants, get check cashing privileges with the supermarket, and open local bank accounts.

⚹ Find a new pediatrician before you need one.

⚹ Mount a street or road map of your neighborhood and learn your way around by studying the map and taking short walking and driving tours.

⚹ Join community groups and establish personal contact with other young families through places of worship, parent support groups, and other family-oriented services. Many busy young parents wait until a depression or crisis brings home their need for a social network. Then they're too miserable to find one. We feel that the best time to make new friends is while you're still on that moving "high."

⚹ Local street fairs, bazaars, garage sales, and other informal gatherings offer an unstructured opportunity to meet new people. If you're not a joiner, be a browser.

⚹ If you're shy about knocking on people's doors, catch them outside, and *you* be the first to break the ice. In the best of all possible worlds, neighbors flock together to welcome new arrivals. In many communities, organizations such as Welcome Wagon serve this purpose. But if you think you've been given the cold shoulder, chances are your neighbor is just as shy as you are. Parenthood is a wonderful common denominator. If you have a child *and* a dog, you're really set.

✓ Remember, you've got a responsibility to your child to make her known to neighbors and ease her way into new friendships. Tell neighbors your child's name. She'll feel more secure knowing those around her don't consider her a stranger.

✓ Never complain about the new community to your neighbors or boast about the old neighborhood's virtues. Even if one of your neighbors is down on the area, refrain from griping about it yourself, at least until you get to know the community and the person better.

✓ Find out about babysitting coops, cooperative nursery schools, daycare centers, and play groups. Enroll your child and yourself in special classes at the local Y. Refer to our directory of parent support groups in the *Help* chapter. If none exists in your immediate area, contact one in a neighboring community. Often, established groups have a file of potential members who are too scattered geographically to form a support group. You might be referred to similarly lonesome new parents near you and start a support group of your own. Two national organizations—The American Society for Psychoprophylaxis in Obstetrics (ASPO) and the International Childbirth Education Association (ICEA)—sponsor support groups nationwide. Contact them for news of new support groups near you. (See our *Help* chapter.)

6

Family and Friends

The Post-Partum Family

Move Over, Everyone. There's a New Baby in the Family

Who says that new parents are the only ones to suffer growing pains when the baby comes? We're convinced that there's at least one universal truth about parenthood: babies shake up family relationships. The tremor may be brief and devastating or barely visible on the familial Richter scale. But the fact remains: *everyone* with an emotional stake in the baby needs time to adjust.

As veterans of family upheavals and realignments, we've come upon another unsettling truth. Though new parents desperately need their family's support and encouragement, it rarely comes prepackaged and ready for consumption. More often than not, we have to *work* at making our family work for us—and that can mean combating jealousy, competitiveness, hostility, meddling, aloofness, criticism, or just plain fear.

Yes, we have become parents overnight, but our transitional problems mirror those of our own parents, who must take on the new identity of grandparenthood. Little brother is no longer the baby of the family. Cousin Betty and her husband, who have been trying to conceive for years, feel bitter and envious despite best intentions. Two sets of parents, now grandparents, compete shamelessly for our attention. A married sister, pushing toward career success, is too busy to come and see the baby. Could she be feeling pressured to start a family, too, now that we've taken the plunge?

We may be too tired and preoccupied to understand our family's often surprising reactions to what is, after all, *our* parenthood. So, for those of us who aren't getting the support and help we expected from our family, the catalog of disappointments begins.

Bottling up these unsettling thoughts and complaints just isn't the answer. "But how can I say what I really feel?" the new parent might ask. "It's hard to find a really willing ear, and embarrassing to pour out my personal woes. Besides, I'm terrible about accepting advice. When somebody tells me what to do, I either immediately think I've made a big mistake that can't be corrected or that I could never be friendly with somebody who knows so much more than I do about being a parent. But I do know that sharing experience is often more important than sharing answers. . . ."

One group of new mothers, members of an informal post-partum discussion group, allowed us to take part in and tape their conversation about family support. Can you identify with any of their experiences?

ERICA: I'm glad we brought up the subject of family, because I'm going through a particularly hard time right now. My mother recently died, and there's so much I wanted to share with her. After the baby was born I got no physical help from her, but I got a lot of emotional support, which I really needed, since my husband and I decided to start our family so late in life. My husband's family—his sister, especially, who lives close by—has given us no support or help whatsoever.

ANNETTE: I've talked to a lot of friends who've felt let down by their families, and frankly I'm amazed. I've always had support and benefited from a very close family network. When I was pregnant I knew they would be there to help. I can't imagine how I would have coped without it.

JEAN: You'd be surprised. Erica's tragedy was pretty unusual, but at least she had spiritual support, which is important. My own mother simply disappeared when Debbie was born. I think she was very upset I didn't have a boy. She already had girl grandchildren. So she didn't come to visit. She wanted a boy to name after my father!

FRANCES: My daughter was my mother-in-law's first grandchild but my mother's fourth. My mother-in-law said to my mother, in no uncertain terms, "This one's mine. Stay away." Just when we really needed everyone's support, Sam and I wound up mediating a childish family feud.

DIANE: Ironically, I'm closer to my mother-in-law than I am to my own mother, who only wants to talk, not listen. When we do talk, we fight. She comes over to help, and I'm waiting for the moment she'll leave. My mother-in-law, on the other hand, lets me be *me*. Maybe because our history together isn't quite so long or complicated.

TRUDY: My parents are both dead, but I have three sisters who are like three mothers to me. None of them has kids, but they all want to babysit whenever they can. They'll drop everything to help me out. A friend of mine got jealous because her own sister hadn't volunteered to sit in three years. So she got brave and called the sister, who said, "Babysit? I'd be glad to. I thought you'd never ask!"

RENEE: Isn't it funny how you sometimes have to "invite" your own family to be a part of your life? My husband's parents saw the baby in the hospital and once after. But the family was so big and the demands on our time so great that weeks went by before they could see the baby again. Finally they blew up. They told us we were deliberately keeping the baby from them. That seemed like a preposterous accusation to us until we realized that they'd just been waiting all those weeks for an invitation. We decided to plan a regular visiting schedule, which has worked out well. They really became grandparents when we told them how much we needed them.

JEAN: You're lucky your in-laws were honest instead of just silently resentful. Mine are like that, I'm afraid. My mother, on the other hand, is painfully candid. When my son was born, she said, "Don't expect me to babysit. I'm too busy with my job, and frankly I don't know anything about babies any more." Much later, after she had fallen in love with him, she admitted how terrified she had been of growing old and being labeled a grandmother. I'm happy to say that in the last few months we've achieved an incredible new friendship. My mother and I have rediscovered each other.

DIANE: That's true for me, too, to some extent. My mother and I do talk more. But let's face it. Babies are a pain in the ass. Some grandparents won't admit it, but they'd be just as happy with a *photograph* of a cute baby, their grandchild, to show everybody at the club. Hassle-free grandparenthood. It's easy to say you love them, as long as you don't have to change diapers or wipe up vomit.

ANNETTE: I just don't relate to that. It's so cynical. I *knew* my family would be there when we had the baby. Both sets of grandparents live nearby, and they get along well. Family functions include everybody. But talking in groups like this, and with friends, I realize my experience isn't the rule. I would say instead that it's *we* who often take advantage of our families.

SALLY: I see those grandmas in the park, sitting with their grandchildren, and I sometimes think it's extremely unfair for them to be there—especially since a few of them have confessed to me they feel their grown children take them for granted.

TRUDY: People in our generation who have careers and babies still see their own mothers as being homemakers who want and need to take care of kids. It's a good old double standard. And then they ask, What's wrong with my mother? Why doesn't she automatically want to stay home and take care of my baby while I work?

ANNETTE: Well, we've done a good job in complaining about how our families let us down, but let's be fair. I think you have to make some decisions about what family can realistically give, and what you want from them. You have to work on these relationships. If it's important to you to have family, you have to nurture relatives, give them time to get used to you as a new family, as grown ups. My son will have 35 relatives at his first birthday party. It's beautiful!

Handling Help and Advice

Do you react to unsolicited advice or meddling by:
a. crying
b. raging
c. getting into an argument with your spouse
d. ostensibly agreeing but secretly doing your own thing when the meddler isn't looking
e. obeying at enormous personal cost—anger, resentment, inadequacy
f. all of the above

Have you noticed? With a baby in tow, we become public property. Shopping bag ladies order us to cover the child's head on an August day; total strangers stop us on the street with observations on child-raising; and, of course, grandparents speak volumes with a lifted eyebrow. Even such phrases as, "You know what's best" can set our teeth on edge, since we are vulnerable and suspicious, way down inside, that we may indeed *not* know what's best but should damn well be given a chance to find out. Like any intangible offense, it's the *principle* that bothers us most. Why can't they treat us like adults, like parents—and that means admitting that some advice deserves consideration, but the rest deserves mature and firm rejection.

But what should we say? Here are some possible retorts to unsolicited advice. See if you can put them in your own words.

✓ "I know it worked for you, but we've given it a lot of thought and feel that this way is best for us."

✓ "I appreciate your advice, but I'll need some time to think it over." Later: "I've thought it over but decided it wouldn't work for us right now."

✓ "I think I understand what you're trying to say, but here are some reasons why we feel the way we do."

✓ "We really need to find solutions that work for *us* as a family, just as you found solutions that worked for *your* family."

Tips on handling advice and interference:

✓ Try not to put down the other person when you defend your own beliefs. Sure, some of their ideas stem from outdated child care fads, but remember that you're as open to parental fashion as previous generations. Swaddling, for instance, has come in and out of vogue with the centuries. Just recently, a major family magazine proclaimed the virtues of the "family bed," a concept long considered anathema.

✓ If you're having a problem, get all the advice you can and try anything that seems remotely helpful, unless it's cruel or dangerous. Especially with colicky babies, where the only *real* solution seems to be time taking its course, the mere fact that you're trying something bolsters morale.

✓ Advice is cheap, but heavy-duty help sometimes carries a steep emotional price tag. If you hand over a "problem" baby to a solicitous grandparent, or let your parent do things for you rather than show you how to do it yourself, don't be surprised if the parent "takes over." There's a difference between seeking support and giving up responsibility, and your average meddler can hardly be faulted for taking advantage.

✓ Once you reject advice, no matter how firmly or maturely, don't be too stubborn to admit when you're mistaken. Give advice a second chance. Let the person know if it works. You'll both reap the benefits.

✓ Try to give involved family members the chance to participate at their own level and capability. Don't force roles on others, such as the grandma-bakes-cupcakes pigeonhole. Maria's grandmother taught her how to play poker, and they had something special between them as a result.

✓ Don't turn away good help when offered. One young mother rejected her mother-in-law's advances toward the infant, believing that "she doesn't hold her right." Who cares? The rebuffed mother-in-law overcompensated for her hurt feelings with criticism. It takes a large "staff" to run a family, and most everybody is willing to pitch in somehow—if you let them.

✓ Allow your child to form his or her own rituals with relatives, even if they don't conform to your way of doing things. You may not enjoy long walks, but a grandparent who feels out of place at the playground should be encouraged to take strolls with the baby if that's what he likes to do.

✓ Sometimes grandparents need private time with the child that is not officially "babysitting" time. Do you always hover during family visits? You might leave the room for brief stretches, or even try something outside as a couple. Let grandparents get to know the child on her turf or theirs, without constant parental intrusion.

✓ There's a difference between practical advice and criticism of our judgment and wisdom. It's necessary to distinguish between the two. Can you point out the difference between "Do you think she needs a sweater?" and "Can't you see she needs a sweater?" Stay away from personal crossfire over little things. If a debate over a sweater is magnified, however, think of an objective answer: "Babies have a higher body temperature than adults. He's usually comfortable with a warm snowsuit and mittens." This shows you're unafraid and aware, and not simply neglectful. Or you could always say, "I don't think he needs one right now, but I'll take one along, just in case."

What to Do about Generous Grandparents: Gifts and Spoiling

Gifts, gifts, gifts. We should be grateful. But occasionally we're convinced that gift-givers are making a statement about the way we should dress, feed, amuse, or otherwise care for our child. Sometimes, if we treat our kids like dolls to dress up and equip in designer finery, a well-meant gift bearing a pop culture slogan rather than a chic insignia makes us angry only because our fantasy and standards have been threatened. What? My child wear an "I Kiss Grandma" T-shirt?

By letting the baby wear the shirt so Grandma can admire him and feel a part of his life, you're certainly accomplishing more for positive interpersonal relations than if you stash the garment in a bottom drawer or designate it for the secondhand sale. If a gift goes against basic principles, that's one matter, but consider the *child's* preferences and feelings. A child will feel special knowing the source of bounty: Grandma's sweater, uncle's train, cousin's book.

According to parents, grandparental spoiling comes in two forms: behavioral, or "letting them get away with murder"; and material, or "giving them anything they want." Occasionally, grandparents are guilty of putting children in danger by not childproofing a house or misjudging a child's ability to do for herself. Some grandparents foist sweets indiscriminately, or overstimulate their temporary charges to the point of hysteria. But the average spoiler is a far less threatening figure. This type of grandparent is simply reaping the benefits of finally being off the hook parentally. Not having to "pay the consequences," grandparents can gorge themselves on the sheer deliciousness of being with a child without the ultimate responsibility for its care: of buying food and goods the child appreciates and of catering to the child's whims without worries about effects on the child's character or emotional development. Grandparents may also be compensating for times and feelings missed with their own children. A busy father, now retired, becomes a doting grandfather. If he only sees his grandchild once or twice a month, the tendency is to cram as much affection and mutual pleasure into the occasion as possible.

We, the parents, react strongly: "They never indulged me like that." "I never had all those dolls." "He never, ever took me to a baseball game, though I asked him every summer. Billy's only five and he's been in the box seats!" One woman at a family reunion found herself enforcing dinner table rules that her own father had imposed strictly during her childhood. She was thrown for a loop when he actually told her to leave his grandson alone. A little mess on the floor and table wasn't anything to get angry about. When pressed to explain his changed behavior, her father admitted that perfect manners were no longer important to him, and that his warm regard for his grandson's typically sloppy eating habits could be regarded as spoiling, but, in his opinion, was nothing of the sort.

Will grandparental "spoiling" undermine all our hard work as parents? In most cases, probably not. Even when grandparents live in the same house, kids tend to see them as friends or allies rather than extra parents. One young father, when he found himself reacting with hostility to his parents' special trip-taking with baby, suddenly recalled how his own grandmother bundled him up and sneaked him out of the house to see movies forbidden by his mother. He realized he'd not been hurt by watching Edward G. Robinson and James Cagney. Instead, he'd developed a lifelong affection for movies. After he made peace with the fact that his own parents just had more time to entertain children than they had 30 years before, the friction subsided.

The "What Our Family Did to Us" Syndrome

Jerry and Martha and Sid and Shirley spent the weekend relaxing in the country. Conversation flowed for three days. The two couples really had a lot in common, including their two five-year-old sons. On the last night of the weekend, Martha excused herself from the lively talk to get a drink of water and overheard the two boys behind their bedroom door.

"What are they talking about?" whispered one voice.

"Same thing they've been talking about all weekend—their families. Don't they ever get sick of it?"

Family shortcomings are a hot topic from adolescence to the time we finally realize that nobody's perfect, a revelation that may very well come with our own parenthood. A baby's arrival leads some of us to reconsider the past, to relive conflicts and fears we had long thought swept under the carpet, or even resolved.

Those who feel content with their own upbringing are more apt to style parenthood on familiar lines. Those who can't escape the notion that they were mishandled as children and young adults may go overboard in the attempt to be different. When new parents vow not to repeat the mistakes of their mothers and fathers, it's a theoretical promise that can't always stand the test of reality.

Nina once harbored a grudge against her mother for ostensibly "abandoning" her to a string of nannies, babysitters, and assorted relatives. She vowed to take total responsibility for her own child for at least the first three years. After one year of intense and ambivalent togetherness, Nina viewed her own mother's choices more clearly and compassionately. Nina was finally ready to admit that her mother, a widow, had many other pressing concerns aside from her child. Nina recognized her own rigidity and began to think not so much about what kind of mother she *didn't* want to be, but what kind of mother she *did* want to be.

How long can we go on being obsessive about and reacting to "what was done to us" years ago? Trying to reconcile past with future, it may help to keep these points in mind:

✔ Yes, parenthood does reopen old family wounds and, if they persist, having a compassionate ear—your partner, a sibling, a friend—to hear you out is essential.

✔ As we begin to understand that *we* don't have ultimate power over the fate of our children, so we must acknowledge that our *parents* may not be solely responsible for who we are today.

✔ If it seems impossible to work through the memories and conflicts, and if this preoccupation overpowers the present, seek professional guidance.

Happy memories fuel our journey into parenthood. Unhappy ones instruct us where we want to be different from our own parents, though that determination is only a small part of the effort to change. "There is a tendency to fall back to the old ways. In some people it's very marked and they're horror stricken when they take a look at themselves and see how much they're behaving like their father or mother," observes Dr. Clifford Sager, a New York psychiatrist. "Things they hated they now see themselves doing. Some have been able to correct this. But others go so far overboard that they become compulsive in another direction. In these reactions they create other problems."

Psychiatrist Sidney Lecker, in his book, *Family Ties*, advises young parents to avoid pursuing an ineluctable "due bill" from their own fathers and mothers—a bill that cannot adequately be repaid. "You don't have to be a slave to your family experiences," Dr. Lecker continues. "You will have many opportunities to reshape your personality. . . . Early family life did create a 'motor' to drive your personality, but the steering mechanism was not irrevocably programmed."

Even having spent years deciphering the emotional hieroglyphics of our past, we don't foresee these sinister intrusions on the new family circle. They're liable to rear up ferociously, though, when we return to our parents' home. Many young parents say this is where their entire coping mechanism breaks down, where the very essence of independent spirit quavers, and we, children again, revert to old patterns. "Each year we spend a week at my parents' house in Florida, and for that week I'm no longer a 32-year-old woman with a husband and son, but a dutiful child again with a two-year-old sibling," one mother admitted.

"When we go back to our childhood nest we fall in very readily," says Dr. Sager. "People come to the big city and become very sophisticated and mature and go back home and, after a day or two, they're infants again. Of course, they're treated as infants and get rewarded for their infantile response. They get sucked into a so-familiar pattern. The neuronal paths have been well greased and they fall right into acting in those familiar ways. By the end of three or four days, they can't wait to leave. Many people rationalize their behavior by saying, 'We only visit two times a year, so what's the difference?' "

The difference is in the cumulative toll taken by passive new parents. How do *you* act?

Recognizing *Real* Family Danger Zones

Some new parents become so bogged down with the nitpicking details of the past that they're unable to see larger potential problem areas in the new family they are shaping. What are some of the danger zones of family life? According to Dr. Salvador Minuchin, a pioneer in family therapy, four behavioral patterns are typical of distressed families.

(1) Exaggerated interdependence of family members. In healthy families, members are tuned into one another's needs, but they also sense when to back off. The troubled family feels threatened by both psychic and physical privacy, and members take "meddling" to absurd extremes. They have no real image of themselves as independently functioning individuals.

(2) Certain members overprotective of others. This usually works from parent to child, creating in the offspring a sense of guilt and unrepayable debt. How can you be honest and hurt someone to whom you owe so much?

(3) A family with a rigid set of rules governing behavior and emotion. Shape up or ship out is the message of this clan.

(4) Avoidance of conflict. This family desires an outward appearance of harmony—whatever the cost.

But Families Do Change

Chances are you have a frozen image of your family, just as other members have a frozen image of you. But it's an illusion to think that families are incapable of altering collective personality. The changes we observe in ourselves as we become parents—enhanced self-image, broader perspective, marital connectedness, increased capacity for affection and tolerance—can have a positive rebound effect within our own extended family.

Loyalties and Rivalries

Perhaps we marry someone from our own neighborhood, of the same ethnic background, striving for the same life-goals. Our parents all play canasta on Saturday night and go to the same church on Sunday. But with the baby come choices: Whose carefully preserved crib is the tot to sleep in? Which grandma will spend the first week with the new family? Whose teddy bear will be the child's favorite?

When two families come together to participate in The Big Event, basic differences emerge, no matter how close they were before. In themselves, these differences may be major or minor—from religion to diaper service—but they are accompanied by a string of associations that leave us in a tangle of loyalties. Our choices in these complex situations often go beyond rational decision making. In other words, we may ram a huge, antiquated pram into cramped living quarters, even if our spouse hates it and the thing doesn't fit. Why? Our parents asked us to. After all, they stored it for thirty years, since our own infancy! It also makes us feel pretty good to see our own child in such a noble contraption, one that we associate subconsciously with the peacefulness we experienced as an infant.

The keener our sense of loyalty to our own family, the harder it is to accept and implement the claims and needs of our partner's clan. In most cases, in-law problems are purely subjective. They are sometimes the result of just how fiercely (or defensively) we're willing to fight for our own way of doing things, and just how fiercely our in-laws are willing to fight back. Bringing a baby into the world can touch off what Dr. Therese Benedek, in her book *Parenthood: Its Psychology and Psychopathology*, calls the "underlying ambivalence" felt for each other by family-members-by-marriage. Battle lines are drawn, with the grandparents usually in spiritual alliance with their own child. "Just as at the time the child went to school, parental narcissism is at work and the fault is seen in the other rather than in one's own child," Dr. Benedek observes.

Though possibilities for conflict are endless when two families unite in marriage, the baby's birth represents the first biological link between these two divergent groups. Whereas before the birth, the husband's family had claim over the husband, the wife's family its claim over the wife, both families must share possession of the infant—and both may vie passionately or discreetly, whichever is their way, for top billing.

Familial love and rivalry flourish side by side. Despite such contrasting feelings, affection for a baby can play a large part in grandparental craving to be involved, to satisfy an instinctive need to perpetuate values and traditions of the ancestral family. One beleaguered mother wrote to Dr. Joyce Brothers's syndicated column: "I love and admire my husband's father but, oh, how I wish he'd stop telling me how to raise my children!" This woman found no ally in her own spouse. "My husband would never dare to suggest that he might know better than his father."

Dr. Brothers's reply was a plea for understanding. The grandfather, she contended, wasn't airing his opinions out of malice. "He just wants to make sure he's noticed and able to put in his two cents."

Some young parents say they don't like the way the in-laws "hold" the baby. Why? Because it's not the way their own mothers held them, or what the latest research prescribes. If we're willing to accept the idea that there is no one "right" way to raise children, then we must also relinquish the nurturing monopoly on our baby. It's the child's birthright to experience and learn from *each* of our families.

While it's difficult to imagine how all contributions will be accommodated, we spend perhaps too much valuable time stewing over the problem. Luckily, the major natural resource of families is *time*. Dr. Therese Benedek reminds us in her book of parent-related essays that "The family is a closely knit organism thriving on a delicate balance of its emotional currents. It is a keenly sensitive balance which must continually be reestablished in adjustment to everyday events. There are always happenings, pleasant and unpleasant, there are always tensions which come and go."

Some grandparents are more comfortable with infants and this is where they will focus their energies; others respond more wholeheartedly to children at verbal age and need time to develop a relationship. The task before young parents is to sort out these divergent demands and needs and, wherever possible, to let our parents approach grandparenthood in the manner with which they're most comfortable, as long as our child is not compromised in any way.

A couple we know was confronted by two sets of grandparents with very different styles. One was younger, active, and always full of energy, while the other was older and more comfortably involved in quiet activities. In time, each evolved a role that was comfortable and gave them a place unique in their grandchildren's hearts. The younger couple became the "outdoor" grandparents, treating the youngsters to zoo and museum trips. The other couple will always be fondly remembered as the "indoor" grandparents, full of fascinating stories of antiquity, delicious teas from far-off places, and a magical attic that became a memorable part of this family's merged culture.

Family Gatherings

Ned and Sheila developed a comfortable lifestyle in their five years of childless marriage. Christmases were enjoyed on warm exotic beaches; Thanksgiving turkeys were shared with family only if they had no better offer; birthdays were celebrated with expensive gifts and a night on the town. Other family occasions were acknowledged with cards, telephone calls, or money. They were usually much too busy to make a personal appearance at family gatherings, which, in fact, they remembered as occasions for too much food and bickering.

Yet, when the baby came, even they found themselves looking at holidays not so much as an opportunity to get away, but as a chance to get involved. After the first self-conscious family Thanksgiving, they realized that many neglected traditions were worth restoring. They also began to see participation in family events as a tacit message to their child: "This is the special society you, and we, belong to. It has values, traditions, and a culture all its own. You will learn of its past and contribute to its future."

Soon Ned and Sheila began instituting celebrations of their own. Their daughter's birthday parties became a focus of attention and expectation for both sets of grandparents, while their return to the Thanksgiving tables of extended family sparked a new sense of belonging.

As the decision is made to recommit to family rituals, how do we handle the logistics if there are two families to please and to honor? If, as Robert Blood says in *Marriage*, "every family has a culture of its own—distinctive ways of living that are deeply ingrained," should we be surprised that both families wish to perpetuate rituals and traditions *their* way? Surprised, no. Prepared, yes. The holiday tug-of-war can set off new ambivalence about the real meaning of celebrations unless couples formulate a policy that encompasses both practice and principle.

✔ Consider which holidays are especially important to each family. Birthdays may not be top priority, while Independence Day might be.

✓ Create a master plan for holidays, including some you'll take responsibility for yourself. Know in advance exactly what form your participation will take. Is a phone call or gift enough, or will anything short of your physical presence result in hurt feelings? Can these hurt feelings be discussed openly?

✓ Don't try to tear yourself in half by attending two events on the same day. Two Thanksgiving dinners is a heavy price to pay to please two groups of people. Consider a rotating plan in which visits are kept to alternate years or consecutive days.

✓ If you feel keenly about beginning your own traditions, don't be surprised if you have to convince skeptics of your ability to carry on the family rituals. Taking on some family events is a symbolic way of assuming your place as an adult in the clan.

✓ Try to bring the spirit and historic traditions of holidays into your celebrations wherever they are held. What is the real meaning of Chanukah, Christmas, Passover, anniversaries, family reunions? Lighting candles, saying grace, hunting for Easter eggs, exchanging anecdotes with distant cousins—these small ceremonies will be remembered by you and your child from year to year, long after the gifts and food have been forgotten.

Rules of the House

When Visiting Maiden Aunt Rosie
or Your Swinging Childless Cousins

1. Don't wait until your host or hostess chastises you about your child for breaking a rule. Ask at the start about general dos and don'ts, and prepare your child beforehand to follow them.

2. Honor house rules, even if it's "only your parents," just as you would expect visitors to honor your own.

3. Don't allow family members to force you into a "henchman" role. If there are lots of regulations that need constant policing, it's best to entertain on your turf. In the case of grandparents or other close relatives and friends, suggest that *they* let their wishes be known and help supervise the kids.

4. Insist that safety measures be enforced when you visit. Urge others to use safety plugs for outlets, lock up poisons, secure terraces and swimming pools.

5. Talk with your host or hostess about meeting you halfway, depending on the age of your child. Most breakables can be easily re-

moved and some stringent laws can be relaxed to suit your child's behavior.

6. Give family members a fair idea of what to expect. Infants aren't intrusive, for instance, but toddlers are.

7. Take toys and activities so your child is not forced to invent pastimes or get into mischief.

8. Give the child safe outlets for curiosity. Maria's mother has a handy what-not box she saves for bored moments. And Nicky's great-grandmother Gi-Gi has reactivated the special surprise drawer she used to entertain her own grandchildren. She calls it "Nicky's drawer" and there's always something special waiting there for him.

9. Try to stress to the child the things he *can* do at a relative's house, that he can't climb on the furniture but *can* roll around on the luxurious wall-to-wall carpeting, explore the attic, or use the yard.

10. Don't feel guilty or repressive about temporarily increasing demands on your children's behavior, within reason. Children learn to understand that different behavior is appropriate in different situations.

Allowing Our Parents to Grow

In times of stress, we still tend to look at our parents from a childhood perspective. We see them as fully matured, therefore static: all-powerful, constant, immutable, and existing *solely for us*. While we don't wish to relate to our parents as if we were children, we still want them to relate to us as parents first. We see one set of values and privileges for ourselves as adults and another for our mother and father. We expect our parents to walk the hazy, impossible line between "taking over" and "abandoning" us, and by doing so we fail to realize our own independence, power, and responsibility.

Jean Nassau, founder and facilitator of Parents Are People, a self-help group for parents of adult children, told us: "An adult child has to understand that Mommy and Daddy no longer exist just for you as they did in your mind when you were a child. When you were young, you felt your parents were there for the basic purpose of *making things all right for you*. This was how you perceived their function long before you could put it into words. But now the focus should shift to seeing them as people in their own right, entitled to live their own lives."

When we recognize that our parents are growing, and not just merely growing old, we may be able to answer for ourselves such questions as:

✓ Why are they spoiling the baby when they were so strict with us?

✓ If my mother enjoyed raising five kids as much as she claims, why won't she sit full-time while I go back to work?

✓ If my father never had time for me, how can he clear his schedule at the mere mention of a visit from his granddaughter?

✓ My parents said they couldn't wait for a grandchild, and now they can't wait to get away from him. They've stepped up their social and travel schedule to coincide with his birth. What are they running away from?

If we find ourselves jealous of the intensity of our own parents' involvement in grandparenthood, or disappointed at their seeming aloofness, we must remember that they, too, experience growing pains. If such acknowledgment doesn't solve the problem, it does begin to put it in the perspective we need for present and future harmonious family living.

Friends

Remember those intense conversations with close friends: Should we have kids? If so, when? Who will be first? Impressions were exchanged about what life would be like with a child. From the outside, parenthood seemed a strange and distant state of being, and it was comforting to know we were not alone in our fears and fantasies. Sometimes our friendships were strengthened by the implicit promise to share experiences down the road, when we—such good friends— would be linked by still another common bond.

Then *you* decide to have a child and tell friends who matter. Their responses run the gamut from coolness and matter-of-fact acceptance to genuine enthusiasm and affection; from derision at your imminent domesticity to envy at the fear of being displaced by the baby as an object of care.

As pregnancy advances, a friend who first seemed indifferent can grow excited and much closer, while another slips away. You are struck by the realization that having a baby is not a self-contained event. Yet it's hard to see that the often unpredictable responses of friends sometimes have more to do with their *theoretical* parenthood than with your *actual* one.

Take the changes experienced by Ginny and Ruth, friends of long standing who had even passed that strenuous friendship test of traveling together peaceably. Ruth followed Ginny's pregnancy with almost obsessive interest and demanded to be named godmother. She bought gifts for the baby-to-be and even read Ginny's natural childbirth books. Then Kathleen was born. After one uncomfortable visit to the hospital, and another to Ginny's home, Ruth was never heard from again. Perhaps Ginny was oversimplifying, but she came to believe her friend's sudden withdrawal of friendship was symptomatic of Ruth's yearning for a child of her own.

After the baby arrives we find ourselves reconsidering relationships and the foundations on which they were built. It's not simply a matter of liking or disliking people more or less. Parental social life involves a great deal of preparation, energy, compromise, and, yes, egocentricity. Sometimes the sacrifices are too great. Each of us has a particular level of toleration and acceptance that may change radically with parenthood. Not surprisingly, a *Psychology Today* magazine survey published in 1979 cited the birth of a child as among the most common causes of the disintegration of friendship!

Why Friends Go

Whatever the causes of lapsed friendship, new parents are less apt to feel discriminating than discriminated against. Nancy Sahlein, a social worker who has counseled new parents at a Westchester, New York, support center, says that "what comes up frequently in our discussions is parents' feelings of how other people view them. They experience feelings of alienation and distance from the 'real world' of their old friends, and express the belief that they have somehow lost stature in the eyes of childless friends and co-workers. Why else would these old acquaintances leave them in the lurch?" Exploration of the causes and effects of friendship shifts at this vulnerable time should encourage parental perspective.

Pressure to Conform

No matter what you say, the mere fact that *you* made the commitment to have a child first puts pressure on others. If your friends seem defensive, or to be peering at you through a microscope, scientifically observing the way you cope with your parenthood, of course they're using you as a guinea pig! Who knows what pressures their families and spouses are applying at this point, and what ambivalence tears at their own souls.

Changing the Ground Rules

Every friendship, including the most intimate and versatile, has a basic theme. Without saying so, each has ground rules, parameters that go beyond how you spend your time together. For instance, with certain friends you never talk about the prospect of raising a family, or your finances, or that you're unhappy with work—or even yourself. On the other hand, friendship may move along comfortably on the shared love of the arts, the great outdoors, gracious living, sports mania, stamp collecting, or being well-dressed. Some friendships are motivated by the shared desire to compete and succeed in chosen work. With the first years of parenthood, you may have to forego valued interests and replace others. In the process, friendships can change to meet your new needs, be put on ice temporarily, or simply die natural deaths.

The Energy Crunch

It's not that the Smiths' parties aren't what they used to be—you're not quite what *you* used to be. Instead of gaining steam at 11 PM, you're looking at the clock and dreading how bushed you'll feel the next morning. There's no way your childless friends can comprehend how tiring the first couple of parental years are. Yet we run the risk of losing friends through complaint if we give them an inkling. So, more often than not, we participate beyond our capability. Many friendships fade through lack of attention, and new parents just have to accept the fact that without full-time help at home, we can't maintain them all, and that having fun can be no fun when we're too tired. This realization often eludes us until we're on the brink of physical collapse. Then we get selective.

A Private Recession

Every time we go out with a friend, we have to figure babysitting fees into the entertainment bill. If Saturday night caps a week of ear infections and doctor's visits, going out for pizza may seem extravagant. The solution is not necessarily to entertain at home, where other hidden costs, both financial and physical, loom up. Short of becoming hermits, we must grapple with cash reallocation forthrightly, before a depleted bank account really hurts. If friends can enjoy our company without frills, fine. If not, the relationship is in trouble.

Turning Off Friendships

Our missionary zeal as new parents—the sheer weight of our joy—causes us to seem incredibly eccentric and insensitive to the needs of friends. No, they don't always realize how immense our experience is, nor should we necessarily hold that against them. If we fail to ask how a friend's new job is going, or whether they've found their dream house, or solved a marital problem, how can we expect them to respond to our main event? New parents run the risk of appearing to gloat if things are going well at home and to wallow in self-pity if they are not. Make some effort to gauge the other person's capacity for details of your baby's and your own development.

Love Me, Love My Baby

Are you insulted if friends show less interest in your child than they do in you? What? She didn't ask how much weight he's gained, or if she's talking yet? Be happy if your friends continue to be primarily interested in *you*. The friend's interest in your child may well increase with his age, but your relationship as adults is a valuable resource now.

Surrogate Family

Although the extended family is a vanishing species, the need for the services and support provided by such a network remains. Friends are our natural resource.

In most cases, close friends step in to help us weather the emotional crises of early parenthood. A friend with an older child can provide a helpful "warm line" telephone contact for solving problems; others invite us over for holiday dinners when we can't get home, or are too tired to prepare one ourselves. But we can't always expect friends to intuit our needs. Nor should they be expected to preoccupy themselves with our sitting and errand chores. Just as we have to think carefully about how to include family members in our life, so we must take into account our friends' personal responsibilities before becoming too dependent.

Soft-Skinned Parenthood

During the transition into parenthood, we're likely to feel emotionally touchy. Maybe friends didn't send an appropriate gift, or over-

stayed their visit to see baby, or are acting much too pushy about seeing us get out in the world again. No matter how well we think we
know our friends, our chances of being hurt at this juncture increase.
Feeling vulnerable, we tend to scrutinize our friendships and may
overreact to real and imagined slights.

In all cases, we should learn to recognize those transient emotions
and obsessions of early parenthood and not let them get in the way of
valued relationships.

Making New Friends

No matter how strong and sustaining our existing relationships with
childless adults, a special loneliness accompanies new parenthood. Often, it's less a physical isolation than a psychic one: we need desperately to make contact with people who understand our new reality
without our having to explain it, people we can talk to about sleepless
nights and high fevers, first steps and first words. People who won't
say, "Why can't the sitter handle it?" when we cancel a dinner engagement on account of infant illness. People who, when they invite us
over with baby, have already put the knickknacks away.

As soon as we feel fit enough to strap the baby into a front or back-
pack or tuck her into the carriage, the search for a peer group com-
mences. We see the father pushing his daughter's stroller Saturday
mornings and wonder who he is. The mother who rides her toddler on
the back of her bicycle intrigues us. We want to know more about the
couple right down the street who have a playpen in their yard. "It
wasn't until I had the baby," one mother told us, "that I began to
sense the need I had to share common experiences. I'd see another
parent blocks away and I'd want to wave and say something. Of
course I didn't. I crossed the street instead. It was as if I'd lost the
ability to be sociable. It was lucky somebody else decided to be
friendly to me!"

"Here I'd spent 15 years in business, taking strangers to lunch. I had
a reputation as a raconteur. New people didn't scare me—until I became a father," one man recalled. "I'd bury my head in a book at the
playground rather than converse with the person next to me, though I
desperately wanted to talk."

These parents and many others realize that a new avenue for friendship and shared services exists but that it will take courage, hard
work, self-evaluation, and a few inevitable false starts before the beginnings of a network are forged. "The parents of young children will

form friendships around babysitting, the PTA, the Little League, and community participation," wrote sociologists Joseph Bensman and Robert Lilienfeld in *Psychology Today*. "These friendships are likely to be based upon residential, social, and personal propinquity, within which, of course, personal preferences operate. They are not necessarily deep, but they may be broadened as people discover more interests in common, and deepened as they serve to satisfy psychological needs."

Here are some suggestions, gleaned from our own experience, for breaking the ice with other new parents:

✓ Check out your pediatrician's office. It's a natural first meeting ground. Some doctors even have special infant checkup hours so that new parents can meet while they wait. Others would be happy to give you the name of other parents you could call.

✓ Check bulletin boards, local newspapers, newsletters from such organizations as ASPO (American Society for Psychoprophylaxis in Obstetrics), La Leche, and the local Y for news of parent support services. (Check our *Help* chapter for a list of support groups around the country.)

✓ Ask parents of older children where the best places are to meet people. Then go there—not once, but several times.

✓ Make the first move because the other person may be shyer than you and may not have read this book. Don't just introduce your baby —introduce yourself.

✓ Try not to let what you are or were before you had the baby make you defensive or disdainful. In the workplace, there's often a stratification of friendships—management hobnobs with management, clerks and secretaries eat lunch together. But where new parents congregate a new equality emerges. We're parents first, and what we have in common is our children, at least at the start. Many of the most productive parental relationships are "working" arrangements in which more services than confidences are exchanged.

✓ Try not to let your approval or disapproval of styles in parenthood interfere with potential friendships. If you don't work, you may think the working mother who is on the playground only on weekends is scornful—yet it is not scorn at all that the working woman conveys, but a self-protective façade to protect her from feeling guilty that she isn't at home like the others. And yes, breast-feeding and bottle-feeding mothers can and should be friends—and so can fathers who are not self-conscious about their varying commitments.

✓ Don't be surprised if the initial level of conversation has more to do with practical, baby-related information than adult topics. Many of us cling to the safety of swapped stories about diaper rash and teething and never allow our need for adult conversation to surface. If it does, we nervously squelch it. Though it can seem like a breach of etiquette to change the topic from baby to *you*, that quantum leap (if successful) can be the first step to *lasting* friendship.

✓ Don't be afraid to extend a favor, or to ask for one, even of new friends. One of the special qualities of child-based relationships is the generosity and tolerance we extend to one another. These friendships have a singularly candid quality, besides. When you watch another parent discipline a child in a ferocious tantrum, you see a demonstration of intimate behavior which isn't all that common, even between good friends. We don't always know how to react. One mother told us of her feeling of utter helplessness when an otherwise controlled mother suddenly burst into tears at her child's uncontrollable behavior. "I realized I didn't know how to comfort her. Though we'd spent countless hours together walking our babies, we hadn't trusted each other with our deeper feelings until this moment. Our children had provided a nice, easy buffer—and yet at the same time a forced intimacy neither of us was prepared to handle. Her tears really broke through the barrier, though. Afterward, laughing again, we felt like kin."

✓ Don't forget your old friends. By making room for the new, there's a tendency to neglect companions we really shouldn't lose. It's essential to maintain a balance between child-related friends and those who affected and stimulated our lives before the baby.

Avoiding Obnoxious Behavior

Instead of trying to socialize and civilize our children, many of us regress to the ill manners and narcissism of preschoolers. We're sure you can think of a number of annoying or insulting parental habits that turned *you* off in the past, from sing-song baby talk to endless parentcraft conversations. Examine your own behavior in adult company. Have you broken these basic rules?

✓ Don't use your child as an excuse for neglecting valued friendships.

✓ Don't complain endlessly about your woeful, overextended existence. It's a turnoff. So is warning your friends against parenthood. Find a support group (see our *Help* chapter) or seek out one or two friends as an outlet for your very real concerns.

✓ Learn some basic parental telephone manners. Don't interrupt your conversations with shrill screams directed at your child: discipline her later. Begin to teach your child that you have a right to use the phone. If she makes too much of a fuss, save your important calls for her sleep hour.

‚ Don't expect your friend to spend the entire time interacting with your child. Do you interrupt adult conversation repeatedly with exclamations about your child's good or bad behavior?

‚ Make an effort to cultivate other than child-related interests. Are your interests varied enough to sustain adult conversation?

‚ Don't give the impression that parenthood is the highest calling in life and the only really meaningful activity known to man or woman, thereby trivializing the interests of childless friends.

Coping with Awkward Moments

Entertaining

"Having friends over for dinner used to be fun. We'd roll out the red carpet—try to outdo *their* last dinner party—and we'd usually pull it off. After they left, when the taste of good food and conversation lingered, we'd sit like contented Cheshire cats in the living room and marvel at our success. These days, though, we not only don't have the requisite energy to prepare such a meal, we have to do all we can to stay awake through the evening."

The experience is a universal one for new parents, who still feel the responsibility to hold up their end of the social calendar but feel increasingly crushed by the very real responsibilities associated with entertaining well. See our *Lifestyle* chapter for ways to modify style without sacrificing substance.

‚ Establish up front what the limitations are to your hospitality. For instance, in your verbal or written invitation, state politely: "Come at 7 PM so we can make it an early evening." If your guests want to see baby, let them know you won't be serving your main dish until the child is fast asleep. By all means, *say* how tired you are by 11 PM; *say* "I'll serve something simple." Good friends won't mind unless they're expecting a gourmet dish.

‚ Arrange beforehand all the details of work-sharing so that you're both not scurrying around at the last minute searching for ingredients. Meanwhile, who feeds the baby? Who gives the bath? Who tidies the living room? And who will wash up after the guests depart? Don't wait until zero hour to make these decisions.

⟶ If you are planning to entertain friends who always stay late, consider asking them for brunch scheduled to coincide with your child's nap. This way, you'll be able to engage in some adult conversation, and you won't be bushed the next day.

⟶ If one of you simply can't keep your eyes open and the clock is approaching midnight, don't be bashful about saying goodnight. Better to make a gracious exit than to be caught snoozing on a chair.

Visiting

Every year since they could remember, John and Anita were invited to spend a weekend at Sara and Richard's country home. So many rich experiences had been shared by the couples that to envision a summer without at least one weekend together was dreadful. The summer afer John and Anita's baby arrived—she was just beginning to crawl—Sara and Richard extended the annual invitation. Only one thing bothered John when he told Anita about it: No direct mention had been made of their daughter. Was she included? Anita interpreted the omission to mean, "Of course she's welcome." John wasn't so sure, and he began to doubt whether the inclusion of so small a person would throw off the perfect balance of personalities he and the others had come to expect.

⟶ When an ambiguous daytime invitation is extended, always ask: "Do you mean all of us, or just the adults?" Never assume a child is invited.

⟶ Consider the pros and cons if your friends do extend their hospitality to include baby, and *insist* that you bring her along. Even if your friends enjoy children, they may discover that the forced intimacy—too many bodies in too small an area—is intolerable. You might not be crazy about it, either. If rain or cold weather intrudes on your weekend stay, your attempts to occupy your child can spoil adult plans. A baby in an unfamiliar environment may not allow you time for that long awaited grown-up dinner. If the outside environment is dangerous, no matter how brief the visit a parent must become an instant policeman, fearful of hidden obstacles behind every tree and over every hill.

⟶ Consider carefully whether your friendship can adjust to the preoccupying demands of a small child who can't even retreat to his own room to play. If your friends already have children, don't necessarily assume your child and theirs will be compatible. Under one roof, parents who are friends can discover that their modes of discipline and emotional breaking points are vastly different.

Being Visited

Living in a major city, Alice and Ed had always put up old friends and family who were in town. They knew how expensive hotels were, and they wanted to be hospitable. But with baby taking up the spare room, their small apartment could no longer easily accommodate visitors. Alice and Ed began to feel put upon when they had to prepare extra meals for guests and wash extra dishes. Some friends expected them to go sightseeing or out to dinner. The pressure to please made Alice and Ted grumpy.

✓ Tactfully question your friends when they first ask to stay with you. Will the visit involve any chauffeuring or transportation duties? Do they mind being awakened during the night when the baby gets up for juice, and as early as 5 AM, which is baby's regular wake-up hour? Will their schedule be a late one, their return to your home at night still another interruption to your abbreviated sleep? How long do they plan to stay?

✓ Ask yourselves these equally direct questions: Are you saying yes to marginal friends who can well afford a few nights in a hotel because you don't know how to say no? Are you prepared to have your baby's schedule and humor less predictable during the stay, and perhaps afterward? Are your friends the kind of people who will put up with a messy house as well as your own divided attention?

7

Work

In a small Southern town the mother of a three-year-old can't find a babysitter when she decides to go back to work because nobody approves of her decision. In New York a laid-off college professor grapples with the demands of full-time parenthood and puts his role-sharing theories to the test while his wife brings in an ample income. A divorced mother at a Minneapolis insurance company drops her kids at the bus stop at 7:05 and gets to her office at 7:30. By taking lunch at her desk, she's home by 3:30, a practical feature of her employer's "flexitime" schedule. A California couple with two children in school resist for the first time the frequent relocations expected by the father's company. In Kansas City, dual-career parents of a two-year-old feel the effects of work/family overload. In Washington, another couple systematically review their lifestyle in preparation for the wife's going back to work.

These are only a few of the work scenarios described to us by parents across the country. Next to sex, work can easily become the biggest readjustment problem facing new parents. U.S. government statistics bear out the complexity of the work question: Less than one-fifth of all families fall into the traditional mold of working father, at-home mother. In addition, U.S. government surveys show that there are more than nine million women and nearly two million men who, as single parents and primary caretakers, work full time to support their families. About half of all married women with preschool children now work, while nearly 250,000 men are full-time "househusbands."

For most of us, the issue is no longer "should or shouldn't" but one of financial and psychological necessity. "Just *having* a paid job meets important human needs: for income, independence, self-respect, belonging to the larger society," psychologist and social research analyst Daniel Yankelovich has written in *Psychology Today*.

As we individually confront the work/family crisis, whatever face it presents to us, there are fundamental arrangements we must make with one another before we even begin to think about babysitters and

151

fringe benefits. In our panic to organize external factors we are apt to neglect such basic questions as:

✓ What is the major function of our jobs in terms of income, self-fulfillment, security, or whatever else matters to us?

✓ How do we view one another's job? With respect? Grudging acceptance? Indulgence? Competitiveness? Disapproval? Admiration?

✓ Is there a cooperative decision-making process, both in the choice of job and its day-to-day long-term demands?

✓ With what label do I feel most comfortable: a family person who works, or a working person with a family? How often am I true to this definition, and how often do I find myself compromising one for the other?

✓ Have my partner and I articulated long- and short-term goals, both material and professional? Have our work decisions to date reflected those agreed-upon aims?

✓ Am I honest with myself about my personal capacity for coping with stress, exhaustion, hostility, and guilt?

✓ Have I done my homework about career possibilities, alternative work patterns, and the particular attitudes of my current or prospective employer toward family obligations?

✓ Have my partner and I evolved sound patterns for dividing responsibilties at home?

✓ Are our theoretical child-raising goals compatible with our decisions regarding work? Do we try, as much as possible, to live according to our principles, or do we blame "the boss" for shaping our lives?

With no up-to-date framework and few *new* models on which to base our lives as dual-career parents, every decision we make about work has to be buttressed by dozens of other personal and highly experimental choices involving our child, marriage, adult relationships, values, and, not insignificantly, self-respect. Yet all working parents confront certain universal questions, and, while there are no universal answers, it definitely helps to compare notes. In this chapter, we'll touch on the most frequently expressed concerns of working families.

Careerism

"The family as a group or institution, and the employer as a group or institution, both want to get everything out of their members that they can. Without defined priorities, there will be conflicts. People must decide where to draw the line.

"The problem of loyalties still exists in general for men—and increasingly for working women—in relation to family versus career advancement. We see in our marriage counseling practice many successful men whose wives complain about their own neglect and their children's neglect because the husbands choose to give priority to the demands of career. That means the family suffers. Conversely, if he chooses to give a greater measure of his time and energy to his family, his career will suffer. There's no way that's ever going to change."

Marriage and family therapist Robert Blood, in his book *The Family*, makes this observation from personal experience. At one point early in his teaching career he was informed that only by accepting additional administrative and peripheral tasks would he be considered for promotion. The father of young sons, Blood was forced to make a pivotal choice. He decided not to give any more than he was already giving to university work, though he told us, "It's very seductive to decide in favor of the employer, because that brings all those rewards of increased money and prestige, responsibility and challenges."

Whether to accept career compromise for at least a few years looms as one of the most agonizing early parental choices. It simply can't be viewed as a self-contained decision for either man or woman: Stepping back from a career entails wide-ranging compromises and sacrifices.

↗ Younger competitors surpass you at work and superiors fail to understand your motives. Though *you* are convinced of the value of your decision, you may begin to feel painfully "out of it."

↗ Career dedication involves no less than a life plan, a mapping out of our future according to where we picture ourselves in the workplace. A career-oriented person sees the compromise of work goals as a compromise of *life* goals and self-image. More of these individuals are consciously opting not to have children. For those who do, the bind of careerism tightens relentlessly.

↗ Because youth is seen as a virtue rather than a liability in the work world, and the twenties and thirties represent "make it or break it" years professionally, the first years of parenthood often painfully coincide with career escalation. "The difficulty at this vulnerable point in life stems from the fact that stresses in both cycles characteristically peak then: both seem to require maximum attention," observes Lotte Bailin in an essay in the book *Working Couples*. For example, the blue-collar worker is more than likely to moonlight upon the birth of the first child, the middle manager to compete harder for that vice presidency, and the corporate executive to accept relocation.

 ⸱ The work ethic has infiltrated even family life: you have to be as busy at leisure as you are at work. Loafing is taboo. "Doing things" counts. Improving your backhand or ski style are "meaningful" leisure activities to be talked about on Monday at the office. The ephemeral quality of lazy Sundays with family is endangered because they show no concrete results, no product. When your co-workers ask you what you did on the weekend, are you confident enough to say, "I spent it with my family"?

 ⸱ Economics increasingly dictate how long and hard we work. Simply staying in place at work means, in some cases, falling behind financially. Like Alice, we're forced to run as fast as we can just to stay put.

 ⸱ Some jobs afford no room for compromise. Competition, expectation, and maintenance of style are so essential in those careers that the worker is compelled to toe the line—or get out.

The key is to organize guidelines for goal-setting that compromise neither work performance nor family unity. Geophysicist David Stewart calls it "a healthy balance" in his pamphlet, "Fathering and Career."

1. Decide on a "minimum level of achievement," as Stewart calls it, that you can live with comfortably. Then ask yourself: Is this schedule compatible with my family needs?
2. Use your time at work to *work*. That means eliminating overlong lunches, most office chatter, coffee breaks, and after-hours "hanging around."
3. Be yourself and try not to let the fear of being different force you into such activities as joining the office softball team (unless you like softball!).
4. Don't be secretive or apologetic about family commitments. By doing so, you'll be telegraphing the message that your home life is secondary to your life at work, and worthy of only second-class respect.
5. Learn to delegate responsibility. Surround yourself with competent people. Have confidence in them.
6. Analyze the components of your job. Which contribute most directly to your success? Concentrate primarily on these.

Work: The Guilt-Edged Sword

The guilt of working parents rarely evolves from broken laws, wrong choices, or clear-cut mistakes. We think we've made the right choice, but what about all those other "right" choices not taken? We think we've used good judgment, but even a casual remark or weighted silence attacks our conscience.

A common but worthless antidote to parental guilt, especially that engendered by work, is super-parent reassurance. "You *can* have it all," say some experts. Maybe our crime stems from a bogus naivete. When have we *ever* had it all, even in a simpler, younger, childless life? Along with the promise of Having It All, we're offered a side order of guilt-reducing remedies. When these don't work we're likely to condemn ourselves further: "Boy, I must *really* be a bad parent if I followed all this good advice and I *still* feel guilty."

Ironically, successful working parents who seem the least guilt-ridden are often the ones we'd least like to emulate: "Sure she's a successful lawyer, but she doesn't *seem to care* about her kids." We may prefer to identify with someone who shows just how much she cares about her kids by how much *guilt* she exhibits. Do you confuse your own feelings of guilt with what psychiatrist Theodore Isaac Rubin calls "a high sense of responsibility and morality"? Guilt, Dr. Rubin suggests in his book, *Compassion and Self-Hate*, is subtly passed off as virtue. As working parents, many of us try to show just how good we are by how bad we feel. This kind of guilt can be easily avoided if we're willing to own up to it.

A predisposition to guilt may also be passed on generationally. Were you raised in a Catch-22 type household, where even the "right" decision was wrong? Maria's mother has a favorite joke to illustrate this point: A doting mother gave her grown son two ties for his birthday. Anxious to please her, he wore one on his next visit. "What, you didn't like the other one?" she cried.

Guilt can be rooted in personal characteristics, or it can flow in generously from disapproving friends, family, or co-workers. These sources can be confronted, if not blocked. "Open criticism is annoying, but it can be dealt with," writes Grace Mitchell in *The Day Care Book*. "It is the invisible 'they' lurking behind the scenes who cause the most trouble. How often we hear: 'They' say that . . . 'They' probably think that . . . 'Everyone' knows that. . . . It is easy to let imagined criticism become reality in one's mind, to be resentful of something that does not exist," Mitchell asserts. We agree. But we've also encountered some common guilt booby traps—situations and sources of guilt which you can't quite put your finger on, and which usually leave you feeling both guilty *and* paranoid. Here are a few you might recognize.

Image Disparity

Co-workers, acquaintances, even some friends may have trouble getting used to your new role. To sustain their original vision of you, they subtly downgrade your new image as parent and worker. A co-worker's laughing statement: "I just can't believe *you* are a mother/father!" frequently implies, "I refuse to believe it; it doesn't fit into my invention of you." Sensing tacit rejection, the new parent actually feels guilty not only for having a child, but for enjoying it. Non-working friends, seeing you on your first day of work, may say, "Aren't you dressed up!", a seemingly innocuous statement that can bowl us over with guilt for having a job and being different.

The Ping-Pong Effect

You've had a bad day at the office, so you're irritable all evening and guilty all night. You're up all night with a sick child? No wonder it's so hard to write that memo the next day. You feel guilty about not doing your best at work. A psychic rivalry develops between home and workplace and, rather than see the fulfillment of both jobs as a matter of balance and compromise, you tear yourself in half with guilt.

Disproportionate Goals

For example, in order to buy a dream house—ostensibly a family goal—parents work overtime and favor work commitments so as not to jeopardize a long-term plan. Family life suffers, but they see the sacrifices as temporary and justifiable. Yet there's a residual and pervasive guilt that can be neither pinpointed nor intellectualized. It's important to frequently weigh long-term goals against current family compromises. Do they stack up?

Peer Pressure

It takes a brave soul to buck the tide. We know a woman who apologized for quitting her job after one year to stay home with her baby. "I would have left my job sooner, but I had talked so much to my friends about the value of work that I felt I would be copping out."

A father in a big accountancy firm confided that he had no desire to go out for drinks after work, yet he went, feeling miserable and guilty about missing his baby's bedtime. Working parenthood forces individuality and tests honesty. We suffer guilt for sins against both.

Husband-Wife Role Tensions

Arthur and Alice had what they thought was a good arrangement. He encouraged her to go to work so as not to be "just a housewife," and she backed his efforts to be more involved at home at the temporary expense of his career. What happened? Each made the other feel guilty—Arthur by criticizing Alice's part-time mothering, Alice by harping on Arthur's missed promotion.

Quality Control

"It's not the quantity, but the *quality* of time spent with children that counts," goes the new adage. Consequently, we as working parents want our end-of-day encounters to be serene, fulfilling, and trouble-free: Grade A quality. Of course the whines and normal chaos encountered at the door are not what we had in mind. Quality home life runs the gamut from tranquil to tantrum, just as the work day is characterized by ups and downs. Yet we often blame work for the inescapable problems of parenthood. If the child wakes up at night, has trouble socially, wears Pampers at four, or seems cranky each evening, we feel guilty for working. Unfortunately, using work as a scapegoat often prevents us from taking a good look at the total situation and judging other possible causes.

We offer no techniques for reducing guilt, and no promise that it *can* be reduced. We do know parents, however, who are able to channel this form of emotional energy. How? By frequently reevaluating and redressing the work/family balance. One highly successful real estate financier and socialite rises at 5:30 AM to spend a prime hour with his toddler son, whom he's not likely to see again that day. A pediatrician and medical school professor brings her own kids into the office when "things get crazy" so that she can be near them and give them a notion of her work demands. Another working couple decide to give up their house in the suburbs and move to the city, reducing commuting time and expanding family time.

Searching for a personal balance and value system can put peer pressure, advice from left field, office ostracism, the babysitter's complaints, and our own masochistic tendencies into perspective. There's

no money-back guarantee, but respondents to our questionnaire reassure us almost unanimously that guilt diminishes as new parents
learn to trust themselves.

Overload

The washer, the dryer, the toaster, and the air conditioner are all on
at once. Suddenly everything stops. The lights go out. Electrical overload has blown a fuse. It's not just a matter of throwing a switch to
reactivate the works. First you must decide which appliance has top
priority and phase out some of the others for the time being. Human
overload is more insidious; the fuse may not blow dramatically. If we
have a tendency to push ourselves, the further we go the further we
think we can go. Working parents are especially vulnerable: all systems are at full juice, and there's no time for refueling, either emotionally or physically.

Nancy Lewis is a vice president with a New York City bank. Her
husband is a corporate executive who travels frequently. Their child
is well cared for by a live-in babysitter. The Lewises' lives hurtle
along by the force of sheer momentum. He's out of town more and
more, while she puts in overtime to keep up with the corporate
Joneses. It's been weeks since they've been together as a family for
more than a morning bowl of cereal. While both Lewises continue to
thrive in their jobs, life as a whole whizzes by in a dizzying blur. For
the Lewises, the fuse blows when the babysitter quits, and they can't
find the time to interview a successor properly.

The crisis is different in every overloaded family, but the manifes-
tations are universal.

Loss of Perspective

There are no report cards at home and no raises if you do a good
job. At work, tangible rewards and prestige reflect accomplishments.
It's easy to believe that your boss needs you more than your family
does, and family obligations begin to look trivial, or at least defer-
rable.

Panic

It arises more from our distorted perception of what is required than from the real demands of home and work. Panic candidates include the young mother who resumes a career and feels she must be a super-achiever in both spheres; the climbing executive who fears that parenthood may dilute job effectiveness and overcompensates; the parent who has too many things going on at home or at work, but has no idea how to steer a reasonable course and therefore speeds up instead of slowing down. Panic is often the sad result of the "you can have it all" promise gone sour: maximum effectiveness in a maximum number of spheres usually boils down to maximum stress and minimal control.

Passing the Buck

"I am a strongly work-oriented person who also has intense commitments to family. If I can't seem to find a workable balance between the two, it's not my fault. Both corporate and family life conspire to place unreasonable burdens on me. Life would be smooth and well-balanced if it weren't for (my wife, the "system," the new baby, that deadline, our mortgage, my in-laws . . .)." Advice to buck passer: Only *you* can prevent burn-out.

Escapism

A "very busy" working parent simply has no time to confront such homely topics as marital stress, child care, self-growth, and health. Escapists believe they have a corner on the busyness market and force everyone else to do double time. In addition, an overloaded parent has no "free hand" to extend to his or her family. Perhaps this is the modern equivalent of an old escapist tradition—the chronically ailing parent who had no strength to deal with family realities.

Fish out of Water

So entrenched is this parent in the workplace that home does not even feel like home. Getting through a family or social outing seems more difficult than preparing a last-minute report. In his book, *The Executive Parent*, psychiatrist Stephen P. Hersh describes this form of alienation from the intimate environment as "a feeling of anomie, of having no importance and no existence without work."

Coping with Overload

Dual-career couples shared with us the following suggestions for avoiding overload.

✓ Have a "meeting" with your partner in which you list, point by point, the ways your lives have gone out of control. Don't try to tackle these issues yet. Just get them down on paper, or at least out in the open. Only then can you reasonably and objectively consider concrete alternatives.

✓ Draw up a balance sheet for those overloaded times if your work is seasonally stressful, like that of an accountant during tax season. List the specific forms your temporary overload will take (i.e., work brought home, weekends at the office, business trips, intense mental preoccupation, physical exhaustion). Then spell out the ways in which you can continue *some* family involvement, no matter how minimal. This might include simply sitting down at dinner three times a week. Finally, agree all around about which activities will have to be totally suspended during the siege, such as chauffering or housework, with the specific understanding that you'll resume full involvement when things ease off. (This is one form of short-term family contracts. For more on contracts, see our *Marriage* chapter.)

✓ Don't become reclusive. Remember the restorative value of being with people you enjoy outside of your work sphere. Stepping away for a few "wasted" hours can increase your effectiveness when you get back to the grind.

✓ Try to keep a handle on how you act toward your family after a tough week at work. The tendency to vent work frustrations on a child or spouse, or to relinquish your responsibility to discipline a child, will only add to your stress in the long run.

✓ Don't lose sight of each other's restorative needs. See if you can accommodate them when possible. These can range from a long, hot, uninterrupted bath to a solo country weekend.

✓ Try to find out why you take work home on a regular basis. Is this a crutch to keep you from having to focus on family? Do you need to improve your on-the-job efficiency? Are you trying to "show and tell" your family how hard you work at supporting them?

✓ Don't be penny-wise and pound-foolish. If you have it, spend the money on the best child care you can find, plus back-up when necessary. Paid housecleaning help, take-home dinners, work-saving appliances all save time that you can channel into family relationships.

✓ Do you feel that you're subtly being edged out of family life?

Actually encouraged to devote *more* time to work? It's possible. We've heard mothers sigh with relief when they know father's not coming home for dinner. Less cooking, clean up, and sexual demands are seen as benefits. If this is the case, you're facing a marital, not a work, problem. Professional counseling might be required if you can't talk it out together.

↗ Review overall career and family goals with your partner. Will the current stress and exhaustion continue indefinitely? Do you think your family life as a whole is endangered? If so, are you willing—and able—to sit down together and work out a new plan?

↗ Don't think of overload as exclusive to working parents. A housebound parent, with full responsibility for home and young children and with no help and outlets, is a prime candidate for overload. The key word to remember in avoiding physical and emotional blackout is balance—a healthy ration of work, leisure, family time, and personal time.

Dual-career parents unanimously agree that some career compromise is essential for family survival, but family-based compromise can go only so far toward avoiding overload. We need help. "The greatest threat to the health of the family . . . is the lack of an underlying social-support system molded around the premise of working parents," wrote working mother Suzanne Schiffman in *The New York Times*. "Western society, particularly ours, is shamefully ill-equipped to assist people in the demanding task of balancing positive parenting with professional achievement. . . . Through well-planned intertwinings of parental and professional responsibilities based on compromise and flexibility, working and parenting can be balanced to benefit career, child, and, ultimately the family."

Home Sweet Home

Mister Rogers comes through the door, puts on his sweater and sneakers, and we are in the presence of a kindly, fatherly spirit. In reality, switching off the work mentality is hard work. We carry with us into our home all the day's baggage—the crises, slights, unfinished business. Unconsciously, we're apt to foist these work concerns on spouse and children, effectively putting the entire family on "overtime." Unintentionally, they bombard us with familial concerns. There's rarely time to "slip into something more comfortable" before we trade one job for another.

Re-entry to home life is, according to psychiatrist Stephen P. Hersh in *The Executive Parent*, "one of the day's major shifts within the daily cycle of families." Most of us need at least two periods of transition, a physical one from workplace to home base and a psychological reacclimation to family life.

With small children it's unlikely that the working parent, nerves rubbed raw, will be given the space he or she needs to unwind. Instead, a harried babysitter, a spouse's tales of domestic woe, tired children, and our own ambivalence greet us. Without thinking, we signal that it's the *family's* responsibility to nurse and restore us in time for the next day in the workplace. If we don't receive the kind of care we require, the family's at fault. Often, families comply with this unspoken request and try to downplay the normal turmoil of domestic life. These families run the risk of generating "silent discomfort, anxiety, and guilt," Dr. Hersh observes. Parents sometimes come to see work as the refuge, or at least as a place where cause and effect are more predictable.

At one time, the home-as-refuge ideal was most often perpetuated by the full-time homemaker who set the stage for a harried, provider father. But what happens when both parents have demanding jobs, and both seek refuge at home? Without compassion and planning, refuge seekers may well turn into refugees. Here are some suggestions for guiding yourself and your partner into easier work/home transition:

↗ Make a conscious effort to relieve your mind of work in the travel period between posts. If you commute, don't shuffle papers; try reading a novel or newspaper instead. If you drive, listen to music or a talk show that doesn't quote Dow Jones. Imagine some of the nice things you'll do when you get home.

↗ Establish a homecoming routine that takes into account some of your personal needs, no matter how briefly. For instance, open the mail, change your clothes, wash your face, before the family onslaught. If you're relieving a babysitter, ask her to stay an extra five minutes to help your transition.

↗ Don't be misguided by the concept of quality time as a time free from conflict. Children will often save their complaints especially for you because they feel comfortable acting out with a parent. It's perfectly normal to have a period of tension when parents return home.

↗ Don't bring your work home with you. Obviously it cuts down on the amount of time you spend with your family, but it also adds an unwanted tension to that diminished time.

↗ Discourage business associates from calling you at home. Invest in a telephone-answering machine to ensure uninterrupted family time, but no missed messages.

↗ Try not to arrive home "starved." Have an energy- and mood-boosting snack before leaving work.

↗ Establish a regular, dependable family time and daily private time with each child and with your partner. Family members are less likely to assail you at the door when they know they'll have your undivided attention later.

↗ Balance the books if there is one working parent who is the first to arrive home every night (and is therefore able to prepare a slightly calmer homecoming for the other), by allowing that parent some extra free time later each evening, or on weekends.

The Changing Workplace

In the recent film, *Nine to Five*, three put-upon women employees of a large corporation kidnap the boss and take over the office. Their aim, largely realized, is to give fellow workers what they really want —a totally humanistic office reorganization. The "revolutionaries" start an on-site daycare center, institute flexitime, promote the concept of shared jobs, and equalize salaries for men and women. The cumulative effect of these changes: a 20 percent increase in productivity.

Sheer Hollywood fantasy? Yes and no. Though the actual American workplace is still far from this celluloid dream, it is a fact that such companies as Northwestern Mutual Life Insurance Company in Minneapolis, which reduced turnover from 38 percent to 12 percent since instituting flexitime in the early 1970s, and the Stride-Rite Corporation of Massachusetts, which provides daycare at the factory, have answered employee needs in a forthright manner.

At General Electric, a counseling office helps workers chart career potential within the organization and from the ground up. At Xerox Corporation, employees can apply for full-year, salaried leaves to work for social agencies of their choice. Some offices of the U.S. government now offer flexitime hours. The reason? "There's a different reciprocity between employer and employee. People are asking themselves, 'What is the company doing to help *me*?,'" Walter Storey, who developed GE's counseling program, told us.

"The period of the 'Me decade' in the 1970s definitely made it all right to be true to yourself. A company couldn't tell you what to do any more," observes Ronald Janoff, director of the career counseling and resource center at New York University. "The sense of self in an employee is very real today, and so, increasingly, is the sense of family."

Milford Jacobson, vice president for personnel at Northwestern Mutual Life Insurance, believes that his firm's radical downswing in turnover after flexitime was instituted is no fluke: "If we see our boss as a good guy who's working in an environment that allows him to be that way, that must mean the company as a whole is a pretty good place. To many of us, the company is how *we* get treated by *our* boss."

A Primer on Work Options

FLEXITIME

Employees choose the hours they will work, within company-imposed limits. For example, one worker could opt for a 7 AM to 3 PM schedule; another for 11 AM to 7 PM. However, all employees must work a "core" schedule—in this case, say 11 AM to 3 PM. Flexitime is currently the most widely adopted alternative work pattern. At least 16 percent of the nation's workforce now participates in flexitime arrangements, according to statistics provided by the National Council for Alternative Work Patterns. (See our *Help* chapter for address.)

COMPRESSED TIME

The 40-hour week is condensed into a four-day (10 hours a day) or three-day (13 hours and 20 minutes a day) schedule. According to the Bureau of Labor Statistics, almost one million jobs fall under this category.

WORK SHARING

Two people divide the duties and responsibilities of one job. They may be husband and wife sharing teaching or small business employment, but job sharers more likely will be total strangers. One works 8 AM to noon, for instance, and the other picks up the 1 PM to 5 PM shift. Job continuity is maintained through memos, telephone calls, and, if necessary, periodic meetings. This is a perfect arrangement for clerical, factory, research, social service, and academic job holders.

CONTINUOUS SERVICE LEAVE

Having put in a certain amount of time with the company, the employee is entitled to a specified leave of absence, at full or partial pay, with the assurance of continued benefits and job resumption upon return. While maternity leave is the most widely accepted form of "sabbatical" in this country, non-sexist personal leave time could benefit new fathers, as well. The Rolm Corporation, a California computer manufacturer, offers employees with six years of full-time service a 12-week leave with pay and benefits. Eligibility is renewed every seven years.

The overriding benefit of these alternative work patterns is that they offer employees a full job with all benefits, vacation time, and nine-to-five status. Or, in the case of shared job holders, benefits are split along with hours.

Going Back to Work

Fewer than 20 percent of American women are now conventional housewives and mothers. Of this number, at least one-third say they will return to work in the future. For an increasing number of new mothers, especially those who left the work force after a decade or more of career engagement, when to return to work becomes a giant issue. "The big question in our house is when I will go back to work," says a mother of two preschoolers who is a teacher by profession. "Every time I think I'm ready, something else comes up, like toilet training, looking for nursery schools, or sleep problems. I think, how can I leave now? To say I'm obsessed and haunted by the work question is to put it lightly."

The work question appears in many guises—practical, philosophical, and intensely emotional. One woman may find all three factors complicating the solution most often suggested by outsiders: to just go back when she's ready. So bogged down by mixed feelings is the average new parent that the stumbling blocks to decision making loom larger by the day. Here are some of the most common.

Logistics

The sheer complexity of arranging for child care, establishing (and maintaining) a smooth work/home schedule, and countless unanticipated nuts and bolts, such as buying a presentable wardrobe, paralyze the decision process. The problem is compounded when individuals who see future work as a probability nevertheless make decisions that undermine that future, such as purchasing a house in an inaccessible area.

Out of Touch

You're out of the work force for three years, in keeping with your promise to immerse yourself fully in motherhood. The fear of having fallen too far behind in a profession demanding continual study, contacts, practice—from medicine to stenography—is overwhelming. So? Keep in touch. Take a refresher course. Subscribe to relevant periodicals. Visit the library. See former colleagues occasionally. And what if the fear of being a mere shadow of your former dynamic self is the real problem? Consider that while your preoccupations are fatigue, divided commitment, and guilt, many childless workers have their own assorted neuroses, real and imagined, including romantic entanglements, housing woes, and tax inequities. In other words, you're not alone.

Feminist Backfire

How could you possibly have predicted that you wouldn't feel like going back to work after six weeks or six months? You never believed parenthood could be this fulfilling. Yet you feel guilty and apologetic. You expected yourself to work. And the modern men and women in whose fishbowl you swim will be distressed at your decision to take additional time off. Then there's your spouse, a fully contemporary fellow who has often said, "My wife's capable of everything and anything. Of course she'll continue working. She wouldn't be happy otherwise."

The Right Time

"When is the right time to return to work?" Many who ask, really want to know when guilt will no longer impede the decision-making process. Most likely, if guilty thoughts about leaving baby clog your mind, *whenever* you resume work you'll experience a sinking and fearful feeling that is often intensfied by the conflicting opinions and warnings of experts and veteran parents you consult.

Inertia

Having set no deadlines for resuming work, you find yourself carried along by the routines of your life as a parent. Every time you even think about work, lethargy takes over. But not before you pose the pregnant question: "Whatever happened to my motivation?" Complaining becomes your main mode of expression. That downtrodden look and its whining vocal counterpart are hardly the personality qualifications needed to sell yourself in the job market.

Finances

"After expenses, we wind up *paying* for me to work," says one mother bitterly. "Though I love my job I sometimes feel it's a luxury we can't afford." So much of her salary is earmarked for daycare and commuting that there's no budget for household help, adult leisure activities, or extra babysitting. Because she loves what she does, this woman feels she's not entitled to any other frills. She teeters on the line between superwoman and superdrudge.

Occupational Malaise

Just because you dedicated 10 hectic years to establishing a career doesn't mean you want to spend the rest of your life in that line of work. Two-thirds of the 23,000 respondents to a *Psychology Today* work survey said there was some likelihood they would switch careers in the next five years. Having a baby gives us marvelous perspective on the meaning and likely course of our work lives. Sometimes the "rewarding" job left behind seems trivial, though it once was the most important element in our lives. The spectre of starting fresh may be intimidating, but remember that you'll no longer be the only oldster in class. And don't forget you've got a good 20 to 35 years of professional productivity before you!

The Two Dust-Rag Family: or, Sharing Housework

"My husband helps me out more with my housework since I took a full-time job."

What's wrong with this statement?

The tip-off phrase is *"my housework."* While current surveys show that men are more willing to do household chores, working mothers still find themselves the victims of what sociologists Rhona and Robert Rapoport call " 'double exploitation' at work and at home, rather than the desired liberation," in their book, *Dual Career Families Re-examined.*

Many women still regard the home as *their* domain. They know best how to keep it clean and functioning. Either through possessiveness or

conditioning, they believe their husbands incapable of handling domestic tasks, so working mothers continue to accept peripheral help
rather than shared responsibility on the home front.

How can we begin to divide up such an abstract assignment as responsibility? By recognizing that every job in the home follows a logi-
cal and practical sequence that *can be learned*. Just as we've come to
accept that both mothers *and* fathers have a nurturing instinct or potential, so we're on the verge of believing that neither sex suffers a
congenital inability to vacuum. When the mystique of housework
goes, so do the excuses for avoidance.

Take a typical household task that is both frequent and important:
the laundry. Unless you've decided to take charge of laundry on a rotating basis, or do it together, the person *not* responsible for the wash
should never have to worry about it, remind anyone, answer how-to
questions, or go without clean underwear. In return, of course, the
launderer could free his or her mind totally of grocery shopping, or
cooking, or whatever else you've agreed upon. Of course there's no
such thing as household Utopia, but we can approach a livable equi-
librium if we keep in mind the basic components of chore division.

Understanding the Relative Importance of a Task

A crucial factor in assuming responsibility for a task is being aware
of how it fits into the household cosmos. People who are used to being
looked after usually have no idea of (and may often be intimidated
by) the complex system of judgment and planning behind simple
housekeeping.

Each task should be weighed objectively, not subjectively. Try going without clean laundry for a week and see what happens. Polishing
the silver, on the other hand, can be avoided or eliminated by storing
the items. Laundry, like grocery shopping, cooking, and dishwashing,
demands regular attention. Window washing can be regarded as seasonal, while as-needed jobs include waxing the floors. To avoid confusion and copping out on important recurring tasks, it helps to keep
the following points in mind when preparing your work contract.

✓ Make a list of all household chores and give them a rating from
one to ten. Make sure you agree upon ratings before noting them.

✓ Next to each job, state an agreed-upon frequency: weekly, daily,
monthly, seasonal, or as needed.

✓ If your family is used to doing everything as needed, life in a
dual-career system might require more scheduling than customary.
Don't fight it—routines are good for your health!

⟡ Be aware of tasks that are important only to *you*. Try to liberate yourself by eliminating some of them. You might consider putting away dry dishes or alphabetizing books on a shelf a must-do. But must you?

⟡ Once you've made up your importance and frequency lists, arrange the tasks in descending order of importance. Then eliminate the bottom third of the list and try to imagine what life would be like with these omissions. In a *Woman's Day* survey of working wives, more than half the respondents said they had cut housework by at least 50 percent. Furthermore, 98 percent no longer regularly cleaned children's rooms; 69 percent had done away with traditional spring cleaning; 34 percent with ironing and making beds.

⟡ Finally, divide the remaining tasks on the list so that each of you has a fair share, but chores that relate to your talents and schedule. The equity of this arrangement is entirely up to you, but it's best to attempt fairness from the start.

Scheduling

Now that the person responsible for a task is aware of its importance and required frequency, he or she has to figure out *when* to do it and *how long* it will take. If necessary, put a notation on your chart: John will do laundry Monday nights from 8 to 10. Or, the chore could be noted in a personal calendar. There should be no room for such excuses as "Why didn't you remind me?" or "I've been too busy."

Couples we know who shared housework before parenthood are baffled by the complexities of juggling domestic and parental responsibilities. "We used to just pitch in on Saturdays and clean the house together like maniacs for about three or four hours, then go out for Chinese food to reward ourselves," said one father. "Now it's 'You take Joshua while I do the floors,' and 'I'll give him a bath while you do the dishes.' At first we resented the bargaining involved, but now we see it as a plus. Since we both work, the barter system helps in two ways—one of us gets a chore done without interruption while the other gets to spend some private time with our son. In the end, we're left with more time to spend *together*, too."

Affinity

Who can tolerate what? Jay was in the Army and is an incomparable latrine scrubber. He's good at grocery shopping, child hair-washing, and all pet-related activities. Neil finds washing dishes therapeutic, and considers it his responsibility. He's made the nightly garbage

patrol a father-son activity during which he teaches Nicky the intricacies of waste disposal.

There are inevitably certain jobs for which neither partner has affinity—and that includes men, like Jay, who hate to fix things, and
women, like Maria, who hate to mend them. In dividing jobs, try to
steer away from stereotypes unless you *really* feel more comfortable
with these. Equally hated jobs can be alternated, or assigned by drawing lots. It's been said that men often take on jobs that show visible
and permanent results, such as fixing, painting, or building things,
while women are relegated to the repetitive and ephemeral, such as
cleaning, cooking, and tidying up. If this is your job division pattern,
it might be worthwhile to revamp it.

Finally, there's the division between so-called "fun" and "drudge"
jobs. Taking the kids to the zoo on Saturday is a responsibility, but it
doesn't stack up against staying home with a week's housework. Obviously, we all have a greater affinity for the fun jobs. The others are, at
best, an acquired taste. It doesn't hurt to take a "try it, you'll like it"
approach, either. Both parents should try each household chore for at
least a week before passing final judgment on affinity.

Competence

Almost any job can be learned, even one with the subtle requirements of laundry. Should I use bleach on your lace bra? Are three
cups of detergent too much? Can I put baby's red tie-dyed shirt in
with my white ones?

Why not do as laundromats do? Post a detailed, step-by-step guide
to laundry procedures, starting with a where-to-find-it list of necessary
tools and equipment. Changing a tire has stymied women as much as
changing diapers has traditionally baffled men. There's no reason why
we can't teach each other what we know. In the process, keep these
tips in mind:

✓ Answer any questions uncritically.

✓ Don't stand around supervising or preparing to step in.

✓ Make sure you have all the necessary ingredients and equipment
in the same place so your partner doesn't have to look or ask each
time.

✓ Allow for and expect improvement over time, but don't judge the
other person's skill by your standards. "Good enough" work should be
acceptable.

⸫ Allow the other person room to bring a personal style to the execution of the task. When one husband we know does the dishes at his usual snail-like pace, his wife stands by tapping nervously on the door frame, having whizzed through her work for the day.

Dependability

A woman's work is never done, goes the old saying, and it remains true today if, when she's finished *her* work, she worries about when he'll get around to *his*. A grudging "helper" is frequently nagged, or quietly resented, by the exploited partner. Sharing home responsibilities should be seen as a commitment over time, like marriage, child care, and work.

Daycare

By 1990, in 75 percent of all two-parent families, both parents will work, according to a projection of the National Daycare Campaign conference held in Kansas City, Missouri, in 1980. That means an increasing number of parents shopping for acceptable and affordable child care. Despite government studies and promises, no national daycare policy has ever been instituted. Daycare standards are left to individual states, including the licensing and inspection of facilities. Quality varies from state to state.

Though we hear today of the usefulness and promise of group daycare, the fact remains that more than 70 per cent of working parents' children are still tended by a relative in a home setting. Another 20 percent, according to the Congressional Budget Office in a 1978 report, spend their week in a family setting with a paid caretaker. That leaves some 10 percent who use group centers or nursery schools. These two broad categories present a number of variables—an intimidating maze to be maneuvered by the working parent who wants to know, simply: "Where and how will my child best be cared for while I am at work?" Here is how we answered the question for ourselves.

Roberta's Story

The first three months of his life, Nicholas, a "perfect baby," slept a lot. During his two four-hour daytime naps I couldn't believe how easy it was to keep up with freelance assignments. Neil arranged to stay home when I needed to go out on an interview. Then, during Nick's fifth and sixth months, Neil, between jobs, was home to share child care. It was with Neil's return to work that the child care dilemma arose. We sat down and explored alternatives available in our neighborhood for a child his age. We decided, since this was our first child care experience, we'd prefer keeping Nicky at home in familiar surroundings. We placed an ad in a large newspaper, but word of mouth on the playground led us to a young nursing student who was a mother herself. Though the part-time schedule we devised fluctuated as her course work changed each semester, the afternoon hours we wanted—12 to 15 hours each week, following Nicky's late-morning nap—suited employer and employee just fine.

In theory, we understood the importance of a back-up sitter, but never did anything about it. When our regular sitter was called away on a family crisis and couldn't be sure when she'd return, we had to start all over again. A neighborhood newspaper ad produced several eager but inappropriate candidates, and a few we seriously considered. After extensive phone and in-person interviews, we hired a college student who remained Nicky's primary sitter for the next four months. When college graduation and impending marriage took her from us, Nicky's original sitter, now returned, was eager to step in. Today, we continue happily with our regular sitter. She would agree with me that it takes time to develop a sensitive working relationship.

When that relationship does flower, parent and sitter seem to be able to read each other's minds when it comes to baby-tending and making decisions and compromises over hours. We also now have a back-up arrangement with a local family daycare home, as well as one regular weekly child swap with another parent. Neil also cut his work week to four days and took responsibility for Nicky's care every Friday morning and on weekend mornings, as well. We occasionally employ a teenage neighbor for short afternoon stints on Saturday and Sunday, if work or housekeeping need attention.

When Allegra arrived we sat down, rethought and renegotiated our joint child care responsibilities. After more than three years of parenthood, equity—for ourselves together, individually, and for our children —remains a vital theme for us.

ROBERTA'S PERSONAL TIPS

✓ Strive for long-term employment arrangements, but steel yourself for the short term. Even the most reliable caretaker needs vacations, and will be called away by family illness or the vicissitudes of life, including transportation breakdowns.

✓ If you work at home as I do, make it clear to your sitter—and this may take more than one conference—that what you do is just as important and carefully scheduled as outside employment.

✓ It is vital for home-based workers to create a separate and reasonably inviolable work space, preferably as far away from the child's play area as possible.

✓ When you are home, inform the sitter of your schedule, and whether she will or will not be responsible for answering the phone or doorbell. If you both run to fill these functions, the child will become confused, and you will lose precious work time. If you do not want to be disturbed, *close the door and absent yourself completely.*

✓ A vital advantage to at-home care is that when your child is ill, the babysitter still comes. Unless he's terribly sick, *let* her come.

✓ Don't make the sitter feel she is second in command just because you are home (except in an emergency). Let her know you have confidence in her and don't interfere. This way she's less likely to interrupt you with questions and problems she's afraid to solve independently.

Maria's Story

The first three months of his life, Jud cried a lot. I'd quit my job in publishing before his birth and was relieved when I pictured what life would have been like with a colicky baby *and* full-time employment. My mother and aunt each came once a week for the first six months to relieve me for a few hours, and my mother cooked and froze main dishes we could eat later on. Otherwise, I was on my own. Jay had just taken a new job and was busy proving himself.

We decided it was vital to have some dependable free time, so a teenage sitter was hired for three hours a week. I had Saturdays off, courtesy of my husband. When Jud was about eight months old, I joined a small play group from which I derived two free mornings a week in exchange for leading the group on a third morning. I was pleased with the arrangement for the second year, but supplemented it with an additional day of child care by a local young mother who took in several children in her nearby apartment. When I look back on it now, I basically eased myself into a situation that made me feel secure, and was then able to start planning and accepting my first freelance writing assignments.

At three, Jud entered nursery school where he spent 15 hours a week. When Jud was four, Jay left the corporate life and began his own business. To help pay the bills, I took a part-time teaching job and simultaneously expanded my writing assignments. Jud was frequently ill during that winter, and Jay got a crash course in role-sharing by caring for our ailing child while I was at work. Today, Jud is in school from 9 AM to 3 PM and Jay and I share child care fairly equally. In fact, Jud's teacher recently remarked that Jud is the only child to go off each day leaving both his parents behind to work at home!

✓ Don't count on a parent-run playgroup for important work time. There are just too many illnesses and unexpected personal complications acting against a dependable schedule.

✓ Be aware that you are responsible for payment even when your child is sick, unless you have negotiated otherwise. Child care is an important source of income for many women and should not be treated irresponsibly by you, the employer.

✓ If you join a playgroup, sit down beforehand, and establish rules and review philosophy. Differences are to be expected, but it's reassuring to know something about other parents' beliefs.

✓ Steel yourself for an onslaught of baby colds if you decide to participate in a group care situation. Parents who have tight work schedules often send sick children on their way. Though it's up to the caretaker of the school to set firm guidelines, there's not much to be done with sickness that appears suddenly after lunch if the parent can't come and pick up his charge.

Taking the Big Step: Hiring a Caregiver

A certain mystique surrounds good sitters who work for other people. They seem to have sprung full blown into their positions for us to marvel at and, let's face it, even envy a little bit. In truth, there are three primary ways to find a sitter, and each of us must try one or more of them at some time if we value our independence.

Word of Mouth

It's not uncommon for good sitters to become disenfranchised when their charges start school. Observe sitters in the neighborhood. Ask them directly if they or someone they recommend needs employment. Discussing your needs with other mothers may also result in part-time sharing of capable sitters, or eventually inheriting trusted sitters. The main drawback of the word-of-mouth method is time and the element of luck.

Agencies

This is a reliable but definitely more expensive tactic. Some parents are happy to pay the higher fee in exchange for the knowledge that the applicant has been carefully pre-screened and is considered a thorough professional (though, of course, not all applicants referred by an agency will fit your needs).

Newspaper Advertisement

If you are a city dweller and place your ad in a large-circulation newspaper, be prepared to receive a flood of calls—as many as 40 or 50 in New York, for instance. If you have many applicants, the initial phone screening becomes exceptionally important. It is here that you should first state your needs and discern that the callers haven't contacted you on a whim.

Community or ethnic newspapers will not elicit as many responses, which may suit you fine. Wherever you advertise, be sure to state your requirements clearly and simply. Here's a sample ad:

> Mature, sensitive woman needed to care for six-month-old child, 8 AM to 1 PM, M-F. Non-smoker essential. Refs required. Call 123-4567, after 6 PM.

Despite specificity in your ad, eager candidates of all ages are likely to call you at all hours. Roberta even heard from a teenage boy looking for manual labor who figured child care was as demanding as construction work. A good way to limit responses to desired hours is to use an answering machine with an appropriate message, such as: "Hi. This is ——. I can't come to the phone right now. If you are responding to our advertisement about daycare, please leave your name and number and I will get back to you tonight."

SCREENING CALLERS

Before the phone starts ringing, you should be prepared with a brief list of questions. Don't be at all surprised if many of your callers have not read your ad carefully, or hope to sway you to another schedule. It's a good idea to be firm and to screen out these callers immediately.

Your explanation of the job, to those who profess interest in it as described in the ad, might go something like this: "Let me tell you a little about the job. The baby is six months old and very active. He needs someone willing and able to keep up with him. He enjoys being outside even when it's cold. Since I work, I need someone who will be thoroughly dependable and I'm not interested in any short-term applicants. The sitter will be responsible for child care only, and for neatening up the baby's room. As stated in the ad, we're looking for a nonsmoker. We're offering $—— an hour to work 8 AM to 1 PM weekdays. Do you have any questions?"

Now comes the second stage of the phone interview. The caller may state some reservations, which you should judge accordingly. Or, she may enthusiastically accept your conditions.

Here are some questions you might ask before committing to an in-person interview:

 ✓ Have you any previous daycare experience?
 ✓ Do you have children of your own?
 ✓ How far away do you live?
 ✓ Do you have references?
 ✓ I'd like someone to start in two weeks. Will you be available?

Keep a chart in front of you on which you write the name of each caller, and mark the date set for the interview. Jot down any phone impressions to compare with the forthcoming meeting. Make sure you repeat the day, date, and time of the interview a few times to avoid confusion.

CONDUCTING AN INTERVIEW

Here are some general pointers to take into account before and during the interview, adapted from Jane Price's valuable book, *How to Have a Child and Keep Your Job*.

 ✓ Prepare your questions together, making sure each of you makes your major concerns known to the applicant at the interview and not at some hazy future date. The candidate should see you as a united team. Bickering over philosophy during an interview might give a responsible applicant instant doubts about working in your home.
 ✓ It's important to interview the applicant together so that you can compare impressions afterward. If you are a single parent, it might help to have an experienced parent or someone who knows you and your child sit in on the interview.

⌁ Remember that this is a business interview, not an inquisition or cocktail party. A brisk and friendly manner is usually most effective.

⌁ Keep in mind that the more interviews you conduct, the better you will be able to judge applicants. The first few sessions will be the most nervewracking.

⌁ Try to cover every foreseeable detail, from vacations to duties expected other than child care, if any.

⌁ Don't try to seduce the applicant into taking a job if you know there may be problems such as frequent overtime, isolated environment, or a problem child. Make any of these possibilities known during your job description.

⌁ Be thorough in your review of the applicant's work history. Don't necessarily be impressed by experience in fields such as social work, nursing, or teaching. A good child care person is one who has taken care of children on a one-to-one basis and is able to convey to you some sense of genuine interest in the work.

⌁ Ask for at least two references. If the applicant has worked in the child care field, at least one reference from a former employer is helpful. Your phone call to this employer should elicit two kinds of information: the applicant's relationship to and treatment of the children and family, and her work habits, including punctuality and attendance. If the other reference is not a child care situation, don't hesitate to inquire about general responsibility and productivity. Hard workers are hard workers.

⌁ Allow the applicant to describe her concept of childraising, including her views on discipline, children's eating habits, pacifiers and thumbsucking, toilet training—whatever is important to her. You can often learn more from what the applicant chooses to talk about than from her answers to specific questions.

⌁ Be firm about your television rules, if any, as well as whether the caregiver will be permitted to take the child on shopping trips in a car or by public transportation. You should let her know how you feel about visiting strange playgrounds and the homes of her friends or people your child meets on the playground, but whom you've never met. These issues will come up again, on the job.

⌁ Try to spot signs of ill health and emotional conflict. Be wary of candidates who use the interview situation to provide you with a blow-by-blow account of a recent personal crisis, especially if you have the tendency to be a do-gooder. You don't want to end up babysitting for somebody else if you can help it!

⌁ No matter how distracting, having your child present during the interview is a wise idea. The applicant should give you spoken and unspoken evidence of interest in the child. Also, she should be able to think clearly through disruption and other typical childhood antics. Obviously, you should note how the child warms up to the applicant, and take that seriously when you decide whom to hire.

↗ Keep notes, especially if you will be talking to several applicants. Later, there will be no confusion about who said what.

↗ You may want to space your interviews more broadly at first— say, one an hour—to get the hang of it. Later, a half-hour may be enough to judge an applicant. Knowing how to end an interview is also important. When you think you've given the person enough time, stand up, thank her for coming, and see her out. Say you have several more applicants to consider, and that you will give her a call later in the week with your decision. Then *do* call, as a matter of courtesy, even if you decide on somebody else. Once in a while, you may want to hire someone interviewed earlier. This is possible only if cordiality and consideration have been maintained.

↗ After the applicant departs, jot down any further impressions next to the original phone comments.

Finally, a word about first impressions and intuition. On the phone, and certainly in person, you will take to certain people and not to others. Unlike stenography, child care is not a technical skill. You should place great value on the human element, sometimes at the expense of a few minor requirements, such as age. A warm, caring caretaker in her twenties who impresses you with intelligence should be taken seriously, even if you had it in your head to hire a mature woman only.

When you've made a decision, plan to have the new sitter come in a day or two *before* you start your job. Stick around and show her the ropes. Let her get a feeling for your style and allow yourself to get a feeling for hers. If you are satisfied with this on-the-job training, for which she will receive full salary, say so. Then go to work with confidence in your choice.

Don't be apologetic or embarrassed if you suffer separation anxiety the first few days or even weeks on the job. It's natural and maybe even desirable to worry about the sitter's handling of your child. You may want to call home frequently at first, but the urge does subside. As one mother told us: "The first day I left, as soon as I got to my job I raced for a phone. I kept calling every day, out of habit, really. Eventually, I had nothing to ask the sitter. I knew she was doing a good job by then. My calls served no purpose. I was quite calm about working and being away occasionally. So I stopped. I only call now when the baby's sick, or if I have a specific comment."

In the beginning, you'll probably also take special notice of the sitter's handling of your child when you leave and come home. If both events continue at fever pitch, nobody's mental health is served. What if your caretaker just doesn't work out; after a month, or even less, you feel a mistake has been made? It's not the end of the world. Most veteran working parents find that, no matter how superb the home care, it's not always permanent. Our greatest fear is that the child will be harmed by the changing caregivers. In truth, children are quite adaptable to new faces, within reason. If the parents remain the stable, primary caregivers, in body and spirit, new faces become part of the necessary expansion of the child's world. Certainly, when sitters are exiting and entering it's unwise to step up your social schedule or to introduce other major changes in family life, such as moving.

Pros and Cons of Individual Home Care

For an infant, or a family with more than one small child, home care is ideal. The developing child matures in a familiar environment, and parents of larger families are spared the inconvenience of dressing and transporting kids every day. Also, when your child is sick, this is really the only working option.

As the infant grows older and he needs to socialize, home care can become isolating and antithetical to the child's intellectual and physical growth. In addition, the ideal infant caregiver may be too protective and strict with an adventurous toddler. We know of one sitter who interpreted the enthusiastic personality of a 13-month-old walker as evidence of "willful misconduct." Another had rigid toilet training ideas which did not surface until her charge was 15 months old.

Just as often, though, a caregiver who pleased you earlier will continue to bring you peace of mind. This person should not be easily cast adrift. In some neighborhoods where parents feel pressured to send young two-year-olds to nursery school, very fine sitters are let go. Think twice about just what you will be giving up when a trusted sitter departs, sometimes prematurely. The alternative is not always better. While a caregiver is in your employ, let her know that the growth and development of your child is very important to you. Frequent conferences, as casual or formal as suits your style, can accomplish this. The most rewarding kind of caregiving experience, for parent and sitter (and child) is one in which the joys and problems are shared. The best home caregivers honestly care about your child.

Remember, though that you are an *employer*, and have certain legal and ethical obligations to your employee should she be full-time. At least one week's vacation with pay after one year, and two weeks thereafter, are traditional. Also, any employee is entitled to some paid sick leave. A five-day-a-week caregiver should expect at least five paid sick days a year and some fair, prearranged schedule of paid holidays. You as the employer are also expected to pay her Social Security taxes, provided she earns more than $50 a quarter. Contact your Social Security Administration office for details.

How to handle your financial commitment to a part-time employee is less clear-cut. Again, questions about terms of payments should be negotiated upon hiring, and these include whether or not to award vacation time, sick days, and reimbursement for work time missed when you are on vacation or for some other reason do not require your sitter's services on a day she is scheduled for work. We've discovered that while most part-time sitters do not expect vacations or sick-time benefits, they naturally perform better and are more apt to remain loyal if you make salary arrangements on days they expect to work but their services are not required. Let's say you expect to be out-of-town for two weeks, during which time your sitter would normally work 28 hours. One equitable solution is to pay her a regular salary each of these weeks, but apply the time she does not work to the weeks before and after your trip. That way she can pay her bills, and you'll have more time to prepare for your trip, unpack, and carry on with other responsibilities.

Family Daycare

It's not uncommon for women, especially young mothers, to open their homes to neighborhood children. The family daycare arrangement usually operates in a ratio of one adult caretaker to four or five (ideally) children of varying ages. Even more ideal is a 1:2 ratio. The children are cared for in the sitter's home, sometimes alongside her own offspring. In some communities, such as Morris County, New Jersey, family daycare *providers*, as they are called, are licensed after completing child care training.

"Family daycare is winning more and more adherents," writes Barbara Kaye Greenleaf in her book, *HELP: A Handbook for Working Mothers*, "because of its unique combination of personal, institutional, and social elements." This is an extremely flexible form of daycare. By prearrangement with the caregiver, you can drop off and pick up your child as needed. Some providers also pick up their charges at school, though this entails taking along other children in their care, unless a second caregiver remains at home with them. A structured learning or activity program usually isn't part of the setup, though plenty of toys, donated by participating families, usually are. Most providers offer a homey, spontaneous environment. Pros: Flexible hours to suit your schedule; social interaction for your child with children both older and younger; personal attention when there aren't too many children; neighborhood accessibility and familiarity; reasonable cost; school pickup service when available; the parent's direct relationship with the provider rather than an institution; overnight/weekend sleep-overs often possible.

Cons: Occasional overcrowding or inadequate facilities and equipment (be sure to check fire safety conformity); a difficult age mix, say if your child is a toddler among active four-year-olds; increased likelihood of illness; necessary dragging along of younger kids when older ones are picked up at school; threat that unlicensed programs may run up against legal entanglements and be forced to close suddenly; if the provider is sick, you're in trouble!

Daycare Centers

Daycare centers are group child care services established to meet the needs of working parents. They fall under three general headings: profit-making enterprises (including franchises) financed by tuition and investor money; non-profit centers organized by community, government, church, or charitable organizations; private non-profit centers run by universities, unions, hospitals, and corporations. When these centers are open to the public, government funding is available. Earnings are put back into the running of the center. Though some people equate non-profit enterprise with reduced rates, this is not necessarily true. All forms of daycare centers are, according to the U.S. Department of Health and Human Services, subject to law: *"In every state all daycare centers must be licensed."*

Pros: Licensing implies meeting minimum space, safety, and adult/child ratio requirements. Caregivers must pass health tests. At least some of the employees are professionally trained in early childhood education. If the teacher is sick, that means somebody else is there to take her place. All this creates a stable, reliable child care option.

Many centers have age-appropriate learning programs. Others are best suited to simple babysitting. Most have outdoor facilities and substantial equipment.

Cons: The very young baby or withdrawn preschooler may be overwhelmed by the hubbub and absence of one-to-one reinforcement. For popular centers, a waiting list of a year or more is not uncommon. The adult-to-child ratio, depending on your child's age, may not be intimate enough. The profit-making franchise centers are apt to strike some parents as too commercial and impersonal. Finally, is a ten-hour day in a group situation, covering two or three shifts of caregivers, too much to ask of a small child?

Parent Cooperatives

Operated and administered by parents, with trained teachers, cooperatives require the services of parents on a rotating basis. In some cooperative situations, all parents put in time in the classroom, while in others, members can choose to donate their time in other ways, including clerical or administrative work, or money.

Paid coops take other forms such as nursery schools with salaried early childhood teachers and parent assistance; home-based play groups with a trained, salaried teacher; and, probably most common, the home-based coop where parents alone take responsibility on a rotating basis for a small group of children.

Pros: Costs are often lower than private daycare centers. Parents have direct input into the policies and programs, as well as pride in community involvement and the opportunity to share preschool experience with their children. A good way to make adult friends, share notes, gain support, or find roots.

Cons: For full-time working parents or busy part-timers, some coops demand more time than is available without hardship. Yet small children feel pride when their parents come to school. If you can't, they may feel inadequate. The parent-run play group also has the disadvantage of being subject to the illness and vagaries of early childhood.

Nursery Schools

While the services offered at most daycare centers are specifically tailored to the needs of working parents—flexible hours, wide age range, fewer holidays, year-round accessibility—nursery schools are designed with the preschooler's developmental needs in mind. That in no way implies that good daycare centers ignore the child's needs; in fact, many centers provide quality educational opportunities. Nursery schools usually take children no younger than 2½. Most have limited and inflexible hours for very young children, long and frequent vacations, and generally do not offer classes for children beyond kindergarten age. Their teachers are specially trained in early childhood education and usually hold degrees in this or related fields such as art, music, or psychology. Like any other schools, nurseries vary in philosophy, quality, and organization. See our *Help* chapter for agencies that will send you free information on daycare, nursery schools, and other child care options.

Choosing a nursery school is one of the most difficult early choices we face. There are many important abstract considerations involved, including the separation from a child from three to six hours a day; goals, fears, and ideals revolving around the child's social and intellectual life; and the personal style and philosophy of parenthood we hope will be supported and enhanced by the school. Then, there are additional practical considerations of accessibility to school, the condition of its physical plant and equipment, and whether you like the people who run it.

Susan Hinkle, educational director of the Grace Church Nursery School in Brooklyn Heights, New York, believes the most important thing for parents to remember is that the nursery school will be a *partner* in parenthood during a sensitive and developmentally complex period in the child's life. "Support and communication are the key words here," she told us. "Visit several schools and sit down with the representative of each. While you are talking, imagine you have a problem or question regarding your child. Is this a person you could come to for guidance?" Susan Hinkle believes, and we agree, that it's not enough to choose a nursery school just for the child—although certain schools are better suited to one child's temperament and learning styles than another. You must also choose a school that is right for you.

Here are essential guidelines for choosing a nursery school.

 ✓ Visit as many schools as you can and talk to the parents of other children currently attending the schools. If you do not know anyone, ask the directors for parents' names. Even a parent's praise can tell you a lot about whether a school is not for you.

✓ Don't discount your gut response to a school. Are the teachers sufficiently involved with the children? Is the atmosphere friendly, warm, and encouraging or disorganized and chaotic?

✓ Take a good look around the classroom. Are there well-defined areas for quiet and active play, with age-appropriate equipment?

✓ Safety is a non-negotiable priority. Is outdoor equipment and play area solidly constructed, sensibly located, and appropriate to your child's age level? Have smoke detectors been installed, and are fire extinguishers located for easy access? Are escape exits clearly marked and kept unlocked?

✓ Is the school licensed? Different licensing laws apply in each state, but general rules for teacher-student ratios, square-footage per child, teacher training, safety and hygienic codes are among aspects of nursery schools monitored by state authorities.

✓ Do your goals mesh with those of the school and are the educational credentials of the director and staff to your liking? If you are an academically inclined parent, emphasis on early reading skills may be important to you. But a nursery school is also a place where a child learns to get along as part of a group. That he simply plays for most of the day is not an indication that a school is failing to do its job. Do some reading about the needs and capabilities of preschoolers before you set your sights on one school.

✓ Don't bring your child on your first exploratory visit. She'll be invited later to get the feel of the place and meet other children.

✓ Don't be afraid to ask questions. If the school is not responsive to your queries now, most likely it won't be later on. Among those subjects you should know about are fees, payment schedules, teacher turnover, toilet training philosophy, availability of nurse, and the way in which separation will be handled during the first days of school.

✓ Which holidays are celebrated by the school, and in what manner (i.e., religious or secular)? Will your child's days off create havoc if you must work and find an occasional but reliable babysitter? What level of participation will be required of you once the school year begins? Some schools insist on parent participation on field trips and at party time. Will you be responsible for any fund-raising?

8

Time

Life is a never-ending stream of possible activities, constantly being replenished by your family, your teachers, your boss, your subordinates, as well as by your own dreams, hopes, desires, and by the need to stay alive and functioning. You have so much to do, but so little time!

Alan Lakein
HOW TO GET CONTROL OF YOUR TIME AND YOUR LIFE

One universal truth about parenthood is the overwhelming lack of personal time. Parenthood not only devours time, it changes its very nature. For the first few months or longer, even private adult moments are mentally shared with your child. Like falling in love, birth is a "magnificent obsession" that colors every waking moment. Later, adapting to the rhythm of parenthood, we gain the capacity for sorting out the various elements of our lives, however changed they might be. But without the skill to restructure our days and nights, getting things done isn't so simple as it seems.

Restructuring and using time effectively during the preschool years is particularly tough because mental gears must literally be shifted every few months or so to accommodate the rapid development of your child. The time patterns of a parent with an infant are very different from those of the parent with a three-year-old. And the time needs of working and non-working parents are obviously not the same.

In those first months we learn to seize haphazard pockets of time between feeding and naps. There's little predictability or flexibility. Parents at this stage are poised to anticipate and respond to the needs of *today*, which may be quite different tomorrow.

At about six months the baby becomes more scheduled and schedulable. Predictable blocks of time—after baby turns in for the night, for instance, or when he takes a regular afternoon snooze—become evident. And oh how we learn to depend on these! Until the bedtime hour is pushed back. Until the afternoon nap dwindles by half. And just as we're about to despair of getting anything done, of distilling some personal time, we suddenly realize it's remotely possible to work alongside our child for ever-increasing productive periods.

While he draws, we sketch; while she plays with clay, we cook dinner. Our description doesn't even take into account the very important time cleared through the use of babysitters, play groups, and nursery schools, and by mother/father time trades. Yet the aim is the same: to balance the demands of parenthood with the demands of a broader adult life.

There is no parental law compelling you to leave all personal or domestic chores to the end of the day when your child is asleep, using daytime hours solely for block building and reading picture books. You will *not* necessarily be a better parent for structuring your day in this way. While it's necessary and fun to play with your child and focus entirely on him for part of each day, it's also necessary—and fun for the child—to know that you are an adult with other adult responsibilities which he or she can sometimes share.

And what can't be directly shared between parent and small child can, at the very least, begin to be understood; children who are treated to plenty of love and attention are quite able to perceive, at a remarkably early age, that there are times when a parent's attention must be devoted elsewhere. The essential point is to *take yourself seriously*, wheher your personal time is spent doing crossword puzzles or preparing law briefs.

Time management expert Alan Lakein inspired us to suggest these personal time tips:

✓ Don't confuse efficiency with effectiveness. "Making the right choices about how you'll use time is more important than doing efficiently whatever job happens to be around," Lakein counsels.

✓ Avoid over-organization, overdoing, and a preoccupation with filling every available pocket of time. It's counterproductive.

✓ Have an overall system directed toward a central goal rather than a series of disjointed, mechanical shortcuts for random tasks.

✓ Clean house of superfluous and outdated social habits which now clutter your life.

✓ Plan. If life seems to be running you rather than the other way around, it's probably because you've abrogated your right to plan. Many parents have foregone that right, and use their children as scapegoats for tasks left undone.

✓ Understand the difference between daydreaming and planning.

Daydreaming means composing pleasant fictions about how you'd like life to be. Planning necessitates definite action. "Writing down goals tends to make them more concrete and specific and helps you probe below the surface of the same old cliches you've been telling yourself," Lakein suggests.

✓ Plan early in the day or late at night and keep a record of past plans. If you're new at plan-making you'll want to review the nature and completion ratio of your plans to see what patterns are being formed and how you'd like to revise future goals.

✓ Learn that doing nothing is sometimes the best thing you can do. Rigid behavior that defines valid time use as time eaten up by tasks deprives the honest worker of pockets of pleasure.

✓ Don't feel that schedules are out of place at home. There are always domestic chores, but they must not take priority over other scheduled activities.

✓ Learn how to delegate. Once aware of your priorities, you'll see that you can't do everything and will need the help of others. Ask for it.

✓ Learn to admit that some jobs don't deserve your time.

✓ Maintain a desk and work area, if only to have a regular place to sit down to make plans.

✓ Face the fact that large blocks of uninterrupted time are a rarity for *everyone*. Use small pockets of time to start projects, however big. Once you start, you'll be more apt to finish.

Time Management for Parents: Shaping Your Day and Beyond

Do you look at your day as an undifferentiated mass without any real parameters aside from waking up, going to work, tending to baby, and falling asleep?

Do you schedule only the "have tos" and not the "want tos"? In other words, do you feel you haven't the right to schedule personal time?

Are you afraid to impose a schedule upon yourself out of worry that you will really have to face up to hidden (or not so hidden) dissatisfactions, frustrations, and "illegal" feelings?

Do you equate scheduling with rigidity?

Do you see schedules as a tool for meeting personal goals, or do you see keeping to the letter of a schedule as a goal in itself?

Do you feel that working parents have no right to schedule personal time, and at-home parents must grasp at it haphazardly?

As a working parent, do you feel schedules belong in the office and have no place in the sanctuary of home?

Do you assume that personal and family leisure time will materialize magically, or that it requires the same kind of thoughtful planning as any other organized activity?

Where Does the Time Go?

The first step to gaining control of your time is recognizing what shape it's in now. Filling out this worksheet will help you determine where the time goes.

Energy Levels: Synchronizing Body and Time

1. When is your highest physical energy level? Morning? Afternoon? Evening?

2. Describe what you usually do during these high-energy periods.

3. Do your activities and energy level mesh in a productive way? For instance, if you feel peppiest in the morning, do you mistakenly take that time to accomplish routine chores that can be done on "half a tank"?

4. When is your highest *mental* activity time?

5. Does that time coincide, or can it be made to coincide, with available pockets of non-distracted time, such as during a child's naps, work commutes, or in the early morning or late night hours?

6. Are you taking good physical care of yourself to make optimal use of energy levels?

Charting Time Absolutes

1. What hours must you spend at home?

2. What hours must you spend at a job?

3. When are you outside the home for schooling, family responsibilities, business-related entertaining, other duties?

4. Have you explored the potential personal time gain during lunch hours, commutes, coffee breaks, and "waiting time"?

Charting Task Absolutes

1. What tasks, inside and outside the home, are not expendable? Be merciless. List only the assignments and responsibilities necessary for maintenance of you, your family, and your job.

Charting Personal Time

1. If you could extract personal time on a regular basis, how would you spend it?
   a. Getting ahead professionally
   b. Reading for pleasure
   c. Participating in sports or other physical activity
   d. Spending more time with your partner and your children
   e. Spending more time with friends or family
   f. Spending more time alone, or simply doing nothing
   g. Pursuing hobbies
   h. Other

2. Do you have any regularly scheduled babysitting time? When? What do you do during this "free time"? Is this what you really want to do?

Organizing Your Time

When Dr. Pamela Newman, textbook author, time management consultant, and vice president of a major management consultancy, spoke on time use to the working mothers of the New York Financial Women's Association, the consensus was: Here is a very organized person who starts her day at 5 AM when she attends to personal projects before her family wakes up. There will be time later to spend with her two children and her husband, with, of course, a large block reserved for professional responsibilities.

Dr. Newman's suggestions for time organization can be applied to parents of both sexes and a wide range of lifestyles.

✓ Try to begin each day with a question: If I get nothing else done today, what is the one thing I want to do? Sometimes it's a major project, sometimes it's very minor but simply has to be taken care of immediately.

✓ Plan out the week on Sunday, and then don't hesitate to replan daily to allow for contingencies. "My calendar includes leisure and family activties alongside business commitments," Newman says.

⌁ Plan family activities ahead of time with the same commitment given to business activities. "When leisure time becomes more manageable it becomes more enjoyable than just waiting around until the last minute to 'do something.' Very few people plan their leisure hours with the same respect afforded professional commitments. Instead, they wake up on Saturday morning, turn to the other person, and say, 'What shall we do today?' "

⌁ Include your child in your leisure plans as often as possible, especially if both partners work. But don't forget to plan specifically for adult time. Get a babysitter on a regular basis so that you can eliminate the debilitating last-minute "arranging" business. Go out on the appointed evenings whether you have something special to do or not.

⌁ Stress and procrastination are the two greatest obstacles to gaining control of your time. A concrete plan of action will help you get past the worrying and putting-off stage. Just seeing what you have to do down on paper will make it seem more manageable.

⌁ Don't let the telephone rule your time. If you get frequent calls that interrupt personal time, politely defer them to a later hour or install an answering device that will allow you to answer when you're free.

⌁ Learn how to shut the door at work and at home so you can get more done.

Goal Statement Test

If you have difficulty setting or sticking to goals, try this goal statement test adapted from a management exercise formulated by Dr. Newman.

1. List three long-term goals, in descending order of importance.

2. For each goal, list three specific and realistic actions you can take, beginning today, to realize the goal. For instance, if one goal is to pursue a college degree, an initial step can be as simple as researching available programs and obtaining applications. Another goal, such as working for yourself rather than a company, can be approached at first by making a list of your personal contacts.

3. If you had a dependable amount of time every day—even if that time were as short as fifteen minutes—what reasonable progress would you like to make toward your goal in the next six months?

4. Spell out exactly what you will have to do in terms of personal scheduling, additional babysitter time, increased efficiency, child care

arrangements with your partner, change in TV and sleep habits—whatever is necessary to ensure reliable personal time.

5. Seal this sheet in an envelope and open it when six months are up. Repeat the process for the next six months, learning from each previous self-inventory. If you feel overwhelmed by the six-months concept, try three months at first.

Parallel Time

The baby is old enough to play in the tub. You're sitting beside her, staring at the tiles. In addition to some child play, why not clean the sink, engage in personal grooming, or move to another activity that allows supervision of the child? Some kids love baths so much that during the summer months they're happy to putter around with toys in inches of water for a good hour. The backyard or playground are good places to jot notes; you can look up frequently while doing your work. Cook dinner while your child eats, rather than breathing down his neck to make sure he finishes his peas.

Parents have to learn to recognize those increasing moments when the child signals: I am going to play by myself; as long as you're in the room with me I'm perfectly happy to concentrate on this puzzle. Many parents arrive at this realization only with the birth of a second child, when attention is necessarily divided. Realize, though, that children become conditioned. They won't automatically allow their parents to read that professional journal; they want their parents to participate in block building—or else. Early recognition of parallel activity possibilities is healthy for parent and child. As the child grows, and begins to trust and respect your activities, certain objects will be recognized as cues to begin games alone.

One professional mother encouraged her 2½-year-old to take out her books when the mother took out her magazines. Roberta found that, from about a year and a half, Nicky recognized that the sight of a pen, the sound of a typewriter, or the mere mention of writing and work meant a change in activity for him, too. Jay provided Jud, at the time a toddler, with his own ample art supplies. Father and son, each at his easel, would embark on separate creative projects.

Making Decisions

Recently, in one of my training seminars, I asked the group

members what they thought about or felt when faced with a decision. They felt decision making was complex, painful, risky, and tiring. They worried about lacking information, acting before feeling confident, giving up the known for the unknown, making mistakes. They were concerned about the time and social pressures involved, and about how their decisions affected other people important in their lives. In short, for the majority, decision making was a chore imposed by a crisis—not an opportunity to shape and control their lives, or to move toward more freedom of action.

Gordon Porter Miller

LIFE CHOICES: HOW TO MAKE CRITICAL DECISIONS

ABOUT YOUR EDUCATION, CAREER, FAMILY, LIFESTYLE

Many of the decisions parents make hinge directly or indirectly on their use or misuse of time. Simply deciding what to put on a to-do list speaks of priorities. And after you've done what you set out to do, expected and unexpected reactions follow. "Once you make a decision, you are not done with it," Gordon Porter Miller reminds us. "You become responsible not only for the results but also for dealing with the impact it might have on other choices." We would add that this is especially true for parents.

Setting short- and long-term goals, planning your day or your life, all require decision-making skills. And decision making is definitely a skill, sometimes intuitive, but more often learned. We've adapted some of Dr. Miller's recommendations for learning to make sound personal choices.

✓ Start with small decisions and examine the way you normally make choices. Let's say you want to buy a stroller. Do you:

1. See what everybody else is using, but fail to ask if they're satisfied with the products?

2. Buy the first stroller you see just to get it over with?

3. Comparison shop for price and quality, and consult a consumer interest magazine to aid in your final choice?

4. Ask your partner or other individual to buy you anything as long as you don't have to be bothered with the chore and the decision—and later complain that he or she made a mistake?

5. Research wisely, then agonize over the choices for weeks rather than going with the facts?

✓ Dr. Miller warns against "self-sabotage" in decision making. Some saboteurs make choices on the basis of what others think; others draw out the decisive moment of truth. The former belittle or ignore their own values; the latter are paralyzed in the face of the responsibility that decision making implies.

↑ Don't confuse *sound* decisions with *successful* ones. "You do not become clairvoyant when you become a skillful decision maker," Dr. Miller points out. By this he means that while all of us hope that how we choose to carry on our lives will necessarily better us professionally and emotionally, we can't actually know this to be true when we make a well-considered decision.

As our parental responsibilities deepen (and threaten to overwhelm us) perhaps with the birth of a second child, and with the great financial burdens most parents now face, more often we decide not to decide, even about something as minute as rearranging our living space for greater practicality. The big changes—jobs, neighborhood, education of our children, enhancement of our own potential—seem insurmountable. We may be obsessive about what to do, but that is hardly as effective as weighing the alternatives and making a choice—taking a stand, no less, and seeing it through.

We earnestly believe that parenthood makes a first-class training ground for goal and decision-making, and the parent who works at it from the start will find the process becomes so much easier even as the day-to-day rigors of family life persist. We also contend that a parent who makes decisions without balancing adult *and* parental needs will ultimately short-change every member of the family. We're all in this together. We all need to be heard.

9

Money

People are uncomfortable talking about their finances," a bank manager and mother of a preschooler told us. "Friends don't discuss their earnings with one another, and within couple relationships, there's all too little sitting down and admitting. 'This is what we can and can't afford.' Money talk just brings out every bad emotion. Most people, afraid to deal directly with their money condition, actually prefer to have outsiders guide them, tell them, 'This is what I should be doing.'

"Having children changes the role money plays in most of our lives because suddenly there's the necessity for many more tradeoffs—from the kind of daycare and schooling your child will need to what kind of vacations can be taken and where the family will live. All of these hinge on the availability of money. Unless parents get a grip on their finances, they'll be in for some rocky times. Much of the time, the un-certainty and fear can be avoided. For some people, good money sense comes naturally. But nobody should be embarrassed by having to learn it."

In a 1981 *Psychology Today* survey on money, 34 percent of the 20,000 respondents to a questionnaire admitted they had recently felt more day-to-day family tension about money, while 28 percent re-ported more arguments about money and 20 percent felt that money stress contributed to a decline in the time they were able to devote to partner and children. Even so, the survey also revealed that "those who are most satisfied with their financial condition are not necessarily those with the highest income." The message was clear: money is only one element in our lives, and not always the key to personal happiness. But for those who keenly react to the absence of adequate funds, de-pression, anxiety, and anger often take over. And parents are no excep-tion. In the magazine survey, almost one-third of the respondents re-ported having to postpone children because of tight pocketbooks. Yet here we are, as parents, struggling with the same money problems, lack of information, and inexpressible fears about how we will get along tomorrow and ten years from now. Anxious to provide the very best for our offspring, we may tend to overspend on early necessities by denying ourselves pleasurable activities and lifestyle. Or we may place great value on savings, but fail to consider the best ways to save. Listen in on an average playground conversation between parents and you'll likely hear talk of money, some of it pretty desperate. Our aim is to alleviate some of this desperation, and perhaps even to make you feel good about your money situation for a change.

Who Needs a Budget?

Denise McLaughlin, banker, mother, and stepparent, believes not everyone needs a budget all the time, but that there are three kinds of situations requiring formal financial planning:

- When your lifestyle changes and your income remains the same
- When your income changes for better or worse
- When your goals and aspirations call for long-term financial administration

"A good way to think about budgeting is to ask yourself, 'How can I control my expenses so that I can manage a household day to day and have the cash on hand when it comes time to pay for essentials big and small?' In addition to your budget, you need a sense of your net assets —what you have in the bank plus whatever you own—and what your liabilities are, so you can come up with how you're doing this year versus a year or a month ago. Only then can you begin to control those aspects of your spending behavior that you're not on top of all the time," McLaughlin told us.

Thomas Tilling, family finance expert and a contributing editor to *Parents*, argues that 999 out of 1,000 family budgets fail—and so, on more than one occasion, have his own.

Greater money consciousness is Tilling's realistic prescription, with the ultimate goal of simply trying to spend less and limit unnecessary outflow. Tilling calls this method "non-budgeting budgeting."

Sara Welles, editor of Citibank's *Consumer Views*, sees "cash leaks for out-of-pocket expenses as one of the most common budget problems." Getting a handle on large expenditures for food, gas, housing, and insurance is only half the battle. Failure to monitor impulse spending on a daily basis is the downfall of many well-intentioned budgeters.

Carole Elizabeth Scott, in her book, *Your Financial Plan: A Consumer's Guide*, writes, "The purpose of budgeting is simply to enable

you to spend money on what you most want to spend it on; not what
others think you should spend it on. . . . Budgeting simply means that
you plan what percentage of your income will be devoted to each possible use on the basis of your priorities. . . . A budget does not have
to be a formal, written document, which allows for no variances. To
budget, all you need to do is plan and control your expenditures. You
do not have to set up an elaborate bookkeeping system. Budgeting may
be as simple as dividing up the money you get when you cash your
paycheck and putting each batch in a labeled envelope to show what
the money will be spent for."

The consensus is that budgets need not be painstakingly kept in
ledgers. Informal notes or even instinctive control of money can work
better than a complex, indecipherable computer printout, but we must
be *aware* and *systematic* in our approach to what comes in and what
goes out.

The starting point for basic organization of family finances is an
understanding of essential financial terminology.

A Parent's Financial Glossary

✔ *Assets* are whatever you own: cash, property, stocks, insurance
policies. *Financial Assets* include cash in savings accounts as well as
personal funds in trusts, IRA, Keogh, UGMA, and pension or insurance
funds. *Tangible Assets* include homes, cars, boats, appliances, and jew-
elry.

✔ *Liabilities* are the debts you owe. Most common liabilities include
credit card charges, money borrowed to finance a car or home, taxes
not withheld by employers.

✔ *Income* is the sum total of the salaries and bonuses, tax rebates,
stock dividends and interest, and accruals from rental of property you
own.

✔ *Fixed Expenses* are the weekly, monthly, or yearly charges you
know you have to pay, such as rent or mortgage.

✔ *Variable Expenses* are the food, energy, and clothing costs that
fluctuate season to season, according to need, and can be controlled,
given your changing financial condition.

✔ *Net Worth* is the difference between what you own, including cash,
and what you owe. If you owe more than you own, you've got a *Negative Net Worth*.

✔ *Avoidable Expenses* are the variable expenses or charges you are
under no obligation to make, though you might like to make them.

✔ *Unavoidable Expenses* may be considered the fixed expenses or charges you must make to maintain your home, lifestyle, and family, and may include certain unanticipated expenses associated with illness and education, to name two.

↙ *Discretionary Income* is the money you have left after paying bills. It can be used for savings, investments, or purchase of something you desire.

Savings

Before the baby, if you and your partner were both working, saving part of two salaries was certainly not as difficult as it is with a child to support. Perhaps one of you works only part-time or is at home all the time, or daycare is devouring your second salary and even some of the old nest egg.

Should savings be forgotten altogether in the tenuous financial time of early parenthood? Financial expert Andrew Tobias, writing in the September, 1980, issue of *Redbook*, believes that's the worst possible solution to long-term liquidity. "Savings may have gone out of fashion in these days of inflation but the absolutely first and eternal axiom of family finance is to try to build a nest egg. Money makes money: savings bring a sense of security, and the only way to get ahead of the game is to spend less each year than you take in." Tobias suggests budgeting some finite amount—however small—exclusively for savings, and sending it right off to the bank when you put your mortgage or rent in the mail. When you've accumulated enough, then you can transfer the savings to a high-interest savings option. Alternatively, you can understate your W-4 tax exemptions, which would mean more of a tax bite into your paycheck during the year, but a bigger refund later on. That "found money" would be earmarked for the savings account.

But saving money, especially when you need it now, can grow to be a chore, especially if you have no savings *motive*. Knowing what your goals are can spur you to put aside something small to start. Once savings become a fixed expense rather than a sometime whim, diverting money into savings will take on meaning.

Shortcuts to Coping with the Credit Impulse

↙ Don't borrow because you can't pay for everyday acquisitions, including food or gas. That means you're living above your means and had better cut back rather than take on more debts.

↙ Take into account the time it will take you to pay back your charges or loan, and whether the interest rate and amount of money you'll owe is in line with the necessity of the purchase. For instance, though it may seem easier to pay off a $2,000 loan for a short vacation over a three-year period, next year, when you yearn for another respite, you'll still owe two-thirds of the present loan. Any additional debt would be foolhardy. Yet signing for a three-year car financing loan is appropriate.

⚊ Don't misuse NOW accounts that let you make overdrafts as a matter of course. While they are lifesaving now and then, once you pretend with any regularity that the overdraft sums are your money, you're in big trouble.

⚊ Never borrow more than you need. On any loan, you want to be saddled with the least burdensome interest rates and principal, no matter how good it feels to have some extra money in your pocket.

⚊ Don't dawdle paying the credit card bills. Failure to pay back the money can mean $300–$500 in interest charges a year.

⚊ Save yourself from the tragedy of over-indulgence in plastic by keeping credit cards in your wallet to a minimum. The urge to charge is even greater when you open that wallet and gleaming out at you are a dozen cards. When the bills come in, indiscriminate use of cards means extra financial juggling.

Families and Houses

A 1981 Louis Harris survey, reported in *Advertising Age*, found that among 25–40-year-olds, "a full 82 percent believe that owning a home is still one of life's most important goals." Owning a home and raising children in it is a great American dream that lately eludes many new families. Interest rates and the scarcity of mortgages, coupled with fewer older homes for sale, fewer new ones being built, and increasing competition from new groups of home buyers, especially single people, all contribute to the despair of young parents who feel they will never be able to fulfill the dream of being homeowners. Others, less sentimental by nature, are caught up in the investment syndrome—owning property is good business—or else the desire to make use of tax advantages through home ownership. Though for different reasons each of these groups feels keenly committed to the concept of owning a house, each often fails to grasp the particular hidden demands that owner-ship makes.

"There is no such thing as a smart, educated person when it comes to buying a house for the first time," Thomas Tilling told us bluntly.

"Everybody underestimates the costs and the responsibility . . . I had determined I would spend 10 percent of my down payment, and at the time it was a substantial 40 percent, to cover hidden costs. For the first year, it turned out to be more like 10 percent of the *total* cost. Until you've actually bought a house, you cannot realize how many unexpected hidden costs there are. One thing always leads to another. . . ."

One not-so-hidden cost today is inflation. Those who purchased homes in the mid-1970s paid about 31 cents for a gallon of heating oil! Those who buy a picturesque Victorian mansion often find they must literally seal off portions of the house in order to cut winter fuel bills (or air conditioning in some parts of the country). In new homes, on the other hand, workmanship may not be everything hoped for. Floors come up. Roofs leak. Flooding permeates the basement. Desperation sets in and bills mount.

We're not telling you that purchasing a home is bad family finance. Experts and laymen agree that purchase of the right property at the right time is one of the few remaining surefire investments. But it's vitally important for young families, especially where funds are limited, to ask lots of questions—of themselves, of real estate consultants, friends—anybody who, from experience, knows that home buying isn't a fanciful pastime.

Familiarize yourself with the type of mortgage you'll be contending with. The *variable-rate* mortgage is considered the "mortgage of the 1980s," and it most likely will almost completely supercede the *fixed-rate* mortgage our parents were issued way back when. As bank interest rates climb, so will your variable-rate mortgage payments; if they fall, so will your mortgage. Sounds fair enough, though the sad fact is that there will probably be more rising of the rates than decline. A limit on how much the mortgage could rise is also part of the arrangement. But, of course, your salary may not be climbing in accordance with the mortgage payments. And that means a potential money crunch at home, at least until you secure that raise.

Also popular today are *renegotiable-rate* mortgages and *shared-appreciation* mortgages. The renegotiable-rate variety works along the lines of the variable-rate mortgage. The bank gives you a fixed interest rate for an agreed upon period (generally three to five years) but reserves the right to change that rate later on. In this respect, this is less risky than the variable-rate mortgage insofar as the borrower knows what the interest rates will be over the initial period.

Shared-appreciation mortgages definitely make it easier to buy a house but eventually undercut the profits you could realize through sale of the home. The lender substantially cuts interest rates when you buy, in exchange for a piece of the resale profit, even though he does not pay for one iota of upkeep through the years you live there. Yet, for some buyers, shared-appreciation mortgages may be the only way to enjoy the benefits of owning a home, especially in a period of economic uncertainty.

Don't buy before appraising a house. You want to know if it is structurally sound, if patch-up jobs have been the pattern in the past, and if the neighborhood surrounding the property is worth investing in. Professional appraisals cost $100–$200. The American Institute of Real Estate Appraisers, 155 East Superior Street, Chicago, Illinois, 60611, can help you locate a good one. So can your local bank. The appraiser should also tell you the condition of the furnace, hot-water heater, roof, walls, plumbing, electricity, problems with flooding and moisture, how the foundation is faring, and if there are any questionable properties in the earth on which the house is built.

What kind of home do you really want? Buying a house is a time-consuming occupation that takes away from whatever family or leisure time you might spend elsewhere. On the average, first-time buyers search for three months and see at least 10 homes before deciding on the one for them. But it's not uncommon for feelings of desperation and paranoia to intrude on the search. People feel they will never find exactly what they want for exactly the price they're willing to pay. They also fear that, by delaying too long, all decent houses will be out of their reach. So they make regrettable choices, perhaps by moving to a neighborhood they don't especially care for, resigning themselves to a structure that needs more work than they are able to put into it, or buying at a higher price than they can afford. They also tend to sacrifice convenience factors, such as accessibility to work, school, family, and friends.

Compute up front whether you have the cash to make the approximately 30 percent down payment now required of a home buyer, and then still possess the liquidity to pay the mortgage while retaining something for inevitable emergencies. Those costs, added up, sometimes are much more than originally thought.

Do you know the property tax assessments in the communities in which you're house hunting? The more services offered, the more you'll probably have to pay, unless industry has offset some of the expense. "Next to your mortgage payment, your tax bill is likely to be your second biggest home ownership cost, and property taxes for years have been among the fastest-rising items in your total living costs," counsels Sylvia Porter. Add the special assessments local governments make to generate capital for improvements, such as roads or a new town hall.

If local authorities plan to reevaluate property taxes, that could well mean a re-evaluation up—and costlier charges to you. Details of the tax trends in the area are public record. Look them up.

Do you know how local zoning affects the ambience of the community under your consideration? If a new mall may be built on a tract of land half a mile from your dream house, this may (or may not) be the environment for you.

Condominiums and Cooperatives

If fewer people are buying houses, more are purchasing condominiums and cooperatives. The major difference between these two is that, when you buy a condo, you own the apartment and have access to common indoor and outside resources; when you buy a co-op, rather than owning the physical apartment you are purchasing stock in a corporation that owns and maintains the building.

Owning a condo or coop means paying monthly maintenance charges *and* the mortgage. As with houses, the joys of ownership are great, but it's important to know some of the pitfalls.

As Sylvia Porter puts it in her *Money Book for the '8os*, owning your apartment in one way or another does not necessarily mean "tax-sheltered easy living, no lawn mowing or snow shoveling, community pools, health clubs, etc." Because you are entering a venture that involves other people, you must be quite certain, not only of the reputability of the developer and management, but of the charges you will really be paying monthly, the cost of a possible default by someone in the corporate "family," or your financial responsibility if a major structural deficiency is discovered in the physical plant.

Coop and condo veterans can't stress strongly enough the importance of asking questions about day-to-day living in these environments (everything from parking and the use of pools and other leisure facilities to whether children can live there on a permanent basis). What are the selling regulations, if any? Does the neighborhood suit your needs? Can you rent your condo if you won't be there to use it? Are the maintenance charges fixed for a certain period of time, or will they rise precipitously and often?

It is also wise to check the financial implications in terms of borrowing to meet mortgage charges. In some states, banks will consider a coop mortgage request under the heading of personal loan, though these are hard to obtain. For young parents who may not have ready cash on a regular basis, purchase of a cooperative or condominium must be

carefully weighed. A good way to find out if you will be able to swing
the cost is to tabulate monthly charges of ownership, including utili-
ties, maintenance, mortgage, and special charges, and compare these
to what you would pay in a rental. What tax breaks will ownership
and the formidable monthly outlay of funds bring you at the end of
the year?

Most banks now offer booklets to help you learn more about coops
and condos. You can also check with the real estate board in your
community for background information, or a local college for possible
courses. The Better Business Bureau will inform you of the reliability
of the people with whom you will be dealing.

Life Insurance and the Young Family

"Make no mistake about it: the main purpose of life insurance—*and
nothing does it better*—is to create an 'instant estate' for your family in
the event of your death," writes Sylvia Porter.

The majority of Americans agree with Porter; more than 90 percent
of U.S. households where the family head is between 25 and 34 years
of age subscribe to some form of life insurance, and their policies pay,
on the average, between $30,000 and $45,000 in the event of death.

The urge to take out an insurance policy grows stronger when a
child is born, and so it should. But if you're shopping for the right
policy, you've undoubtedly found the jargon confusing and the choices
complex. High-powered, mystically persuasive insurance agents simply
confuse the situation more. If you're shopping for insurance for your
young family needs, advance preparation for the visits of prospective
agents is essential. Most important, know what you're getting into before you sign on the dotted line.

Women and Insurance

"The notion that a breadwinner needs a lot of insurance is based on
the assumption that he has a dependent wife and children who'll need
a lot of money if something happens to him," Jane Bryant Quinn states.
But she contends that as more families go the dual-income route, insurance needs for a family change. Other factors pointing to the need for
women to get insurance protection are the escalating threat of divorce
and the statistical likelihood that the wife, by outliving her husband,
may profit from a special nest egg generated through management of
her own insurance policy. And more women are deciding that they've

left insurance to men far too long. "They no longer tell me that they must consult their fathers or husbands before deciding what kind of policy to purchase," writer Nadine Brozan quoted Jane Boswell, an Equitable Life Assurance Society of the United States underwriter and representative, as saying in *The New York Times* of May 30, 1981, "They're coming to realize that they have the same need to protect themselves financially as men, and, in fact, they are better than men at long-range planning."

Insurance and the At-Home Parent

Thomas Tilling believes that a woman at home with children, who is working at childraising, needs an insurance policy every bit as much as her spouse who is engaged in another kind of job. (Or, perhaps it's the husband who's at home and the wife who's working: the rationale is the same.) Were the at-home spouse to die prematurely, the burdens of replacing her work would be great—to start, at least $10,000 a year in 1980, and probably a lot more, to pay a surrogate at-home worker to care for the children and maintain the home.

How to Insure

According to Thomas Tilling, "a husband should never insure himself, and neither should his wife. If either of them does, the proceeds from the policy could end up being taxed as part of the deceased's estate." Instead, says Tilling, cross-insure, each spouse taking out a policy on the other, establishing a separate bank account from which to pay for the policy. If the wife has no present income, the husband can give her enough money each year to pay the premium when it comes due—again, after she has deposited it in her account. The separate accounts assure that each partner has no claim to the money in the other's account. That's an essential quality of the cross-insurance technique.

Where to Go for Insurance

The consensus of financial experts is to shop around before deciding on an insurance company. Sylvia Porter recommends finding a "strong" insurance company. By that, she means financially strong. *Best's Insurance Reports* or *Best's Insurance Guide* authoritatively rate companies from A plus to C (or, Excellent to Fair). *Consumer Reports* also rates insurance companies periodically. Companies in the excellent range do not necessarily charge more for their policies. Because they are big, some can afford to charge less.

Wills

"Remember that for the family's future, any old will is not enough," Thomas Tilling contends in *Parents*. "Estate planning requires a good will and game plan that disinherits the tax man as much as legally possible."

Then why do 70 percent of all Americans fail to leave wills behind them? Fear of death, guilt about dying, or the belief that you own too little of use to beneficiaries cause many people to neglect writing wills. But whether or not you leave an up-to-date will can affect the following substantial issues:

- Who will care for your children if they are minors when you die and you leave no spouse?
- Will your children be financially secure in your absence?
- Who will benefit from the possessions you leave behind?
- Who will be appointed executor of your estate?
- What federal and state taxes you will pay on your assets?

A will expedites these matters and lessens the possibility of arguments among survivors. But most important for a family man or woman is the knowledge of a relatively smooth transition for survivors. If husband and wife are killed and guardians are appointed by the court in the absence of a will, expenses may be so great that money intended for the children's future is squandered for court costs. If one parent dies leaving a complex network of assets and bills, the surviving parent may find there is no money for daily living on the short term, and that the process of untangling the mess is an extremely protracted one. Sylvia Porter isn't overstating the issue when she argues in her *Money Book for the '80s* that "next to your birth certificate and marriage license your will may be the most important document of your life."

The Uniform Simultaneous Death Act

A common statute on the state level, USDA protects survivors from a hair-splitting death situation that goes like this: you and your spouse have wills stipulating that should the wife die first, her $200,000 insurance policy goes to the husband. If she dies first, his $200,000 goes to her. And if the deaths are simultaneous, the kids get everything. But if the Internal Revenue Service can prove that one spouse died even a few seconds after the other, the assets of the spouse who survived longer will be subject to taxes *without the benefit of the standard marital deduction allowed by law*. Experts advise that a lawyer draw up specifics for parents who wish to avoid this bizarre deathbed controversy and save the children from needless emotional and financial strain.

Do It Yourself?

Forms are easily available at any good stationers, but the price of error in a do-it-yourself will may be higher. Certain rules must be followed when wills are drawn up, and these are hardly common knowledge.

✔ Any writing appearing after the will is signed is automatically void: the will, itself, may not be worth the paper it's written on if writing appears after your signature.

✔ A handwritten will must be totally handwritten—no stamped, printed, or typewritten sections permitted.

✔ A missing, replaced, or mispaged portion of a will may void the entire will.

✔ Failure to initial a section of a will that has been crossed out or added later may void all or part of the will. Writing "void" on sections of a will is ineffectual; you must tear up the will and start over if you wish to change the wording or meaning of a section.

Your Children's Guardian(s)

You come from a large family and believe that in the event of your deaths the children will be well taken care of; you particularly admire the ability of your brother Fred to relate to kids. He has three of his own and is a wonderful parent; so is his wife, Renate. So when you're sitting in the lawyer's office and he asks who will become your children's guardian in the event of your passing, you casually say, "Fred and Renate Jones." But you never actually consult with them. A horrible accident befalls you and your wife. The will is read and Fred and Renate, middle-class people struggling to get along, find themselves, quite without warning, the parents of five, not three, children. Moral of the story: Ask those people whom you wish to become your children's guardians if they're up to the task. Not only do you want your offspring to be humanely treated, you want them to be wanted. Sometimes, even close relatives cannot promise this, for they are already overextended. The time to explore other avenues is when you're still very much a part of this world.

Money and the Two-Career Family

Dual-career couples have some 55 percent more money to spend as they wish than couples in which only one person works. Nevertheless, the strains on two incomes in the same household are heightened considerably by the arrival of a child. The illusion of wealth and self-sufficiency causes many two-career couples to continue spending as they always have, though, in fact, their incomes now fail to generate adequate funds for everyday expenses. Left unmanaged, two incomes in parenthood can seem as slight as one. Marlys Thomas recently reported in *Money* magazine that the two-income household "is in many cases richer than it ever dreamed, yet poorer than it thinks. For when wives work, the family's finances undergo a range of adjustments that few households are adequately prepared for, or even explicitly aware of. Costs tend to be higher, spending freer, and time at a premium. In such an atmosphere, the future is all too often left to fend for itself."

One of the prime reasons for the inability of dual-careerists to make extra money work positively for them is the pattern of spending developed before baby. Two-income householders eat out twice as frequently as one-earner families; they spend 33 percent more on transportation and twice as much on education. They purchase prepared foods more often, require larger outlays for professional wardrobes, and must often resort to hiring people to clean their homes, mow their lawns, till their gardens, and walk their dogs.

Dual-career couples, unless committed to long-term savings goals, experience immense pleasure in *not* having to pay attention to finances. They know they have more than enough money for now, so frugality seems absurd. As one bank executive put it: "Two-income couples are terrible spenders, not savers."

The dual-income couple with child should begin to think of a strategy of survival to combat the eerie depreciation of salaries. It starts with the realization that after-tax incomes rather than the pre-tax salaries dictate how much the couple has to spend. Two people pulling in $80,000 may feel rich until they acknowledge that only half this amount is available for them to spend or save.

Additionally, dual-careerists must agree on whether the money they earn belongs to both of them, or whether only part is to be shared. Will there be his, hers, and ours accounts, or a traditional joint account?

"When we set up our joint household, we set up individual accounts for each of us and a joint account between us. He's got an ex-spouse and children. His payment of his alimony is his business. And I feel a nice comfort to know that I have some private money, too. It's not that we have any secrets, because he usually balances my account. And we run the house from a joint account. This procedure works for us," one working parent told us.

Another said: "We have a money jar. Each time we spend money for the house we put our initials on the receipt and drop it in the jar. At the end of the month, charges are apportioned according to a formula which takes into account that one of us makes slightly more than the other. That person pays a lower proportion of the joint expenditures, while some of the expenditures are perceived as separate. Yes, we're parents, and we've owned real estate together, and are an emotional partnership. So why do we use this method to run our home? It helps us get along as working people and as a couple, and it forces us to monitor what we spend more efficiently."

Family finance writer Thomas Tilling and his wife, an illustrator, maintain separate accounts for one particular reason—life insurance where each partner takes out insurance on the other's life. The Tillings and their three children live day to day by a joint account. "We are probably an oddball remnant type family in this respect," he says. "Having a joint account is an oddball situation in the urban environment, particularly in the sophisticated centers where there is an increasing tendency to believe that what's mine is mine and what's yours is yours."

Jane Bryant Quinn, financial columnist, and her lawyer husband maintain separate accounts so that she can pay the mortgage and expenses on a home she purchased alone. In an interview with *Money* she said: "It's important in order to keep estate taxes minimized that the property I own be financed clearly out of the money I make, and that's easier if it comes out of a separate account." Quinn and her spouse have other jointly owned real estate and market investments, and for daily living expenses they prefer the "one pot" system.

"I know some households where the husband borrows from the wife if his expenses run over budget one month," she told *Money*. "Then she says, 'You owe me.' That's not the way a marriage should work. When you say, 'These are your bills,' and 'These are my bills,' you run the risk of quibbling unnecessarily about money."

Tips for Two Careerists

✓ Start building a money reserve equal to three to six months of your joint, after-tax income. One of the pitfalls of living well on two incomes is that, if one salary suddenly dries up, the family is put under enormous pressure to maintain a high-living lifestyle. Treasury bills, money market funds, and cash in the bank are all easily obtained in a pinch.

✓ Avoid committing more than 20 percent of your after-tax income to installment buying (excluding mortgage). If you can't do away with short-term debts within a year, you're simply charging too much.

✓ Begin slotting 10 to 15 percent of your joint gross income for investments and savings, even if this means cutting down on enjoyable pastimes like eating out or spending weekends away. Later on you'll be able to resume these activities but with the knowledge that you've the savings to support them.

✓ Share the burden of borrowing rather than following the traditional route of having the husband borrow alone.

✓ Consider the benefits of separate credit cards. This will help both spouses develop independent credit ratings; in the event of divorce, having established such ratings can mean a shortcut to buying the things you need to start a new life.

✓ Make sure you're not paying for more life insurance than you need. One alternative is to divert some insurance-bound cash into other investments or high-interest savings. But don't stint on health insurance. Unexpected illness can debilitate the two-income family as severely as the one-income household. Traditionally, disability coverage has been mistakenly overlooked by working women, who need it just as much as men.

✓ In the event of the husband's death in a two-career household, the wife must prove to the IRS that she has contributed to the family assets, including purchase and upkeep of property. It's necessary for the wife to keep records of any money she's made which is so used, or else the IRS is more than willing to count all property as the husband's. But remember that you'll be taxed only if the estate is worth more than $400,000. (The blanket marital deduction is $250,000, and other credits total $157,000.) Yet financial experts counsel that, while it may be hard to imagine assets of this magnitude, they do add up, and inflation helps them do so.

✓ The Economic Recovery Tax Act of 1981 has done away with the marriage tax penalty. That means that two working spouses will not pay a higher rate of tax than they would have as individuals, which was the case before. Under the new law, two-earner married couples filing joint returns will receive a gross income deduction of 5 percent in 1982, and 10 percent in 1983, for the lower-earning spouse. If the spouses earn the same amount, the deduction can be computed on either spouse's income.

10

Nutrition and Exercise

Nutrition and the Expanding Family

Ruth and Henry had always been fairly conscious of their health and physical appearance, but never more so than when Ruth became pregnant. Ruth paid special attention to diet and exercise, knowing that her own and her baby's wellbeing depended on sound eating habits. Henry too saw fit to keep fit. He considered himself "in training," not only for his eagerly awaited role as birth coach and father, but also for his private long-term fantasy of remaining lithe and energetic, the kind of youthful father a son could look up to.

Ruth gained about 29 pounds by the time of her baby's birth, which was long but problem-free. By the time Ruth and Henry came home, in a mixed mood of elation and exhaustion, Ruth had lost all but seven pounds of the weight gained during pregnancy, while Henry had shed about five pounds through sheer nervous energy. In the flurry of the first weeks Ruth concentrated on establishing her milk supply, coping with post-partum physical changes, and generally getting her strength back while caring for the newborn. But when things settled down she took that long postponed look in the mirror. She looked as lumpy and haggard as she felt. Of course, her breasts were larger because she was nursing. It was only natural (wasn't it?) to attribute the extra five or six pounds gained since delivery to the nursing. Her stomach had a way to go before returning to its flat, tight, pre-pregnancy shape. That would take time and energy—both of which were in short supply. In the upheaval of her life, Ruth felt she had lost her grasp of many things. Yet she wasn't quite prepared to face this ungainly and unfamiliar body, whose maintenance seemed entirely out of her control. Her infant daughter now called all the shots; sleeping, eating, and resting were all determined by the baby's erratic schedule. Constantly exhausted through lack of sleep, Ruth turned to coffee and sugary snacks as pick-me-ups. Concerned about her needs as a lactating mother, she conscientiously drank glasses of whole milk, ate high-fat cheeses, and treated herself to ice cream and milk shakes. Dinner was frequently a take-out or convenience-food affair, as meal planning was difficult and cooking a drag.

Henry wasn't doing much better. Preoccupied with the double responsibilities of work and fatherhood, Henry hit the office snack wagon, soda dispenser, and candy machine with greater frequency. He was determined not to work late more than absolutely necessary, so he usually had a quick lunch while working at his desk. When he did go out, he really indulged, knowing it would be many a moon before he'd eat fettucine Alfredo at home. Feeling guilty about the inevitable Saturdays and weekends he had to work, Henry gave up playing squash and jogging in the morning to be with his daughter, now six months old. After all, he was a father now, and that came first. Henry saw himself as a solid citizen. Maybe a little too solid, but. . .

By the time their little girl was a year old, Henry and Ruth had a more comfortable and predictable lifestyle, two jobs, and about twenty-five extra pounds between them. They'd slipped off the nutritional track somewhere, but when and how? Ruth tried a grapefruit diet, but failed miserably after a nervewracking week. Henry would skip lunch only to come home ravenous and irritable. Obviously, they thought, parenthood and dieting (as they know it) were mutually exclusive. The strict regimes of weight loss diets were much too demanding to integrate with the responsibilities of work, child care, social life, cleaning, and so on. Besides, they reassured themselves, all their friends with children were in the same boat, so they could sink into inertia together . . . and have a sundae to celebrate!

Of course Ruth and Henry are a fictionalized composite of many parents we've known (including ourselves). Most of us don't run the gamut of dietary woes but, with rare exception, as parents we've all had to struggle at one time or another to take charge of our eating habits. While parenthood itself does not automatically signal the end of good nutrition and sensible weight control, it presents its own problems and boobytraps.

First, parenthood represents a major revolution in lifestyle, at least in the short term. Most of us are unaware of just how instinctive our eating habits are. Over the years we've come to associate food with certain activities and moods: dinner after work, coffee break at 10:30, chocolate cake when depressed, coffee when tired, and so on. We may be unconscious of the patterns, but we miss them when they're replaced by the unfamiliar rhythms of parenthood. Since good nutrition relies heavily on self-awareness and planning, it's easy to see where we go wrong, whether our lives are suddenly unstructured, overstructured, or merely upside-down.

Children also do the devil's work in putting temptation before their parents' eyes. Sooner or later, you give in to a Mister Softee cone, a fast-food orgy, candy, and other forbidden fruit. You might find yourself finishing those toddler bananas, the half-empty bag of potato chips, the hamburger or hot dog doused in ketchup. And, for the homebound parent, there is the eternal temptation of the nearby fridge.

More subtle but equally devastating to the physique is the negative reinforcement of society and the parental peer group. What mental images do the words "maternal" and "paternal" conjure? Without thinking, many of us identify with the portly, nurturing beings who symbolize all good things on the homestead. We sit in playgrounds munching coffee and doughnuts, telling each other how good we look even with the added pounds, commiserating over the impossibility of losing them. We nod in agreement as we blame parenthood itself for our woes.

Finally, most of us have grown up thinking that there's a difference between good nutrition and dieting, that maintaining health and weight are two distinct goals, the first calling for health foods and a learned background in nutrients, the second requiring short-term tests of self-punishment and deprivation. We unhappily consign ourselves to the ranks of the undernourished and overfed.

The good news is this: Permanent weight loss and good eating are synonymous and don't really require nutritional contortions. With the help of our nutritional consultants Cheryl Corbin, director of the Nutrition Information Center at New York's Memorial Sloan-Kettering Cancer Center, and Michele Fairchild, Associate Director of Nutrition Programs for the American Health Foundation, we'll show how to fit good nutrition and gradual, *permanent* weight loss into the parental lifestyle. We suggest, however, that you check with your doctor before altering your diet in any way.

Self-Awareness: First Step to Good Nutrition

As new parents we're often too preoccupied to notice what's wrong with our eating behavior. Knowing *how* you eat is just as important as knowing *what* you eat. Ask yourself the following ten questions. Pinpointing bad habits is the first step toward changing them.

How Do You Eat?

1. *Do you skip meals?* Some parents are "too busy" to eat during the

day, relying on snacks instead of balanced meals to keep them going. Others look forward to dinner after the baby's bedtime as their one quiet meal, or as part of a fad diet. Dinnertime overdosing on calories usually means that more fat is deposited. Three balanced meals are a must.

2. *Do you use food to counteract boredom, anxiety, anger, or frustration?* About one-third of all Americans are overweight, but most of the excess calories result from boredom or stress rather than hunger. Physical exercise is a far better cure for the doldrums.

3. *Are you getting too little rest?* Eating more, or more frequently, doesn't give needed energy when the root of fatigue is lack of sleep or emotional overdrive. In addition, coffee and tea often act as appetite stimulants (and a source of extra calories when sweetened).

4. *Do you rush through meals?* Often when we eat with our children we tend to gobble food in order to finish quickly and attend to our parental duties. Eating fast usually means eating more and feeling less satisfied. If you rush through meals with your child, try eating alone. Schedule your meals so you won't be pressed for time.

5. *Do you snack with your child, or finish leftovers?* There is nothing immoral about garbage or leftovers. One mother we know ate two dinners nightly while her toddler was going through his food-refusal stage. Munch on a carrot stick or other healthy snack while your child is eating cookies, if you can't bear to watch.

6. *Do you know your vulnerable points?* Do you salivate at the sound of the coffee wagon? Do you treat yourself to sweets during the baby's nap, or accept cookies at play group? Try to anticipate those times and situations that are dangerous for you, and substitute. Bring low-calorie snacks to work, for instance. Anticipate your low-energy or low-resistance points, and have fruit or juice on hand to tide you over.

7. *Do you eat while carrying out other activities?* Snacking in a TV daze, or while reading, or concentrating on work, is an unconscious route to overeating. Make eating an exclusive occupation. If you usually eat in the kitchen or dining room, limit all eating to that place only. Pay attention to what you eat and you'll eat less.

8. *Do you use food as a reward?* We've been taught since childhood that if we're good, we'll be rewarded with ice cream; if we finish our dinner, we'll get dessert. Parenthood reawakens that subliminal need, and we find ourselves seeking edible rewards when the parental ones are less evident.

9. *Are you reasonably in control of your day?* Eating well requires advance planning. If you haven't yet established a daily and weekly

routine for shopping, menu planning, and meal preparation, you should start now.

10. *Are you in this together?* Whether both parents are working or one is home with the baby, good nutrition requires as much teamwork and mutual support as good parenting. This includes not only sharing the work of eating well, but encouraging one another's good eating habits. Bring home roses instead of sundaes to show your love!

What Do You Eat?

Once you have some idea of your eating *personality*, you're ready to zero in on your eating *preferences*.

1. *Do you have a basic knowledge of good nutrition?* We'll offer fundamental information, but further reading is a good idea. We recommend two excellent books: *Nutrition* by Cheryl Corbin, and *Jane Brody's Nutrition Book* by Jane Brody. See our *Help* chapter for free nutrition information from government and health agencies.

2. *Do you limit sweets?* We all know that candy is dandy but bad for us, but are you aware of the hidden sugars in some fruit juices, processed foods, cereals, and condiments? Read the ingredients list on food labels. If sugar or other sweeteners are high on the list, they are a major ingredient in the product.

3. *Do you limit your intake of sodium?* The salt shaker is an obvious source of sodium, but "hidden" sources include processed and canned foods, including soups, pickles and relishes, dehydrated soup mixes, packaged snacks, luncheon meats, MSG, some cheeses, and frozen dinners.

4. *Do you eat whole grain breads, cereals, and baked products rather than highly refined substitutes?* Minerals, vitamins, and necessary fiber exist in whole grains but are lost in the refining process. Even when flour, grains, and cereals are "enriched," only selective nutrients are reintroduced. You still miss out on bran and trace minerals.

5. *Do you limit the amount of fat in your diet?* Bite for bite, fat is more fattening than anything else you're eating. Be aware of the *amount* of fat you're eating, as well as its *type*. Red meats, cheese, butter, cold cuts, baked products using lard, butter, or palm oil, nondairy creamers, ice cream, and puddings are high in saturated fat, which has been tied to heart disease. Oil, margarine, mayonnaise, and shortening are low in saturated fat and cholesterol, but they are also calorie-high and should be limited.

6. *Do you include fish and chicken in your menus frequently, and have at least two meatless days a week?* Avoidance of fat is only half the battle. The other half includes restructuring your family's eating patterns to include the above low-fat protein sources regularly. Besides chicken and fish, meatless combinations of beans and grains, or grains and low-fat dairy products, provide necessary protein with much less fat.

7. *Do you eat plenty of fresh fruits and vegetables?* Substitute these for high-calorie snacks and you're on the right track. See our Daily Food Guide (later in this chapter) for recommended portions, and remember that raw or lightly cooked, unpeeled fruits and vegetables are highest in nutrients.

8. *Are you a teetotaler or light drinker?* Liquor and beer are high in calories and low on the health scale. Drinks mixed with sweet sodas or syrups are even worse. No more than one a day is the rule for good health.

9. *Do you have some knowledge of the caloric content of foods?* Calorie charts are available in most bookstores, stationery stores—even candy stores. You don't have to memorize the chart to have a general awareness of which foods are worth the calories they provide.

You gain weight when more calories are consumed than expended, and lose weight when that ratio is reversed. How many calories do you need daily? The following formula, from the book *Nutrition*, will help you establish your caloric level. But remember, you'll only get a ball-park estimate here, and the formula is not for pregnant or lactating women.

"To *maintain* your body weight, calculate 15 calories for each pound that you weigh. This is the average for a moderately active person. For example, if you are moderately active and weigh 150 pounds, you would require approximately 2,250 calories per day to maintain this weight (15 calories/pound x 150 = 2,250 calories). If you are sedentary or get very little exercise, multiply your weight by 13. In this case the 150-pound person would require only 1,950 calories (13 calories/pound x 150 pounds = 1,950 calories) for weight maintenance. To *lose* weight, a deficit of 3,500 calories per pound per week is required. Subtract 500 calories per day to lose a pound a week or 1,000 calories per day to lose two pounds per week."

10. *Have you learned to substitute similar foods with fewer calories for their high-calorie counterparts?* Our calorie substitution chart will show you the painless way to cut calories without "dieting."

COOKING THIN

For This   Substitute This

Beverages	Calories		Calories	Calories Saved
☐ Milk (whole), 8 oz.	165	Milk (buttermilk, skim) 8 oz.	80	85
☐ Prune juice, 8 oz.	170	Tomato juice, 8 oz.	50	120
☐ Soft drinks, 8 oz.	105	Diet soft drinks, 8 oz.	1 *	104
☐ Coffee (with cream and 2 tsp. sugar)	110	Coffee (black with artificial sweetener)	0	110
☐ Cocoa (all milk), 8 oz.	235	Cocoa (milk and water), 8 oz.	140	95
☐ Chocolate malted milk shake, 8 oz.	500	Lemonade (sweetened), 8 oz.	100	400
☐ Beer (1 bottle), 12 oz.	175	Liquor (1½ oz.), with soda or water, 8 oz.	120	55
Breakfast foods				
☐ Rice flakes, 1 cup	110	Puffed rice, 1 cup	50	60
☐ Eggs (scrambled), 2	220	Eggs (boiled, poached), 2	160	60
Butter and Cheese				
☐ Butter on toast	170	Apple butter on toast	90	80
☐ Cheese (Blue, Cheddar, Cream, Swiss), 1 oz.	105	Cheese (cottage, uncreamed), 1 oz.	25	80
Desserts				
☐ Angel food cake, 2" piece	110	Cantaloupe melon, ½	40	70
☐ Cheese cake, 2" piece	200	Watermelon, ½" slice (10" diam.)	60	140
☐ Chocolate cake with icing, 2" piece	425	Sponge cake, 2" piece	120	305
☐ Fruit cake, 2" piece	115	Grapes, 1 cup	65	50
☐ Pound cake, 1 oz. piece	140	Plums, 2	50	90
☐ Cupcake, white icing, 1	230	Plain cupcake, 1	115	115
☐ Cookies, assorted (3" diam.), 1	120	Vanilla wafer (dietetic), 1	25	95
☐ Ice cream, 4 oz.	150	Yoghurt (flavored), 4 oz.	60	90
Pie				
☐ Apple, 1 piece (1/7 of a 9" pie)	345	Tangerine (fresh), 1	40	305
☐ Blueberry, 1 piece	290	Blueberries (frozen, unsweetened), ½ cup	45	245
☐ Cherry, 1 piece	355	Cherries (whole), ½ cup	40	315
☐ Custard, 1 piece	280	Banana, small, 1	85	195
☐ Lemon meringue, 1 piece	305	Lemon flavored gelatin, ½ cup	70	235
☐ Peach, 1 piece	280	Peach (whole), 1	35	245

For This   Substitute This

	Calories		Calories	Calories Saved
☐ Rhubarb, 1 piece	265	Grapefruit, ½	55	210
☐ Pudding (flavored), ½ cup	140	Pudding (dietetic, non-fat milk), ½ cup	60	80

Fish and Fowl

	Calories		Calories	Calories Saved
☐ Tuna (canned), 3 oz.	165	Crabmeat (canned), 3 oz.	80	85
☐ Oysters (fried), 6	400	Oysters (shell w/sauce), 6	100	300
☐ Ocean perch (fried), 4 oz.	260	Bass, 4 oz.	105	155
☐ Fish sticks, 5 sticks or 4 oz.	200	Swordfish (broiled), 3 oz.	140	60
☐ Lobster meat, 4 oz. with 2 tbsp. butter	300	Lobster meat, 4 oz., with lemon	95	205
☐ Duck (roasted), 3 oz.	310	Chicken (roasted), 3 oz.	160	150

Meats

	Calories		Calories	Calories Saved
☐ Loin roast, 3 oz.	290	Pot roast (round), 3 oz.	160	130
☐ Rump roast, 3 oz.	290	Rib roast, 3 oz.	200	90
☐ Swiss steak, 3½ oz.	300	Liver (fried), 2½ oz.	210	90
☐ Hamburger (av. fat, broiled), 3 oz.	240	Hamburger (lean, broiled), 3 oz.	145	95
☐ Porterhouse steak, 3 oz.	250	Club steak, 3 oz.	160	90
☐ Rib lamb chop (med.), 3 oz.	300	Lamb leg roast (lean only), 3 oz.	160	140
☐ Pork chop (med.), 3 oz.	340	Veal chop (med.), 3 oz.	185	155
☐ Pork roast, 3 oz.	310	Veal roast, 3 oz.	230	80
☐ Pork sausage, 3 oz.	405	Ham (boiled, lean), 3 oz.	200	205

Potatoes

	Calories		Calories	Calories Saved
☐ Fried, 1 cup	480	Baked (2½" diam.)	100	380
☐ Mashed, 1 cup	245	Boiled (2½" diam.)	100	140

Salads

	Calories		Calories	Calories Saved
☐ Chef salad with oil dressing, 1 tbsp.	180	Chef salad with dietetic dressing, 1 tbsp.	40	120
☐ Chef salad with mayonnaise, 1 tbsp.	125	Chef salad with dietetic dressing, 1 tbsp.	40	85
☐ Chef salad with Roquefort, Blue, Russian, French dressing, 1 tbsp.	105	Chef salad with dietetic dressing, 1 tbsp.	40	65

Sandwiches

	Calories		Calories	Calories Saved
☐ Club	375	Bacon and tomato (open)	200	175
☐ Peanut butter and jelly	275	Egg salad (open)	165	110
☐ Turkey with gravy, 3 tbsp.	520	Hamburger, lean (open), 3 oz.	200	320

For This		Substitute This		
	Calories		*Calories*	*Calories Saved*
Snacks				
☐ Fudge, 1 oz.	115	Vanilla wafers (dietetic), 2	50	65
☐ Peanuts (salted), 1 oz.	170	Apple, 1	100	70
☐ Peanuts (roasted), 1 cup, shelled	1375	Grapes, 1 cup	65	1305
☐ Potato chips, 10 med.	115	Pretzels, 10 small sticks	35	80
☐ Chocolate, 1 oz. bar	145	Toasted marshmallows, 3	75	70
Soups				
☐ Creamed, 1 cup	210	Chicken noodle, 1 cup	110	100
☐ Bean, 1 cup	190	Beef noodle, 1 cup	110	80
☐ Minestrone, 1 cup	105	Beef bouillon, 1 cup	10	95
Vegetables				
☐ Baked beans, 1 cup	320	Green beans, 1 cup	30	290
☐ Lima beans, 1 cup	160	Asparagus, 1 cup	30	130
☐ Corn (canned), 1 cup	185	Cauliflower, 1 cup	30	155
☐ Peas (canned), 1 cup	145	Peas (fresh), 1 cup	115	30
☐ Winter squash, 1 cup	75	Summer squash, 1 cup	30	45
☐ Succotash, 1 cup	260	Spinach, 1 cup	40	220

The Parent's Survival Exercise Program

Attention sufferers of Stroller Hunch and Toddler-Induced Back Pain! Just as there's more to parenthood than parenting, there's much more to exercising than slimming thighs. For new parents, especially, the *therapeutic* effects of a sensible exercise program are just as important as its *cosmetic* value.

The exhaustion and, for some, the tension of the post-partum months can be overwhelming. The right exercises can both refresh and relax you. Later, as the sheer physical demands of the growing child increase, exercise can counteract such common parental ills as lower back pain and round shoulders, and increase your stamina.

Exercise can combat more subliminal problems as well. It can ease the post-partum blues, take the edge off those normal negative emotions, and provide a new physical outlet for the home- or office-bound. And, of course, exercise will slim your thighs and help you feel better about the way you look.

The exercises in this chapter were developed for us by Blair Gorsuch, an exercise physiologist at Yale University who works with athletes, faculty—and new parents. His pregnancy and post-partum exercise classes have become a popular and vital service of the Yale University Health Services Parent Support Group, which supplements its valuable discussion groups and infant care classes with good physical self-care through exercise.

Fitness

Fitness is a vague term and it's different for each individual. For some, fitness is being able to run a marathon in world-record time. For others, fitness is simply feeling better. In determining your immediate goals, be realistic. How fit were you before your pregnancy? Were you active or fairly inert during your "confinement"? Set small goals first. Think *only* of achieving these. As you realize each goal, set new ones— literally inching toward your overall target.

The Four Components of Fitness

FLEXIBILITY

Flexibility refers to the degree to which a joint moves through its maximal normal range of motion. The loss of flexibility in the joints often contributes to postural difficulties, crowding of internal organs, and lower back pain. One example is round shoulders, in which short-ening of the muscles and connective tissue in the chest draws the shoulders forward. Also, 80 percent of all back pain is caused by either inelastic or weak muscles. The need, then, for adequate flexibility is obvious.

BODY COMPOSITION

Body composition is the relative percentage of fat and fat-free weight in your body. Body fat can be measured scientifically through hydrostatic, or underwater, weighing and skinfold measurements taken with special calipers. Since most of us lack sophisticated equipment, we've devised this simple test: look at yourself in a mirror. *If you look fat, you probably are.* This excess weight can cause the body, that is, the cardiovascular and musculo-skeletal systems, to work harder with every movement.

Body fat can be eliminated by a combination of sensible dieting and an exercise program geared to strengthening and toning the unused muscles, especially in the areas of accumulated fat.

STRENGTH

Stronger muscles offer protection to the joints that they cross. With adequate strength an individual is less susceptible to strains, muscle pulls, and soreness. Better tone of the muscles in the trunk helps prevent some of the more common postural problems, such as round shoulders, low-back pain and sagging abdomen.

CARDIOVASCULAR FITNESS

This is probably the most important component of a total fitness program. A regimen to improve the functioning of your heart and circulatory system must satisfy three minimum requirements:

Duration. A minimum of fifteen minutes of uninterrupted activity.

Frequency. A minimum of three days per week, preferably every other day.

Intensity. Vigorous enough to elevate the heart rate—your heart should be beating faster than it normally does—but not so vigorous as to cause over-exhaustion or strain. An easy way to discover whether your exertion is within healthy bounds is to take the "talk test." While exercising vigorously, if you gasp for breath and can't carry on a normal conversation, you've been working too hard for now. Exercise within a comfortable range, within your limits.

Type. The exercise should be continuous and rhythmical in nature and involve the use of large muscle groups. For example: cycling, walking/running, jumping rope, cross country skiing, ice and roller skating, and racquet sports.

Spot Reducing

Contrary to the claims of various health spas, one cannot "spot" reduce; that is, reduce this area and not that. Exercise and diet will reduce body fat and increase muscle tone, but the *fat patterning* will remain the same. Fat patterning—where the fat is deposited in the body—is determined by age, sex, and heredity. Exercising a specific area improves the appearance of that area through an increase in muscle tone, but the fat pad remains there. For example, if a person does sit-ups for the abdomen, there will be an improvement in the waist measurement due to an increase in muscle tone, but unless there is an overall weight loss there will be no further improvements. (See our *Nutrition* section for diet guidelines.)

The use of sauna suits, or rubberized warm-up suits, is discouraged. Body dehydration is the only result and the weight loss temporary. Exercising in a rubberized suit places extreme demands on the cardio-vascular systems, and the effects can be dangerous.

Cellulite

By whatever name you call it, fat is fat. And cellulite (fat) is handled in the same manner as the other fat in your body.

Fat is used first for the normal functions of the body and then the excess is stored. Cellulite is fat deposited along the thighs, the back of the upper arms, and in the lower abdomen. It takes its name from its cellular appearance.

Changing Bust Measurements

The breasts are made up of glands, fatty tissue, and connecting ligaments, and are not likely to change as a result of exercise. Exercise can improve the strength and tone of the pectoral muscles and muscles in the upper back, and, with better posture, the bustline will naturally improve.

Before You Exercise

1. Talk with your physician and obtain his or her approval and advice before you begin.

2. Don't attempt too much exercise at the start. Begin slowly, progress gradually. Set small goals. Think in terms of months, rather than days or weeks. Be patient. Improvement comes slowly.

3. Do as many repetitions of each exercise as you feel comfortable with. Suggested repetitions are provided here merely as a guideline, not as a challenge.

4. Start with the stretching exercises, work through the more strenuous exercises, then repeat the stretching in *reverse* order.

5. Do not hold your breath while exercising. Breathe normally, exhaling while applying force and inhaling when relaxing it.

6. Exercise often during the week and during the day.

7. Stop or cut back for a while at signs of overexertion. These include extreme tiredness, breathlessness, dizziness, and nausea. Should you experience any of these symptoms, rest. If they persist, contact your physician.

8. Perform the exercises slowly, making sure you follow a full range of motion with each.

9. Exercise with others whenever possible. See our couples exercises later in this chapter. Enlist your partner, or a friend, or start your own exercise group. You'll be less likely to give up if you have support and company.

How to Stretch

Stretching will help you relax, reduce muscle tension, and feel generally refreshed. To do their job properly, *stretching movements should be gradual, never forced.* Bob Anderson, author of *Stretching*, favors going "into each stretch slowly and controlled, so that the proper stretch feeling can be found, used, and enjoyed."

Hold each stretch for 15 to 30 seconds, and breathe slowly. Don't hold your breath. Stretching can be done casually and spontaneously. Stretch while watching TV, sitting for extended periods, waiting for a bus or train.

Do It Together: Exercises for Partners

Involvement of your partner in an exercise program adds incentive and enjoyment. Young fathers are not exempt from the physical challenges of the first parental years. They're likely to eat poorly or on the run, spend less time on regular participation in sports, and have more on their minds. Finally, on a family outing it's usually dad who gets to carry the tired toddler through the zoo.

We'll start with stretching exercises for two. Do the entire series, then reverse roles to give your partner a turn.

Inner Thigh Stretch

1) Lie on back with soles of feet together. Your partner should be on his knees at your feet, with his hands on your inner thighs.

2) Your partner will exert gentle downward pressure until you feel the muscles along the inner thighs begin to stretch. Hold 15 counts and relax.

Groin and Lower Back Stretch

1) Sit with legs wide apart with your partner behind you, resting his chest against your back.

2) Your partner should exert slow, forward pressure until the stretch is felt in the groin and lower back area. Hold 15 counts and relax.

Hamstring (Rear Thigh) Stretch

3) a. After you straighten up, your partner should exert gentle pressure toward either leg to stretch the hamstring (rear thigh) muscles. Keep the legs straight.

b. Move to the point of the stretch, hold 15 counts, relax, and repeat with other leg.

c. Stretch the tighter leg first.

Strengthening Exercises for Partners

Your strengthening program will combine isometric and eccentric isotonic exercises with partners.

In isometric exercise, the muscle attempts to shorten as you apply force against a resistance, but does not in fact shorten. Isotonic contraction involves the expenditure of energy while the muscle is gradually lengthening (eccentric) or shortening (concentric).

The main point to emphasize here is to breathe. *Do not hold your breath while you are attempting these exercises.* When exercising, always breathe out while applying pressure, breathe in while relaxing. Breathe normally.

The technique for each of these exercises is similar. Your partner will apply resistance while you attempt to move against it. For the first six counts your partner will allow no movement as you apply pressure. On count 7 through 10, your partner will gradually decrease the pressure, allowing you to move the muscles worked through a range of motion.

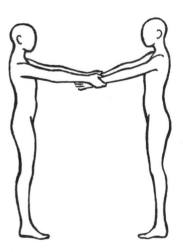

Upper Chest Strengthening

1. Arms outstretched, shoulder-width apart at shoulder height, your hands outside your partner's.

2. Apply pressure, pushing hands together for six counts. Keep arms straight.

3. On count 7, your partner will relax slightly, allowing you to gradually move your hands together.

Upper Back

1. Face each other, arms outstretched at shoulder height, your hands inside your partner's.

2. Apply outward pressure, attempting to force partner's hands apart.

3. On count 7, partner should decrease pressure, allowing movement of your arms backward.

4. Good for improving and preventing round shoulders (optional).

Rear Shoulders (Rx for Shoulder Slump)

1. Bend at the waist, keeping your back straight, arms hanging down, feet apart.

2. Partner should be on knees, facing you, hands on the outside of your arms and elbows.

3. Apply upward and outward pressure against his resistance, lifting arms to your side.

4. On count 7, your partner should decrease resistance so that you may gradually raise your arms to shoulder height.

Shoulders

1. Stand arms at side, hands open.

2. Partner stands at your side with hand on outside of your arm.

3. Exert outward pressure and attempt to raise arm to your side.

4. On count 7, partner decreases resistance, allowing you to raise the arm to shoulder height.

5. Repeat with other arm.

Biceps/Upper Arm Strengthening

1. Stand facing each other, arms bent, palms up, elbows into your side.

2. Partner should be in same position with palms down, resting on your palms.

3. Exert upward pressure, keeping elbows into side.

4. On count 7, partner will allow you to bring hands to shoulders gradually.

5. Note: Reverse hand positions with spouse to work the triceps, or back of upper arm.

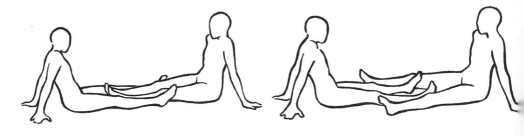

Inner-Outer Thigh Strengthening

1. Seated on the floor, extend legs on the outside of partner's. Feet should be at knee level.

2. Exert inward pressure as your partner attempts to force the legs apart to exercise inner thigh.

3. On count 7, partner will allow you to bring your legs together gradually.

4. Reverse leg positions to exercise muscles of outer thigh.

How to Avoid Backache

Lifting

ɤ Avoid bending at the waist when lifting heavy objects or children. The legs are much stronger than the muscles of the lower back and should be used when lifting to avoid injury.

ɤ When you pick anything up off the floor, assume a squatting position. With the back held straight, and without twisting, lift from the knees holding the object or child in close to the body.

ɤ Children who want to be carried and who are old enough to stand should step up on a chair or stairstep to avoid your having to squat lower than necessary.

Walking

ɤ As you walk, carrying the object, hold it in close to the body.

ɤ Back packs and/or front carriers are best for carrying your baby any distance. Carrying a child over your shoulder or resting on the hip for a long period can lead to lower back problems.

ɤ Strollers should be at a height that doesn't cause you to bend excessively at the waist in order to push it. Most umbrella strollers, although convenient, are hard on your back. Use them in addition to, not in place of, a standard stroller that moves easily, in order to prevent what we call "stroller hunch."

Standing

ɤ When standing for long periods of time, e.g. ironing or working at a counter, prop one foot up on a stool. Shift often from one leg to the other.

ɤ Sit on a high stool with a back support whenever possible.

Sitting and Kneeling

ɤ Work on all fours when scrubbing the floors or looking for that lost Tinker Toy under the couch.

ɤ Kneel at the edge of the tub when bathing your child.

ɤ Put a foot rest under your desk and the child's crib.

✓ Diaper the baby sitting next to him on the bed.

✓ Use a rocking chair, as rocking relaxes the back by changing the muscle groups used.

✓ Use your abdominal muscles. Weak abdominal muscles rob your back of needed support.

✓ Chairs should be low enough so that you can sit with both feet on the floor with the knees higher than the hips.

✓ Sit with your back firmly agains the chair. Don't slump.

Sleeping

✓ Sleep on a firm mattress that will give you support. Sleep on your side with your knees bent, or on your back with a pillow under your knees.

Driving

✓ The driver's seat should be close to the pedals, so that your knees are bent and higher than your hips. Reaching for the pedals will cause lower back strain.

Low-Back Relief

✓ Lie on your back with your feet on a chair. Relax and breathe slowly. This position should be held 10 to 15 minutes for maximum relief.

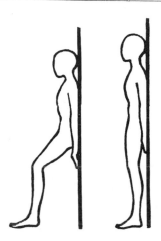

Posture

✓ Good posture is essential for a healthy lower back. Find the correct posture by standing one foot from the wall. Sit back against the wall, bending the knees slightly. Tilt the pelvis to flatten the lower back against the wall by tightening the abdominal muscles. Then, holding this position, slide up the wall into a standing position. Walk away from the wall, maintaining the same posture. Move against the wall to see if the lower back rests against it.

✓ Maintain this good posture while walking. Keep your head high, pelvis forward.

✓ Make sure you wear comfortable shoes with low or moderate heels. Many women's shoe sizes change after pregnancy. If your old shoes hurt, don't be surprised. Have your feet remeasured when buying new shoes, and see a podiatrist for treatment of foot problems that can interfere with good posture.

11

The Developing Family

Remember the fantasies and promises of the pre-birth months? A made-to-order baby and perfect parents. Then, just as you were reconciling yourself to baby colic or adult inadequacy, your best friends, the parents of a toddler, said: You think that's hard? Wait until the Terrible Twos! And that was your introduction to the eternal parental riddle: how to reconcile the challenges of the moment with the warnings, promises, and predictions of the future.

In the first years, it's hard to imagine the future beyond the next developmental stage. But as the child's personality and independence—and your own self-perception—come into focus, so does your curiosity and need for information about parent-child milestones ahead.

In the following pages we reflect on some of the common themes of family life as parents strive for a changing ratio of adult needs and parental responsibilities, and their children strive for a balance between belonging and independence. The choice both parents and children make will sometimes intersect and sometimes conflict in the natural course of time and events. We can muse endlessly about where we or our children will be ten, twenty, or thirty years down the line. We can fortify ourselves against the Terrible Teens just as we did against the Terrible Twos. We can prepare for the empty nest by keeping other interests afloat during the intense nurturing years. But we shouldn't forget the first parental lesson we learned with the onset of labor: education, awareness, and control can help us *prepare* for the future, but not *predict* it.

Power and Responsibility

Parent-child relationships begin with the dependency of infants, but they do not stay there. At the beginning the child is incapable of negotiation because he cannot talk. The parents necessarily control him 100 percent. By the time he is launched from the family he must be capable of controlling himself 100 percent.

Therefore parents must do a complete about-face. Nor can this be
a simple one-step change. From the time the child begins moving
toward independence at around age two until he finishes that
process of launching, a whole series of steps must be taken. . . .
In a sense the family must continually readjust the balance of power
between parents and children throughout this entire period.

Robert Blood and Margaret Blood
in THE FAMILY

The awesome power of the early months is so absolute as to be intimidating. Looking at the infant, parents know that they are fallible
and unprepared. Later, when the child starts to test parental power,
with bedtime rebellions, the perennial "no," dinnertime miseries, and
physical aggression against peers, we're forced to try out half-formu-
lated or untested beliefs and to scale down Utopian goals. In short, even
if we secretly imagined never having to limit or correct our child, we've
begun the *process* of discipline that ideally leads to a transference of
power and responsibility from parent to child.

The recurrent parental task is to redefine and renegotiate the balance
of power between parent and child. This is not a smooth or predictable
process. The pace at which we transfer responsibility to the child, hop-
ing to create a responsible adult, depends, say Robert & Margaret Blood
in their book, *The Family*, "on the child's increasing knowledge, his
understanding of human relations, his increasing socialization and developing conscience. . . . Parents must repeatedly reassess their child in
relation to his environment in determining how fast they can safely
relax their controls and transfer power to him."

If our goal in disciplining and shifting power and responsibility is
what Selma Fraiberg calls the "education of character" in her book,
The Magic Years, then we must be prepared to examine and expose our
own "character"—the goals, standards, and double standards that influence our behavior.

We must also be prepared to see our values translated in ways we
hadn't anticipated. The adolescent taught the value of independence
may shock her parents by choosing to travel and work abroad for a
year rather than enter college. Another, who was taught the importance
of hard work, may work very hard in a rock and roll band, to the dis-
may of his conservative parents.

The final shift of power from parent to child can leave us in a vacuum or offer much-needed breathing space. Elinor Lenz, author of
Once My Child . . . Now My Friend, told us: "Frankly, I didn't enjoy
my daughters as much when I was a parent as I do now that I am a

friend. As a parent, joy was always tinged with worry and anguish, with a sense of 'What have I done wrong?' Now I'm free of all that, free to just enjoy them without adopting a critical parental attitude— no big shoulds or oughts. They ask my opinion, I give it; if they don't ask my opinion, I don't give it. They give me advice about what I should do. Sometimes I think they're parenting me more than I'm parenting them—and we laugh about that."

Growing Pains and Separation

In the first two years or so, we're preoccupied by "what comes next." We anticipate and encourage each developmental phase. We state the age of our child in months, so aware are we of the velocity of change and growth in the very young person. But parents can become overwhelmed by the more profound changes that occur as the child matures and strives for independence, individuality, and, ultimately, separation. At some point most of us yearn to *slow down* the process. The more realistic of us accept the inevitability of change and try to learn the art of letting go. We as parents experience growing pains in ourselves when confronted with change in our children.

In parent-child relationships, growth is synonymous with separation. The parent's job is to prepare the child for survival on his own, though it's natural to cling to the hope that the ultimate independence will include a degree of attachment. In *Between Generations: The Six Stages of Parenthood*, Ellen Galinsky describes the meaning of parent-child separation in this way: " 'Separate' means that the parent understands the ways in which the child is unique. It doesn't preclude an appreciation of the ways in which the child is similar . . . separateness is always linked with connectedness."

Beginning at birth, the complex process of separation gains momentum when the child enters preschool or first grade. Parents not only learn to share their child with teachers and peers, but help them learn to respect and value these "outsiders." Increasing independence in the child eventually makes the *parent* feel an outsider in his child's universe. This society of children, which gains strength in the years preceding adolescence, has its own language, jokes, dress code, value system, and secrets that many parents find hard to understand and accept.

Equally distressing to parents is the realization that the child's own world is not a Utopia, but a scale model of the actual human condition, where cruelty, injustice, frustration, loneliness, and physical violence exist in tandem with learning, sharing, and trust. It's not always possible for parents to intercede on behalf of their own child even when he suffers before their eyes. When Maria's son was hit by an otherwise good friend, she had to consider the following: At six, Jud was old enough to either fight back or walk away. When he did neither —choosing instead to cry in front of the perpetrator, and try repeatedly and unsuccessfully to make up—Maria felt the pain as keenly as if it were her own. Should she step in and chastise the friend? Should she ignore the incident altogether? Should she talk with the other child's mother? Should she talk to her own child about pride or give him boxing lessons?

In the school years, parents will ask themselves similar questions about intervening or encouraging independence as they see their child struggling with homework, disagreeing with teachers, feeling left out or misunderstood, coming to terms with personal strengths and weaknesses.

The "Terrible Teens"

Anticipating the teenage years has become the primary task for parents in what Ellen Galinsky calls the "rehearsal period" of preadolescence. Here's the common parental spectre Galinsky describes in her book, *Between Generations: The Six Stages of Parenthood*:

> These preadolescent years mark the end of childhood per se and the approach of a new stage. Parents think about this coming venture with a melange of emotions—sorrow, fear, nostalgia, and anticipation. The teenage years, in American culture today, have an awesome reputation. . . . Some parents, remembering their own teenage years, picture the worst—their children transformed, surly, turning their backs on their parents, ungrateful, speeding dangerously down highways, hot-rodding, hitchhiking, drinking, metamorphosed by drugs, enmeshed in sex. They imagine that the remaining umbilical cords tying their children to them will be severed—not gently, but chopped off, leaving wounds. They have been warned by the parents of teenagers: "You think it's nice (or hard) now—well, just wait."

As parents sense they are beginning to "lose their children," psychoanalyst E. James Anthony writes in his book, *Parenthood, Its Psychology and Psychopathology*, "the attempt to recapture the vanishing object can be strenuous. With every artifice at their command, certain parents will attempt to close the doors and raise the drawbridges and dig deep moats to keep their burgeoning offspring in, for they cannot bring themselves to realize that the loss entailed is almost as inevitable as death and almost as irreversible. They may offer themselves as apparently new objects, disguised as adolescent playmates, but the adolescent readily detects the old object in the new and struggles to escape even more strenuously. They may attempt to keep pace with the young and wear themselves out in doing so, or, at least for a while, they may successfully deny entrance to any new object."

Perhaps sadder, from the adult viewpoint, is the misguided effort of some parents to keep up with their teenage children's activities and even to compete with them. The middle-aged father who was a star athlete in his own youth, may alternately encourage and envy similar accomplishments in his teenage son. One mother in her early forties, who had thrived on her attractiveness, couldn't bear to look in the mirror with her teenage daughter—an identical but far younger version of herself. For this mother and many others, accepting the child's right to sexual development is devastating. Fathers and mothers caught in what Yale University professor Daniel Levinson calls "the young/old polarity" of midlife have to find some balance between denying and overcompensating for the inexorability of the life cycle.

Today, of course, as the parental age range grows ever wider, parents in their early forties may be running after an active toddler, while their contemporaries are coping with a teenage daughter's dating life, and feeling quite "over the hill." The toddler parents are likely to identify with their more youthful peers in parenting, while the teenager's parents run the danger of stereotyping themselves as middle-aged.

For parents engaged in the push-pull behavior of adolescence, growing pains indicate what's still to come. Not far down the road is the final leave-taking for the child—going to college, deciding to live alone, with friend or lover, joining the armed forces, traveling, getting a job. And childless parenthood begins, even if you have other children still at home.

The "empty nest" still exists, however remodeled by new attitudes about women, work, middle age, relationships, and life expectancy, and the acknowledgment that men as well as women suffer when kids leave home. Author/psychologist Eda LeShan, in her book, *The Wonderful Crisis of Middle Age*, points out that among her own friends, all career women, childless parenthood was not feared, but "almost all of us have been shocked to discover that no matter how prepared we thought we were, there have been major adjustments and upheavals. . . . The most common pattern seems to be a period of unacknowledged mourning for what has passed, which the couple does not share with each other.

Perhaps this is even more characteristic of couples who *do* have many interests, for what seems to happen is a period of growing apart, during which neither partner is fully aware of what is happening."

"When the children leave," writes Eda LeShan, "marriage faces a moment of truth; is there strength enough to sustain it without the excuse of parenthood? . . . Once the children are gone and there is no child sleeping in the next room, and no kids underfoot of a lazy Sunday afternoon, the lack of mutual pleasure and gratification becomes a clear and present problem, hanging in the air, palpably, and can no longer be avoided."

The child's leave-taking has traditionally coincided with parental middle age, which some parents see as a "last chance" stage in their own lives. It's not surprising, then, that so many "grown-ups" are becoming as experimental as their offspring in exploring new commitments and rediscovering sexuality, thus astonishing grown children, with their own eagerness for change.

Have We Done a Good Job?

Parental self-evaluation usually begins in the labor room. Is the father participating? Is the mother breathing correctly? Will she deliver "naturally" or require medication or an unexpected Caesarian? Early bonding, nursing, and infant nurturing experiences all go into the first report card.

In the preschool years, we're told, our influence is crucial. We find ourselves repeatedly taking our parental pulse as toilet training, nightmares, discipline, nursery school, and other tests confront us. By the time the child enters school, we're used to asking ourselves: "How are we doing?" But that doesn't mean we're ready to be evaluated by others.

Karen Brody, a school psychologist counseling parents and children of kindergarten through high school age, told us: "Parents feel vulnerable when a child enters school. Their adequacy and his are being questioned. Some of the questions parents begin to ask, and expect immediate answers to, are, 'Is my kid smart enough, strong enough, competitive enough? Is he well liked by friends and teachers?' "

The scope and nature of behavior in the preadolescent years is, of course, different for every family and depends a good deal on how quickly a child blossoms. But the questions parents ask at this point are universal: Have we given our child a good foundation of family life as insurance against the negative influences outside? How much control do we dare exercise, and in what manner? How can we walk the line between sheltering and exposing our child to new influences? Will we be hated or rejected for clinging to values which may seem outmoded? How can we reach out to this child, who looks and acts like a different person, but is still very much our own?

Even with parental soul-searching, and no matter how much "insurance" you buy, the child's entry into the teen years is liable to shake the family to its roots. Often the adolescent's developmental brooding about "where am I going" is mirrored by his parents' "Where have we gone wrong?"

While scrutiny is nothing new to parents, the standards have suddenly become much more exacting, especially as our culture puts ever more emphasis on beauty, success, achievement, competitiveness, and being best. When we look back, we see how clearly the collective expectations of society have drawn us in: when our infant was born, the important thing was to have a healthy, normal baby. By the early school years, normal and healthy have been supplanted by yearnings for gifted, popular, handsome, athletic, creative, independent, and self-assured. Here again we are judged by the quality of our "product."

Problems and disappointments that even the healthiest of families encounter can easily be interpreted as the parents' failure to make the right decisions, even when the decisions are not theirs to make.

Kenneth Keniston and the Carnegie Council on Children, in the book *All Our Children*, trace the propensity of American parents to blame themselves for the normal vagaries of childraising on "the feeling of not being in control as parents, and the widespread sense of personal guilt at what seems to be going awry. For when the right way to be a parent is not clear, almost any action can seem capricious or wrong, and every little trouble or minor storm in one's children's lives can be the cause for added self-blame."

If the parent hasn't realized it already, this is about the time when the lingering fantasies of the ideal parent and typical child are put into mothballs—to be recalled perhaps as distant memories by aged parents and grown children, many years down the line.

Did we do a good job as parents? Many parents believe the final answer hinges on the adaptation of the grown child to adult life. A good job, sound relationships, healthy self-image, acceptable living environment are all seen as indirect "returns" on the years of parental effort. But what if our children do poorly at work and at personal relationships? What if they aren't happy in ways we find acceptable? Have we failed as parents? Have we done a bad job? Maybe. The unanswerable question reflects what the committee of psychiatrists who wrote

The Joys and Sorrows of Parenthood call "the true dilemma theory of parenthood," in which "the parent may be the best kind of person he can be, but the final product is not entirely within his control, no matter how much of his life he devotes to the children. . . . There are no simple formulas on how to rear an individual child to reach parents' expectations. . . . Parents care terribly whether the consequences are good or bad, but the intensity of their *wishes* does not influence the outcome."

The leave-taking may bring into painful focus the knowledge that your children have defined your existence at least as much as you have theirs. This is the day of reckoning for parents who have used children as an excuse for postponing their own lives. Or, if getting to know your kids has taken a back seat to career, as it traditionally has with many fathers, the leave-taking underscores a missed opportunity. "Many men find their careers not all that satisfying in middle age. And all of a sudden they discover they have these interesting adult children, but that the children don't need them," observes Elinor Lenz.

For both parents, the entry into childless parenthood is a period of marital, personal, and professional stock-taking. Despite the loneliness and nostalgia parents feel at a child's departure, there *are* good things to look forward to—more leisure, more privacy, time for yourself, and a chance to foster adult relationships.

Ironically, today the "empty nest" sometimes fills up again with grown children unable to support themselves in economically unstable times. Some parents are surprised to find that they need distance as much as the child, and that they can't figure out just what the relationship should be between all these adults living under the same roof. Some find themselves wishing that this new "extended" family will be only temporary, and that they will soon pursue their own new lives unencumbered.

"Good" parenting is so subjective that it defies definition. If we view parenting as a job apart from the other functions of our lives, then perhaps we can stand back and rate ourselves objectively. But if we think of *parenthood* as a state of being as well as a matter of doing, can we honestly evaluate how we did apart from the context of who we are?

"The aim in being a parent is not to succeed, since no one knows what success would look like," historian and literary critic Garry Wills wrote in a recent issue of *Parents* magazine. "It [parenthood] is a bond that exists no matter what one does about it—one that can be abused or shirked, but never effaced. Once a parent, one is a parent for life, as we are all somebody's children for life. We have entered the social texture through one particular mesh; and we must struggle along with these primary ties.

"In this struggle we afflict each other, do secret damage, hurt with love," Wills continues. "But the inviolable mystery of each person's identity does not allow us to keep experimenting with others until things 'come out right.' The only duty is to keep on *being*. . . . It is a way of becoming human in the company of others—the only way that is ever done."

12

Help

Resources for New Parents

This directory offers the names and addresses of agencies, support groups, counseling services, periodicals, and other resources for new parents. If you write for information, remember to include a self-addressed, stamped envelope to facilitate prompt response. Materials available without charge have been noted in the listings; however, many services and subscriptions are not free, so be sure to ask about fees when contacting the organization.

Adoption

Adoptive Parents Committee, Inc.
210 Fifth Avenue
New York, N.Y. 10010

Committee for Single Adoptive
Parents
P.O. Box 4074
Washington, D.C. 20015

North American Council on
Adoptable Children
Suite 229
1346 Connecticut Avenue, N.W.
Washington, D.C. 20036

Open Door Society
P.O. Box 536
Ronkonkoma, N.Y. 11779

Car Seats

Action for Child Transportaiton, Inc.
P.O. Box 266
Bothell, Washington 98011

Write for a copy of "Kids Are
Fragile—Travel With Care."
Include 25¢ and a large, stamped,
self-addressed envelope.

U.S. Department of Transportation
National Highway Traffic Safety
Administration
400 7th Street, S.W.
Washington, D.C. 20590

Send for "Early Rider" packet, containing free pamphlets on buying,
using, and renting car restraints
nationwide.

239

Childbirth

American Society for Psychoprophylaxis in Obstetrics (ASPO)
1411 K St., N.W. Suite 200
Washington, D.C. 20005

Local chapters nationwide offer
classes for expectant mothers in
the Lamaze method of prepared
childbirth. Many chapters also
offer post-partum support groups.
Write to national headquarters for
address of chapter nearest you.

International Childbirth Education
Association (ICEA)
Post Office Box 20048
8060 26th Avenue So.
Minneapolis, Minn. 55420

International clearinghouse for information and support, stressing
family-centered childbirth. Inval-
uable mail-order book service for
literature on family life and
childbirth. Post-partum support
groups nationwide. Write to main
office for address of chapter
nearest you.

National Association for the
Advancement of Leboyer's Birth
Without Violence, Inc.
P.O. Box 28455
University of Miami Branch
Coral Gables, Fla. 33124

Information on Leboyer method of
gentle birthing.

Read Natural Childbirth Foundation, Inc.
1300 S. Eliseo Drive, Suite 102
Greenbrae, Calif. 94904

Information on natural childbirth
methods and philosophy of
Grantly Dick-Read, M.D.

Child Care

Daycare

Day Care Council of America, Inc.
Suite 507
711 14th St.
Washington, D.C.

Contact for up-to-date information
on daycare nationwide.

For a free copy of "A Parent's Guide
to Day Care," publication No.
(OHDS) 80–30254 write to:
LSDS
Department 76
Washington, D.C. 20401

Parents Cooperative Preschools
International
20551 Lakeshore Road
Baie D'Urge, Quebec, Canada
H9X 1R3

Information on all aspects of parent-run preschools.

Quality Child Care, Inc.
P.O. Box 176
Mound, Minn. 55364

For a national directory of child care information and referral services, reprinted from the January 1981 issue of *Working Mother*, send 35¢ to:

Working Mother Magazine
Department DD
230 Park Avenue
New York, N.Y. 10169

Nursery Schools

National Association for the Education of Young Children
1834 Connecticut Ave., N.W.
Washington, D.C. 20009

Association for Childhood Education International
3615 Wisconsin Ave., N.W.
Washington, D.C. 20016

Consumer Information and Support

Consumer Reports
P.O. Box 1000
Orangeburg, N.Y. 10962

Monthly publication of the Consumers Union

Consumer Information Catalog
Consumer Information Center
Department Y
Pueblo, Colo. 81009

Free or low-cost government pamphlets covering consumer affairs as well as general family topics.

Product Safety

To report a product hazard or product-related injury, write to:

U.S. Consumer Product Safety Commission
Washington, D.C. 20207

Toll-free hotline: 800–638–8326
Maryland residents: 800–492–8363
Alaska, Hawaii, Puerto Rico: 800–638–8333

Travelers Insurance Co. of Hartford
Hartford Conn. 06101

Send a stamped, self-addressed envelope for a free Home Safety Checklist.

Counseling/Mental Health

American Association for Marriage
and Family Therapy
924 W. 9th St.
Upland, Calif. 91786

Maintains listings of thousands of
qualified family counselors
throughout the United States.
Send self-addressed, stamped
envelope for referrals in your area.

Family Service Association of
America
44 East 23rd St.
New York, N.Y. 10010

Source of information and literature
on a variety of local social service
agencies. Referrals to local marriage counseling services.

National Association for Mental
Health
1800 North Kent St.
Rosslyn, Calif. 92209

Information on local agenices involved in the prevention and
treatment of mental illness. Broad
range of family mental health
literature.

National Institute for Mental Health
5600 Fishers La.
Rockville, Md. 20852

Government agency providing information on all aspects of family
mental health, including child
abuse and depression. Publishes
directory of local mental health
services and mental health
pamphlets.

National Council on Alcoholism
733 Third Avenue
New York, N.Y. 10017

Public Affairs Committee, Inc.
381 Park Avenue South
New York, N.Y. 10016

Inexpensive, supportive pamphlets
on family wellbeing and problem
solving.

Fathers

Dads Only
P.O. Box 340
Julian, Calif. 92036

A monthly resource newsletter for
fathers and husbands. Send for
current subscription rates.

Nurturing News
187 Caselli Avenue
San Francisco, Calif. 94114

A quarterly newsletter with information and insights from and
about fathers and other men in
the lives of young children.

Single Dad's Lifestyle
P.O. Box 4842
Scottsdale, Ariz. 85258

Support, information, and resources
for the divorced father.

Single Dad's Hotline: (602)
998–0980

The Fatherhood Project
Bank Street College of Education
610 West 112th Street
New York, N.Y. 10025

National resource center and clearinghouse for information about
fatherhood and men in nurturing
roles.

Health

Center for Medical Consumers and
Health Care Information, Inc.
237 Thompson St.
New York, N.Y. 10012

Free medical library for laypeople;
consumer newsletter.

National Health Federation
211 W. Colorado Blvd.
P.O. Box 686
Monrovia, Calif. 91016

Monthly health consumer bulletin.

National Women's Health Network
224 7th St., S.E.
Washington, D.C. 20003

Offers information on all aspects of
women's health, and referral list
of health centers thoughout
nation.

Birth Control

Planned Parenthood
810 Seventh Avenue
New York, N.Y. 10019

SIECUS
(Sex Information and Education
Council of the U.S.)
1855 Broadway
New York, N.Y. 10023

Breastfeeding

Health Education Associates
520 School House Lane
Willow Grove, Pa. 19090

International Childbirth Education
Association
(ICEA)
P.O. Box 20048
8060 26th Ave. So.
Minneapolis, Minn. 55420

La Leche League, International
9616 Minneapolis Avenue
Franklin Park, Ill. 60131

Publications, support groups, clearinghouse for information on
breastfeeding. Local chapters
nationwide.

Caesareans

Caesarean Birth Association
125 N. 12th St.
New Hyde Park, N.Y. 11040

The Caesarean Connection
P.O. Box 11
Westmont, Ill. 60559

C/Sec, Inc.
15 Maynard Road
Dedham, Mass. 02026

Nutrition

The American Health Foundation
320 East 43 Street
New York, N.Y. 10017

Center for Science in the Public
   Interest
1755 S. St., N.W.
Washington, D.C. 20009

Consumer advocacy and information.

National Nutrition Consortium, Inc.
9650 Rockville Pike
Bethesda, Md. 20014

Society for Nutrition Information
2140 Shattuck Avenue
Suite 1110
Berkeley, Calif. 94704

Free or low-cost government pamphlets on nutrition are available from:

Consumer Information Center
Department Y
Pueblo, Colo. 81009

or:

U.S. Department of Agriculture
Office of Governmental and Public
   Affairs
Washington, D.C. 20250

Home

House Swapping

Vacation Exchange Club
350 Broadway   Rm. 1110
New York, N.Y. 10013

Moving

Interstate Commerce Commission
Office of Consumer Protection
Washington, D.C. 20423

Complaint Center: 800–424–9312
   and 800–424–9313

Magazines, Newsletters & Pamphlets

Low-cost or free publications on a multitude of family topics can be tained from:

Consumer Informaiton Catalog
Consumer Information Center
Department Y
Pueblo, Colo. 81009

Fifty Ways to Help You Be a Better
  Parent
Friends of the Family
P.O. Box 40845
Washington, D.C. 20016

Public Affairs Pamphlets
381 Park Avenue South
New York, N.Y. 10016

Superintendent of Documents
U.S. Government Printing Office
Washington, D.C. 20402

General Parenting Magazines & Newsletters

American Baby
10 East 52 St.
New York, N.Y. 10022

Family Journal
RD 2, Box 165
Putney, Vt. 05346

Mothers Manual
Box 243
Franklin Lakes, N.J. 07417

Newsletter of Parenting
2300 W. Fifth Avenue
P.O. Box 2505
Columbus, Ohio 43216

New Parent Adivsor and *Parenting
  Advisor*
13-30 Corp.
505 Market St.
Knoxville, Tenn. 37902

Parents
685 Third Avenue
New York, N.Y. 10017

Practical Parenting
18318 Minnetonka Blvd.
Deephaven, Minn. 55391

Redbook
P.O. Box 2027
Rock Island, Ill. 61207

Single Parents

Many parent support groups have special services for single parents, as do local YM and YWCAs and other community service groups. The following organizations were founded specifically to meet the needs of single, widowed, and divorced parents.

Divorced and Divorcing Men's
    Support Groups
6723 W. Lloyd St.
Wauwatosa, Wis. 53213

Divorced Men's Association of
    Connecticut
P.O. Box 723
Waterbury, Conn. 06720

National Association of Separated
    or Divorced Catholics
Paulist Center
5 Park St.
Boston, Mass. 02108

Parents Without Partners
7910 Woodmont Avenue
Washington, D.C. 20014

National organization with many
    local chapters and publication,
    Single Parent. Write to headquar-
    ters for address of group nearest
    you.

Single Dad's Hotline
(602) 998–0980

Information and support for single
    fathers.

Single Parent Family Project
16 W. 23rd St.
New York, N.Y. 10010

Divorce/Arbitration

American Academy of Matrimonial
    Lawyers
200 Garden City Plaza
Garden City, N.Y.

American Arbitration Association
140 West 51st St.
New York, N.Y. 10036

Family Mediation Association
5018 Allan Road
Bethesda, Md. 20816

Publications

Co-Parent
P.O. Box 92262
Milwaukee, Wis. 53202

Single Dad's Lifestyle
P.O. Box 4842
Scottsdale, Ariz. 85258

Single Parent
Parents Without Partners
7910 Woodmont Avenue
Washington, D.C. 20014

Single Parent Families
(No. OHDS 79–30247)
Library and Statutory Distribution
    Services
Dept. 76N–1
Washington, D.C. 20402

Free booklet for single mothers and
    fathers from the government's
    Health and Human Services
    Department.

Stepparents

Remarried Parents, Inc.
Box 323
Times Square Station
New York, N.Y. 10036

Step Family Association of America
900 Welch Road
Palo Alto, Calif. 94304

Step Family Bulletin
Human Sciences Press
77 Fifth Avenue
New York, N.Y. 10011

Step Family Foundation
333 West End Avenue
New York, N.Y. 10023

Special Circumstances

Bereaved Parents

The Compassionate Friends, Inc.
Box 3247
Hialeah, Fla. 33013

Support for families who have lost
a child. Local chapters nationwide
provide discussion groups, warm
lines, and information. For the
address of chapter nearest you,
write to national headquarters.

The National Sudden Infant Death
Syndrome Foundation
310 S. Michigan Avenue
Suite 1904
Chicago, Ill. 60604

Child Abuse

Parents Anonymous
22330 Hawthorne Blvd.
Torrance, Calif. 90505

Hotline:
   In California: 800–352–0386
   Elsewhere: 800–421–0353

Handicapped Children

Closer Look
The National Information Center for
the Handicapped
Box 1492
Washington, D.C. 20013

Free information and advice for
parents of mentally, physically, or
emotionally handicapped children.

National Easter Seal Society
2023 Ogden Avenue
Chicago, Ill. 60612

Practical information and support
for parents of handicapped children. Send for booklet, "Your
Child Has a Future."

Hospitalized Children

Children in Hospitals, Inc.
31 Wilshire Park
Needham, Mass. 02192

National information, support, and
   advocacy organization for families
   of hospitalized children. For a list
   of local chapters, send self-
   addressed, stamped envelope to
   above address.

Premature

*The Premature Infant: A Handbook
   for Parents* is available for $3.00
   from:

The Hospital for Sick Children
Room 1218
555 University Avenue
Toronto, Ontario, Canada M5G 1X8

Twins

Double Talk
P.O. Box 412
Amelia, Ohio 45102

National Organization of Mothers
   of Twins Clubs, Inc.
5402 Amberwood Ln.
Rockville, Md. 20853

Nationwide network of support
   groups; publication dealing with
   the care of twin children.

Women's Groups

(See Work and Health Sections for more resources)

National Commission Against
   Domestic Violence
1728 N Street
Washington, D.C. 20007

National Congress of Neighborhood
   Women
11–29 Catherine St.
Brooklyn, N.Y. 11211

National Organization for Women
(NOW)
Action Center
425 13th St., N.W.
Washington, D.C. 20004

Rural American Women
152 K Street, N.W.
Washington, D.C. 20005

Women's Action Alliance
370 Park Avenue
New York, N.Y. 10017

Work

American Women's Economic
Development Corp. (AWEC)
1270 Avenue of the Americas
New York, N.Y. 10020

Business and Professional Women's
Foundation
2012 Massachusetts Avenue, N.W.
Washington, D.C. 20036

Careers: The Women's Bureau
U.S. Department of Labor
Washington, D.C. 20210

Catalyst
14 E. 60 St.
New York, N.Y. 10022

Clearinghouse of information and
career counseling for women.
Local offices nationwide.

Displaced Homemakers Network
755 Eighth St., N.W.
Washington, D.C. 20001

Over 300 career counseling centers
nationwide offer practical and
emotional support to divorced or
widowed homemakers who are
reentering work force.

National Council for Alternative
Work Patterns, Inc.
1025 K Street, N.W.
Suite 308A
Washington, D.C. 20001

Information on new work patterns
such as flexitime, job sharing, etc.

Project Re-Entry
14 Beacon St.
Boston, Mass. 02108

Wider Opportunities for Women,
Inc.
1511 K St., N.W.   Suite 700
Washington, D.C. 20006

Women's Action Alliance, Inc.
370 Lexington Avenue
New York, N.Y. 10017

Parent Support Groups: A Directory

National Organizations

The following organizations serve as support clearinghouses for new
parents. If you are unable to find a group near you (and remember,

new groups are forming, and others disbanding, almost daily) consult your local Y, ASPO, ICEA or La Leche chapter, or the newly organized Family Resource Coalition.

American Society for Psychoprophylaxis in Obstetrics (ASPO)
1411 K. St., N.W.   Suite 200
Washington, D.C. 20005

Family Resource Coalition
230 North Michigan Avenue
Suite 1625
Evanston, Ill. 60601

International Childbirth Education
  Association (ICEA)
P.O. Box 20048
8060 26th Avenue So.
Minneapolis, Minn. 55420

La Leche League, International, Inc.
9616 Minneapolis Avenue
Franklin Park, Ill. 60131

YMCA (Young Men's Christian
  Association)
National Headquarters
291 Broadway
New York, N.Y. 10007

YWCA (Young Women's Christian
  Association)
National Headquarters
600 Lexington Avenue
New York, N.Y. 10022

California

Postpartum Education for Parents
Sharon Eastman
370 Orlena Avenue
Long Beach, Calif. 90814

Postpartum Education for Parents
Jane Honikman
927 N. Kellogg
Santa Barbara, Calif. 93111

The Family League
Debra English
P.O. Box 840
Santa Maria, Calif. 93456

WARM LINES

ABC Warmline
Riverside, Calif.
(714) 781–4816

PEP
Santa Barbara
(805) 964–2009

PIPS
Los Angeles
(213) 652–3122

Colorado

Westside Parents' Group
Susan Mosier
40 S. Allison St.
Lakewood, Colo. 80226

Connecticut

The Childbirth & Family
Development Institute
57 North Street   Suite #403
Danbury, Conn. 06810

Florida

Mothers' Support Groups
Childbirth Education Assoc.
1501 Whitehall Rd.
West Palm Beach, Fla. 33405

Georgia

COPE
3177 Peachtree Road, N.E.
Atlanta, Georgia

Illinois

Family Focus
2300 Green Bay Road
Evanston, Ill. 60621

Indiana

Director
Continuing Parent Education
Maternity Family League
705 E. 61st St.
Indianapolis, Ind. 46220

Parents Together
Judy Fain
2407 Chestnut St.
Portage, Ind. 46368

Iowa

D.C.P.E.A. Parents Discussion
    Group
P.O. Box 54
Dubuque, Iowa 52001

Louisiana

P.A.C.E.
P.O. Box 7076
New Orleans, La. 70186

Maine

Parenting Committee
Maternal & Child Health Council
46 Columbia Street
Bangor, Me. 04401

Massachusetts

COPE
37 Clarendon Street
Boston, Mass. 02116

Michigan

Sandra Hermann
Psychological/Social Services Dept.
Midland Hospital Center
4005 Orchard Dr.
Midland, Mich. 48640

Human Understanding for Growth
  (H.U.G.)
Sue Hornby
9460 Spring Valley Dr.
Traverse City, Mich. 49684

Minnesota

Child Oriented Parent Education—
  C.O.P.E.
109 Second St., N.W.
Aitkin, Minn. 56431

Parent-Child Center
Bloomington Early Childhood/
Family Education Program
8900 Portland Ave. S.
Bloomington, Minn. 55420

For a directory to parent education
  and support groups in Minnesota,
  write to:

Council on Quality Education
Room 722 Capitol Square
  Building
St. Paul, Minn. 55101

Missouri

Parent and Child St. Louis
Member I.C.E.A.
P.O. Box 9985
Kirkwood, Mo. 63122

New Hampshire

Concord Parents and and Children,
  Inc.
P.O. Box 576
Concord, N.H. 03301

New Jersey

CLASP
c/o Marian Wattenbarger
18 Elmwood Lane
Fair Haven, N.J. 07701

Mothers Center of Central New
  Jersey
P.O. Box 7
Scotch Plains, N.J. 07076

New York

Bellmore-Merrick Mothers Center
United Methodist Church
Royale St. at St. Marks Ave.
Bellmore, N.Y. 11710

Families First
250 Baltic Street
Brooklyn, N.Y. 11201

Family Life Center
Riverdale Neighborhood House
5521 Mosholu Avenue
Bronx, N.Y. 10471

Parenting
c/o Anne Siegel
35-25 160 St.
Flushing, N.Y. 11358

Mothers Center of Queens
Hawthorne Adult Center
81-15 Oceania St. and Horace
   Harding Expressway
Fresh Meadows, N.Y. 11364

Hicksville Mothers Center
United Methodist Church
Old Country Road at Nelson Ave.
Hicksville, N.Y. 11801

Consultation Center:
   help in organizing new Mothers
   Center
   (516) 486-6614
   800-645-3828

Mothers Center of Suffolk
P.O. Box 92
Holbrook, N.Y. 11741

Mother and Child Center

YMCA
175 Memorial Highway
New Rochelle, N.Y. 10801

Mother and Child Center
11 Wilmot Road
New Rochelle, N.Y. 10804

Parenting Center
92nd St. Y
1395 Lexington Avenue
New York, N.Y. 10028

Parents Resources, Inc.
Box 107, Planetarium Station
New York, N.Y. 10024

Parents & Friends
c/o Jean Filipowski
21 Readonna Lane
Penfield, N.Y. 14526

Mothers Center of Rockland County
4 Deltic Road
Spring Valley, N.Y. 10977

Parents Place, Inc.
3 Carhart Avenue
White Plains, N.Y. 10605

WARM LINE

(212) 598-3174
The Children and Infant Parenting
   Service (CHIPS) of the New York
   University Psychoeducational
   Center counsels parents on non-
   medical childcare questions.

Ohio

Center for Human Services
Early Childhood Community
  Consultation
2084 Cornell Rd.
Cleveland, Ohio 44106

Mothers Offering Mothers Support
  (MOMS) Inc.
2578 Queenston Rd.
Cleveland Hts., Ohio 44118

Parents Educating Parents
129 Sheppardson Ct.
Granville, Ohio 43023

Parents After Childbirth Education
  (PACE)
Branda Ellner
14908 Shaker Blvd.
Shaker Heights, Ohio 44120

WARM LINE

(216) 831–BORN, Inc.

A telephone support service offering
  counseling and non-medical, non-
  judgmental advice and information for parents of children under
  one year.

Pennsylvania

Childbirth Educ. Assoc. of Greater
  Philadelphia
Parenting Program
129 Fayette St.
Conshohocken, Pa. 19428

Texas

Houston Organization for Parent
  Education
3311 Richmond   Suite 330
Houston, Texas 77030

Virginia

PEP (Parenthood Ed. Project of
  No. Va.)
Alexandria Community Y, Inc.
418 S. Washington St.
Alexandria, Va. 22314

Wisconsin

Childbirth and Parent Education
  Assoc. of Dodge Co.
701 West St.
Beaver Dam, Wis. 53916

Family Enhancement Program
605 Spruce St.
Madison, Wis. 53715

APPENDIX
The Questionnaires

QUESTIONNAIRES were disseminated to more than 500 mothers and fathers across the United States, the majority of whom are members of parent support groups. Unlike professional surveys based on sophisticated demographic and psychographic information and larger samples, we sought only personal insights and shared experience from parents of diverse backgrounds living in different places. One-third of the questionnaires—and there were two types, one for parents of both sexes and a second directed specifically to fathers—were returned to us complete. They gave us inspiration for many of the concrete tips and home truths that are at the heart of this book.

The respondents live in Manhattan, Long Island, Buffalo, Brooklyn, and in Westchester County, New York, in Chichester and Concord, New Hampshire, Portland, Oregon, St. Louis, Missouri, Santa Barbara, Oakland, Berkeley, and Napa, California, Westfield, New Jersey, Durham, North Carolina, Chicago, Illinois, Atlanta, Georgia, and other towns and cities. In packets of 25, our questionnaires were sent to ten parent centers, while friends and friends of friends distributed them elsewhere. Most of the respondents were white, middle-class parents (though we did not ask them to identify themselves as such) ranging in age from late twenties to early forties, and were all with children under the age of ten. A majority of these people were married, and most of the women were taking some time out from established careers to raise their children. Of the 50 father questionnaires distributed for us by David Giveans, editor of the California-based *Nurturing News*, half were returned to us.

These respondents ranged in age from mid-twenties to early fifties, their children from newborns to adults. In some cases, the candid comments from respondents of both questionnaires led to longer personal interviews by phone or in person. In all cases, we were careful to honor requests for anonymity from participants.

Dear Father:

Under contract from a publisher, we are researching a book to help new parents care for themselves—and each other—while nurturing their young children. We would like to learn how mothers and fathers throughout the country perceive the needs, problems, challenges, and rewards of parenthood, and would appreciate your answers to the questions below. Your views will be a vital resource for us, but will remain completely anonymous.

255

We are most interested in your frank, personal insights—perhaps even those you've never talked through with others—into issues that interest you. You do not have to answer all of our questions. All replies are strictly confidential.

Name _____ Age _____

Occupation _____ Marital Status _____

Number and ages of children _____

May we contact you again for further discussion? If so please provide address, phone number, and best times to be reached.

1. In the first months of parenthood, did you have any serious doubts about your ability to cope as a parent? As a functioning adult? As a spouse? What were the major post-partum adjustments you experienced (i.e., physical—lack of sleep; emotional—confusion/disorientation; practical—reduced mobility, overcrowding)?

2. Many parents feel they have less time to communicate and less inclination for sex after the baby is born. Do you have a personal insight on parental sex and marriage? Advice?

3. Did you find your relationship with family changed when you became a parent? Please share any significant experiences with your own family or in-laws.

4. Have you made any conscious alterations in your work pattern (i.e., cutting back to spend more time with family, or increasing work responsibilities to be a better provider)? Does this situation please you?

5. Did the nature of your friendships change with fatherhood? If so, how?

6. What are your perceptions of the role and status of the working father in the marketplace?

7. Is your fathering situation special in any way? If you are a single, divorced, or over-40, first-time father, do you have any concrete advice for other men like you?

8. Do you or your partner have a reliable and mutually acceptable system for sharing house and childcare? If so, please describe.

Dear Parent:

Under contract from a publisher we are researching a book to help new parents care for themselves—and each other—while nurturing their young children. We would like to learn how mothers and fathers throughout the country perceive the needs, problems, challenges, and rewards of parenthood, and would appreciate your answers to the questions below. Your views will be a vital resource for us, but will remain completely anonymous.

We are most interested in frank, personal insights and anecdotes pertaining to issue that interest you. You do not have to answer all of the questions.

Name (optional) _____ Age _____

Sex _____ Occupation _____

Number and age of children _____ Marital Status_____

1. In the first months of parenthood, did you have any serious doubts about your ability to cope as a parent? As a functioning adult? As a spouse? Please give concrete examples of problems you may have had.

2. What solutions to these emotional upheavals would you offer new parents, based on your own experience?

3. In the initial months of parenthood, what person(s), if any, provided the help and support you needed?

4. What was the specific nature of this help and support? Help with the infant? Housework? Long talks? Physical and emotional nurturing of you, the new parent?

5. What appliances, luxuries, and necessities would you recommend for the care of *parents* during the first weeks and months of parenthood?

6. Did you and your partner suffer from post-partum depression? If so, how long after the birth of the baby did it begin, and what form did it take?

7. Do you believe that both parents (if there are two) should share the responsibility as well as the work of parenthood? If so, how do you suggest new parents evolve a sharing pattern from the start?

8. Can you describe how baby-related responsibilities are shared (or not shared) in your household? Are you satisfied with this arrangement?

9. If you were forced to leave your newborn behind in the hospital, what were some of the things you did (or didn't do, but wish you had) to make the experience more bearable?

10. Did you or your partner make any other major life changes around the time of the birth (job change, move, marriage, divorce, or major shift in outlook)? Can you describe the change and its effect on you as a parent?

11. Did you find your sex life improved or hampered by new parenthood? If it was hampered, were the reasons physical or emotional? Was the conflict resolved? How long did it take to re-establish sexual relations?

12. Do you belong to any groups or organizations offering resources and support for new parents? If so, can you provide name and address and a brief description of program?

13. Have the ways in which you have fun as a couple changed? Do you have any tips on how not to lose sight of adult pleasure?

14. Did the arrival of baby shake up or complicate existing family relationships? Can you share an example of family complications or improvements? If dismaying problems have been encountered, do you blame yourself, or feel guilty?

15. Did the nature of pre-baby friendships change when you became a parent? How? Please give examples if you can.

16. Do you have any suggestions on how to take a successful vacation with a small child in tow?

17. Do you consider yourself a "good" parent? How do you think you measure up against implied ideals of childcare books?

18. What are the major sacrifices or compromises you feel you've had to make for your child's, or your family's welfare?

19. What kind of resource material would you like to see in a parents' self-care book?

BIBLIOGRAPHY

Abarbanel, Karin, and Siegel, Connie. *Woman's Work Book.* New York: Praeger, 1975.

Africano, Lilian. "Dating and the Single Parent." *Woman's Day.* February 20, 1979, p. 60.

Ahrons, Constance. "The Binuclear Family: Two Stepfamilies, Two Houses." *Stepfamily Bulletin.* Summer, 1981, p. 5.

Alter, Stewart. "The Facts of Life Insurance." *Parents.* January, 1979, p. 90.

Anderson, B. Ray. *How You Can Use Inflation to Beat the IRS.* New York: Harper and Row, 1981.

Annas, George. *The Rights of Hospital Patients.* New York: Avon Books, 1975.

Anthony, E. James, and Benedek, Therese. *Parenthood: Its Psychology and Psychopathology.* Boston: Little, Brown, 1970.

Bailin, Lotte. "Accommodation of Work to Family." *Working Couples.* Robert Rapoport and Rhona Rapoport (Ed.) New York: Harper/Colophon, 1978.

Bane, Mary Jo, et al. "Child Care in the United States." Monograph from Wellesley College Center for Research on Women, December, 1978.

Banks, Ann and Evans, Nancy. *Goodbye House.* New York: Harmony Books/ Crown, 1980.

Barber, Virginia, and Skaggs, Merrill. *The Mother Person.* New York: Bobbs-Merrill, 1975.

Barnhill, Laurence, et al. "From Generation to Generation: Fathers-to-be in Transition." *The Family Coordinator.* April, 1979, p. 229.

Bennetts, Leslie. "Guidelines for Stepfamilies Suffering from Togetherness." *New York Times,* August 28, 1979, p. C11.

Bensman, Joseph, and Lilienfeld, Robert. "Friendship and Alienation." *Psychology Today.* October, 1979, p. 56.

Benson, Herbert. *The Relaxation Response.* New York: Morrow, 1975.

Berman, Claire. "The Art of Being a Stepparent Today." *Woman's Day.* March 11, 1980, p. 46.

———— *Making It As a Stepparent.* New York: Doubleday, 1980.

Berman, Eleanor. *Re-entering: Successful Back-to-Work Strategies for Women Seeking a Fresh Start.* New York: Crown, 1980.

Bernstein, Anne C. "Jealousy in the Family." *Parents.* February, 1979, p. 47.

Bing, Elizabeth, and Coleman, Libby. *Having a Baby after 30*. New York: Bantam Books, 1980.
Blood, Robert, and Wolfe, D. M. *Husbands and Wives: The Dynamics of Married Living*. Glencoe, Illinois: The Free Press, 1960.
Blood, Robert. *Marriage*. Glencoe, Illinois: The Free Press, 1978.
Blood, Robert, and Blood, Margaret. *The Family*. Glencoe, Illinois: The Free Press, 1972.
Bohannan, Paul. "Stepping In." *Psychology Today*. January 1978, p. 53.
Boston Women's Health Book Collective. *Our Bodies, Ourselves*. New York: Simon and Schuster, 1976.
——— *Ourselves and Our Children*. New York: Random House, 1978.
Brazelton, T. Berry. "Coping With a Colicky Baby." *Redbook*. June 1974, p. 72.
——— "It's Twins." *Redbook*. February, 1980, p. 80.
——— "When a Baby is Born Too Early." *Redbook*. November, 1979, p. 53.
——— "The Unexpected Cesarean Delivery." *Redbook*. January, 1980, p. 42.
Brewer, Gail Sforza, and Greene, Janice Presser. *Right From the Start: Meeting the Challenges of Mothering Your Unborn and Newborn Baby*. Emmaus, Pa.: Rodale Press, 1981.
Brewster, Dorothy Patricia. *You Can Breastfeed Your Baby . . . Even in Special Situations*. Emmaus, Pa: Rodale Press, 1979.
Brody, Jane E. *Jane Brody's Nutrition Book*. New York: Norton, 1981.
——— "What Does a Diet Actually Do?" *New York Times*. February 24, 1981, p. C1.
Brooks, Andree. "Families Smaller, Housing Adjusts." *New York Times*. Section 8, Sept. 14, 1980, p. 1.
Brozan, Nadine. "Learning to Accept Financial Responsibility." *New York Times*. May 30, 1981, p. 15.
——— "Men and Housework: Do They or Don't They?" *New York Times*. November 1, 1980, p. 52.
——— "Twins or Triplets: How Families Cope." *New York Times*. Sept. 14, 1981. p. B12.
Burck, Frances Wells. *Babysense*. New York: St. Martin's, 1979.
Byrne, Susan. "Nobody Home: The Erosion of the American Family—An Interview with Uri Bronfenbrenner." *Psychology Today*, May, 1977, p. 40.
Chess, Stella. *Your Child is a Person*. New York: Viking, 1965.
Clarke-Stewart, Alison, *et al. Child Care in the Family*. New York: Academic Press, 1977.
Cohen, Nancy Weiner. "Minimalizing Emotional Sequellae of Cesarean Childbirth." *Birth and Family Journal*. Fall, 1977, p. 114.
Cole, K.C. "Can Natural Childbirth Survive Technology?" *New York Daily News Sunday Magazine*. January 14, 1979, p. 6.
——— "Controversy Rises with the Rate of Cesarean Sections." *Newsday*. Sept. 18, 1978, p. 9A.

———— *What Only a Mother Can Tell You About Having a Baby.* New York: Doubleday, 1980.

Collins, Glenn. "Fathers Get Postpartum Blues Too." *New York Times.* April 6, 1981, p. 14.

Coons, Mary. "Premature Baby." *Baby Talk.* January 1981, p. 11.

Cooper, Kenneth. *The Aerobics Way.* New York: M. Evans, 1977.

———— *The New Aerobics.* New York: Bantam, 1970.

Corbin, Cheryl. *Nutrition.* New York: Holt, Rinehart and Winston, 1981.

Dallas, Gus. "Bankruptcy's Too Often in the (Credit) Cards." *New York Daily News.* October 12, 1980, p. B1.

Daly, Margaret. "A Family Budget That Works." *Better Homes and Gardens.* May, 1980, p. 23.

———— "Life Insurance: Planning Protection for a Growing Family. *Better Homes and Gardens.* May, 1980, p. 23.

Daniels, Pamela, and Weingarten, Kathy. "Late First Time Parenthood: The Two Sides of the Coin." Paper of the Wellesley College Center for Research on Women. October, 1979.

————. *Sooner or Later: The Timing of Parenthood in Adult Lives.* New York: Norton, 1982.

DeFrain, John. "Androgynous Parents Tell Who They Are and What They Need." *The Family Coordinator.* April, 1979, p. 237.

Delli Quadri, Lyn, and Breckenridge, Kati. *Mothercare.* New York: Pocket Books, 1980.

Deutsch, Ronald M. *The Family Guide to Better Food and Better Health.* Des Moines, Iowa: Creative Home Library/Meredith, 1977.

Donovan, Bonnie. *The Cesarean Birth Experience.* Boston: Beacon Press, 1977.

Dullea, Georgia. "Nursemaid Versus Mother." *New York Times.* March 15, 1982, p. B5.

———— "Parent's Dating: A Child's Reactions." *New York Times.* February 16, 1981, p. B6.

———— "Parents Who Go It Alone Decide to Stick Together." *New York Times.* June 5, 1978, p. D8.

———— "Weighing the Impact of a Joint Custody Law." *New York Times.* April 27, 1981, p. C19.

Eberle, Nancy. "The Importance of Couple Time." *Glamour.* February, 1981, p. 208.

Edelson, Edward. "The Nursing Mother." *New York Daily News Sunday Magazine.* February 4, 1979, p. 7.

Einstein, Elizabeth. "Stepfamily: Chaotic, Complex, Challenging." *Stepfamily Bulletin.* Fall, 1980, p. 1.

Eisenberg, Richard, "How Employers Can Help." *Money.* November, 1980, p. 89.

Elkind, David. *A Sympathetic Understanding of the Child: Birth to Sixteen.* Boston: Allyn and Bacon, 1978.

Farran, Christopher. "The Crying Baby Blues." *Parents.* July 1981, p. 56.

———— "What Mothers Say About Colic." *Baby Talk*. March, 1981, p. 28.

Fein, Robert A. "Men's Entrance to Parenthood." *The Family Coordinator*. October, 1976, p. 341.

———— "The First Weeks of Fathering: The Important Choices and Supports for New Parents." *Birth and Family Journal*. No. 2, 1976, p. 53.

———— "A Research on Fathering: Social Policy and an Emergent Perspective." *Journal of Social Issues*. 1978, p. 122.

Feldberg, Roslyn, and Kohen, Janet. "Family Life in an Anti-Family Setting: A Critique of Marriage and Divorce." *The Family Coordinator*. April, 1976, p. 151.

Ferretti, Fred. "Reducing Child Custody Fights." *New York Times*. January 1, 1981, p. 15.

Flower, Joe. "Is There Sex After Parenthood?" *Couples*. November 1980, p. 103.

Fraiberg, Selma. *The Magic Years*. New York: Scribner's, 1959.

Frank, Elizabeth Pope. "Who's Minding the Children?" *Good Housekeeping*. February, 1979, p. 111.

Freeman, Castle, Jr. "Trusts: More For Your Kids, Less for the Feds." *Family Journal*. January, 1981, p. 46.

Freudenberger, Herbert J. "Treatment and Dynamics of the Disrelated Teenager and His Parents in the American Society." *Psychotherapy: Theory, Research and Practice*. Fall, 1969, p. 249.

Friedan. "Feminism Takes a New Turn." *New York Sunday Magazine*. November 18, 1979, p. 40.

Friedman, Max. J. "Twins." *Parents*. November, 1980, p. 76.

Forst, Elizabeth. "Grandparents: The Other Victims of Divorce." *McCalls*. September, 1980, p. 42.

Galinsky, Ellen. *Between Generations: The Six Stages of Parenthood*. New York: Times Books, 1981.

Galper, Miriam. *Joint Custody and Co-Parenting: A Source Book for the Separated or Divorced Family*. Philadelphia: Running Press, 1980.

Gatley, Richard, and Koulack, David. *Single Father's Handbook*. New York: Doubleday/Anchor Press, 1979.

Gaylin, Willard. *Feelings: Our Vital Signs*. New York: Harper and Row, 1979.

Giges, Nancy. "Study Follows Baby Boom Spenders." *Advertising Age*. May 11, 1981, p. 53.

Gilberg, Arnold L. "The Stress of Parenting." *Child Psychiatry and Human Development*. Winter, 1975, p. 59.

Gill, John Edward. *Stolen Kids: Why and How Parents Kidnap Their Kids . . . And What to Do About It*. New York: Seaview Books, 1981.

Gould, Deb, *et al*. *Playgroups: How to Grow Your Own from Infancy Onward*. Boston: Child Care Resource Center, 1974.

Greenberg, Martin, and Morris, Norman. "Engrossment: The Newborn's Impact Upon the Father." *American Journal of Orthopsychiatry*. July, 1974, p. 520.

Greenleaf, Barbara Kaye, and Schaffer, Lewis A. *HELP: A Handbook for Working Mothers.* New York. Crowell, 1978.

Greenleaf, Barbara Kaye. "What Not to Settle For: Tips on Divorce Negotiation." *Working Mother*, March, 1981, p. 63.

Group for the Advancement of Psychiatry, *The Joys and Sorrows of Parenthood.* New York: Scribners, 1973.

Hammersmark, Judy, and Guess, Lee Ann. "Handle With Care: The Premature Baby." *Baby Talk.* May, 1979, p. 20.

Harris, Marlys. "Divorce's Friendly Persuaders." *Money.* April, 1980, p. 85.

————— "Keeping a Working Marriage Working." *Money.* January, 1979, p. 44.

Hausknecht, Richard U., and Heilman, Joan Rattner. *Having a Cesarean Baby.* New York: Dutton, 1978.

Heffner, Elaine. *Mothering: The Emotional Experience of Motherhood After Freud and Feminism.* New York: Doubleday, 1978.

Heiser, Verda. *A Handicapped Child in the Family.* New York: Grune and Stratton, 1972.

Hersh, Seymour P. *The Executive Parent.* New York: Simon and Schuster/ Sovereign Books, 1979.

Hetherington, E. Mavis, *et al.* "Divorced Fathers." *Psychology Today.* April, 1977, p. 42.

Hinds, Michael deCourcy. "Discipline Problems With a Stepchild." *New York Times.* March 22, 1981, p. 15.

————— "No One Should Be Without a Will." *New York Times.* May 30, 1981, p. 15.

Hite, Rodney. "How to Choose a Pediatrician." *Parents Resources Newsletter.* Spring, 1980.

Hobbs, Daniel F., Jr., and Cole, Sue Peck. "Transition to Parenthood: A Decade of Replication." *Journal of Marriage and the Family.* November, 1976, p. 723.

Hochstein, Rollie. "Home-Style Child Care: Answering Mothers' Needs." *Woman's Day.* November 25, 1980, p. 36.

Holmes, Kay. "My Child is in the Hospital." *Parents.* September, 1980, p. 42.

Honig, Judy. "A Parents' Primer on Hospitals." *Parents Resources Newsletter.* Winter, 1981.

Howard, Jane. *Families.* New York: Simon and Schuster, 1978.

Howe, Louise Knapp. *The Future of the Family.* New York: Simon and Schuster, 1972.

Johnson, Beverly L. "Single Parent Families." *Family Economics Review.* Summer/Fall, 1980, p. 2.

Johnson, Sharon, and Leishman, Katie. "Round Two." *Working Mother.* November, 1980, p. 47.

Jones, Suzanne Y. "Service Supports For Single Parent Families." Paper presented to the Groves Conference on Marriage and the Family, April, 1978.

Keniston, Kenneth, and the Carnegie Council on Children. *All Our Chil-*

dren: The American Family Under Pressure. New York: Harcourt Brace, Jovanovich, 1977.

Kennedy, Mopsy Strange. "Surviving Ambition and Competition." *Savvy*. May, 1980, p. 32.

Kennell, John H. "Birth of a Malformed Baby: Helping the Family." *Birth and Family Journal*. Winter, 1978, p. 223.

——— "Parenting in the Intensive Care Unit." *Birth and Family Journal*. Winter, 1978, p. 23.

Klaus, Marshall. "Future Care of the Parents." *Birth and Family Journal*. Winter, 1978, p. 246.

Klaus, Marshall H., and Kennell, John H. *Maternal-Infant Bonding: The Impact of Early Separation or Loss on Family Development*. St. Louis: C.V. Mosby, 1976.

Klemesrud, Judy. "Conflicts Facing Women Without Jobs" *New York Times*. May 7, 1981, p. C1.

——— "Learning to Mix Love and Money." *New York Times*. February 16, 1981, p. B6.

Kosner, Alice. "What Sex Therapists are Learning." *McCalls*. August, 1979, p. 85.

Kracoff, Carol. "Careers: Flexing Time." *Washington Post*. October 9, 1979. p. C5.

Lake, Alice. "The Day Care Business." *Working Mother*. November, 1980, p. 143.

Lakein, Alan. *How to Get Control of Your Time and Your Life*. New York: New American Library, 1974.

Lally, J. Ronald. "Some Common Concerns of Mothers Who Work Outside the Home." *Zero to Three*. Washington, D.C.: The National Center for Clinical Infant Programs, March, 1981, p. 10.

Landers, Ann. *Family Circle*. February 10, 1978, p. 3.

Lasch, Christopher. *The Culture of Narcissism: American Life in an Age of Diminishing Expectations*. New York: Warner Books, 1979.

Lazarre, Jane. *The Mother Knot*. New York: Dell, 1977.

Lecker, Sidney. *Family Ties*. New York: Wyden Books, 1979.

Lein, Laura. "Male Participation in Home Life: Impact of Social Supports and Breadwinner Responsibility on the Allocation of Tasks." *The Family Coordinator*. October, 1979, p. 489.

Lenz, Elinor. *Once My Child . . . Now My Friend*. New York: Warner Books, 1981.

LeShan, Eda. *In Search of Myself and Other Children*. New York: M. Evans, 1976.

LeShan, Eda. *The Wonderful Crisis of Middle Age*. New York: David McKay, 1973.

Levine, James A. "Breaking the Day Care Stalemate: The Prospects and Dilemmas of I and R." Monograph from Wellesley College Center for Research on Women, undated.

——— *Who Will Raise the Children?* Philadelphia: J. B. Lippincott, 1976.

Lewis, Robert A., *et al.* "Fathers and Postparental Transition." *The Family Coordinator.* October, 1979, p. 514.

Linscott, Judy. "The Workplace is Changing . . . But Not Too Fast." *New York Daily News.* March 10, 1981, p. 19.

Lofas, Jeanette, and Roosevelt, Ruth. *Living in Step.* New York: Stein and Day, 1976.

Lopata, Helena Z. *Marriages and Families.* New York: Van Nostrand, 1973.

Lyon, Shari, and Perreault, Kelle. "Notes on Feeding Twins." *Baby Talk.* February, 1979, p. 32.

Macauley, Ian T. "Varieties of Mortgage Plans Offered By Lenders Grows." *New York Times.* September 21, 1980, Section 8, p. 1.

Mace, David. "Marriage and Family Enrichment—A New Field?" *The Family Coordinator.* July, 1979, p. 409.

Mangurten, Henry H., *et al.* "Parent-Parent Support in the Care of High-Risk Newborns." *Journal of Obstetrical and Gynecological Nursing.* September-October, 1979, p. 275.

Margolius, Sidney. "Family Money Problems." New York: Public Affairs Pamphlet No. 142, 1979.

Marieskind, Helen I. "An Evaluation of Cesarean Sections in the United States." Report issued by the Department of Health, Education and Welfare, U.S. Government, 1980.

Maslow, Abraham H. *The Farther Reaches of Human Nature.* New York: Viking, 1972.

Masnick, George, and Bane, Mary Jo. *The Nation's Families, 1960–1990.* Boston: Joint Center for Urban Studies, 1981.

Mason, Diane, *et al.* "How to Grow a Parents Group." Minneapolis: International Childbirth Education Assn., 1979.

Masters, William H., and Johnson, Virginia E. *Human Sexual Response.* Boston: Little, Brown, 1966.

———— *The Pleasure Bond—A New Look at Sexuality.* Boston: Little, Brown, 1974.

McCleary, Elliott. *Your Child Has a Future.* Chicago: Easter Seal Society, 1978.

McNamara, Joan, and McNamara, Bernard. *The Special Child Handbook.* New York: Hawthorn, 1977.

McNiff, Veronica. "The News About Grandparents." *Parents.* November, 1979, p. 51.

Mendes, Helen A. "Single Fatherhood." *Social Work.* July, 1976, p. 308.

Miller, Gordon Porter. *Life Choices.* New York: Crowell, 1978.

Miller, Neil. "The Father and Child Reunion." *Boston Phoenix.* December 12, 1978, p. 5.

Minuchin, Salvador. *Families and Family Therapy.* Boston: Harvard University Press, 1974.

Money. "A Professional Advisor's Personal Advice." November, 1980, p. 56.

Montgomery, James E. "Impact of Housing Patterns on Marital Interaction," *The Family Coordinator.* July, 1970, p. 267.

Mitchell, Grace. *The Day Care Book*. New York: Stein and Day, 1979.

Moore, Coralie B., and Morton, Kathryn Gorham. *A Reader's Guide for Parents of Children with Mental, Physical or Emotional Disabilities*. U.S. Department of Health, Education and Welfare Publication No. (HSA) 77–5250, 1976.

Muenchow, Susan. "Sex and the Single Parent." *Parents*. June, 1979.

Murdoch, Carol Vejvoda. *Single Parents are People, Too!* New York: Butterick, 1980.

Nance, Sherri. *Premature Babies—A Handbook for Parents*. New York: Arbor House, 1982.

Newman, Pamela. "Master Time Lest It Master You." *Management Controls*. May-June, 1977, p. 20.

Noble, Elizabeth. *Essential Exercises for the Childbearing Year*. Boston: Houghton Mifflin, 1976.

———— *Having Twins: A Parent's Guide to Pregnancy, Birth and Early Childhood*. Boston: Houghton Mifflin, 1980.

Noble, June, and Noble, William. *How to Live With Other People's Children*. New York: Hawthorn, 1977.

Norman, Michael. "The New Extended Family." *New York Times Sunday Magazine*. November 23, 1980, p. 26.

Nugent, Jean, and Stefan, Julia. "Child Care Solutions." *Mother's Manual*. October, 1980, p. 54.

Parents Resources Newsletter. "Suggested Groundrules for a Cooperative Playgroup," Fall, 1979, p. 1.

———— "How to Choose a Childcare Person." Spring, 1980, p. 1.

———— "How to Start a Babysitting Co-op." Spring, 1980, p. 1.

Parke, Ross D. "The Father's Role in Infancy: A Reevaluation." *Birth and Family Journal*. Winter, 1978, p. 211.

Parlee, Mary Brown. "The Friendship Bond." *Psychology Today*. October, 1979, p. 42.

Pennwalt Pharmaceuticals. "Are you really serious about losing weight?" Rochester, N.Y., 1979.

Pleck, Joseph H. "Men's Family Work: Three Perspectives and Some New Data." *The Family Coordinator*. October, 1979, p. 461.

Porter, Sylvia. *Sylvia Porter's New Money Book for the 80s*. New York: Avon Books, 1980.

Porterfield, Kay Marie. "There's No Such Thing as an Ex-Grandparent." *Working Mother*. January, 1981, p. 92.

Price, Jane. *How to Have a Child and Keep Your Job*. New York: St. Martin's, 1979.

———— *You're Not Too Old to Have a Baby*. New York: Farrar, Strauss and Giroux, 1977.

Quint, Barbara Guilder. "Are You Paying Too Much for Your Life Insurance?" *Family Circle*. May 31, 1977, p. 34.

Rakowitz, Elly, and Rubin, Gloria. *Living With Your New Baby*. New York: Franklin-Watts, 1978.

Rapoport, Rhona, and Rapoport, Robert. *Fathers, Mothers and Society: Towards New Alliances*. New York: Basic Books, 1977.

———— *Working Couples*. New York: Harper and Row/Colophon Books, 1978.

———— *Dual-Career Families Re-examined: New Integrations of Work and Family*. New York: Harper and Row, 1976.

Raymond, Louise, and Dywasuk, Colette Taube. *Adoption and After*. New York: Harper and Row, Revised, 1974.

Renwich, Patricia A., and Lawler, Edward E. "What You Really Want From Your Job." *Psychology Today*. May, 1978, p. 53.

Roberts, Francis. "Stepfamilies: Stresses and Surprises." *Parents*. March, 1981, p. 108.

Roby, Pamela. *Child Care—Who Cares?* New York: Basic Books, 1973.

Roman, Mel, and Haddad, William. *The Disposable Parent*. New York: Holt, Rinehart and Winston, 1978.

Rosen, Benson, et al. "Dual Career Marital Adjustment." *Journal of Marriage and the Family*. August, 1975, p. 570.

Rosenblatt, Paul C., and Russell, Martha G. "The Social Psychology of Potential Problems in Family Vacation Travel." *The Family Coordinator*. April, 1975, p. 209.

Rossi, Alice. "The Mystique of Parenthood." *Family in Transition*. Arlene Skolnick and Jerome Skolnick ed.) Boston: Little, Brown, 1971.

Rozdilski, Mary Lou, and Banet, Barbara. *What Now? A Handbook for New Parents*. New York: Scribner's, 1975.

Rubin, Theodore Isaac. *Compassion and Self Hate*. New York: David McKay, 1975.

Rubinstein, Carin. "Vacations: Expectations, Satisfactions, Fantasies." *Psychology Today*. May, 1981, p. 29.

Russell, Candyce Smith. "Transition to Parenthood: Problems and Gratifications." *Journal of Marriage and the Family*. May, 1974, p. 294.

Sager, Clifford, and Hunt, Bernice. *Intimate Partners: Hidden Patterns in Love Relationships*. New York: McGraw-Hill, 1979.

Sarrel, Lorna, and Sarrel, Philip. "How Couples Can Learn to Share Their Inner Feelings." *Redbook*. March, 1980, p. 46.

Sawin, Douglas, and Parke, Ross D. "Fathers' Affectionate Stimulation and Caregiving Behaviors with Newborn Infants." *The Family Coordinator*. October, 1979, p. 509.

Schiffman, Suzanne. "Making It Easier To Be A Working Parent." New York Times. Nov. 24, 1980, p. 27.

Scott, Carole Elizabeth. *Your Financial Plan: A Consumer's Guide*. New York: Harper and Row, 1979.

Segal, Julius, and Yahres, Herbert. "Bringing Up Mother." *Psychology Today*. November, 1978, p. 90.

Seixas, Suzanne. "Singing the Bankruptcy Blues." *Money*. November, 1980, p. 56.

Shepro, David, and Knuttgen, Howard. *Complete Conditioning: The No-*

Nonsense Guide to Fitness and Good Health. Reading, Pa.: Addison-Wesley, 1976.

Sherrard, Jane. *Mother, Warrior, Pilgrim.* Kansas City: Andrews and Mc-Neel, 1980.

Shosenberg, Nancy. *The Premature Infant: A Handbook for Parents.* Toronto: Sick Children's Hospital, 1980.

Skolnick, Arlene, "The Myth of the Vulnerable Child." *Psychology Today,* February, 1978, p. 56.

Smilkstein, Gabriel. "The Family APGAR: A Proposal for a Family Function Test and Its Use By Physicians." *Journal of Family Practice,* No. 3, 1979. p. 557.

—— "Why and How to Use the Family APGAR: A Family Function Questionnaire." *Consultant,* September, 1980, p. 246.

Smith, William M., Jr. "Family Relationships: Communicating a Concept." *Journal of Marriage and the Family.* February, 1968, p. 12.

Sones, Melissa. "A Divorce Trauma: Telling the Parents." *New York Times.* March 12, 1981, p. C3.

Stafford, Linley. "Bankrupt and Wiser." *New York Times.* July 23, 1981, p. A27.

Stechert, Kathryn B. "At Last! Help in Collecting Child Support." *Woman's Day.* April 28, 1981, p. 42.

Stepfamily Bulletin. "Stepmother Stress Documented." Summer, 1981, p. 12.

Stephen, Beverly, "Single Parents and the Empty Nest." *New York Daily News,* Jan. 5, 191, p. 28.

Stewart, David. *Fathering and Career.* Seattle: Pennypress, 1979.

Stigen, Gail. *Heartaches and Handicaps: An Irreverant Survival Manual for Parents.* Palo Alto: Science and Behavior Books, 1976.

Stiles, David. *Easy-to-Make Children's Furniture.* New York: Pantheon, 1980.

Stone, Elizabeth. "Mothers and Daughters: Taking a New Look." *New York Times Sunday Magazine.* May 13, 1979, p. 14.

Streich, Corrine. *Let's Lunch.* Englewood Cliffs: Prentice-Hall, 1981.

Switzer, Ellen. "The Sex Problem Nobody Talks About." *Family Circle.* November 15, 1977, p. 54.

Theroux, Rosemary T., and Tingley, Josephine F. *The Care of Twin Children.* Chicago: Center for the Study of Multiple Gestation, 1978.

Tilling, Thomas. "Save for College: A Tax-Free Plan." *Parents.* February, 1979, p. 94.

—— "Going for Broke: The Bankruptcy Option." *Parents.* December, 1980, p. 35.

—— "Insurance: What You Need." *Parents.* June, 1981, p. 40.

—— "Is Our Credit Card World Crumbling?" *Parents.* October, 1981, p. 36.

—— "Twenty Great Income Tax Deductions." *Parents.* April, 1981, p. 38.

—— "The Mortgage Game." *Parents.* May, 1981, p. 34.

———— "Your $250,000 Baby." *Parents*. November, 1980, p. 83.

———— "Where There's A Will There's A Way." *Parents*. March, 1981, p. 34.

Tobias, Andrew. "The Ten Most Common Money Mistakes." *Redbook*. September, 1980, p. 25.

Tognoli, Jerome. "The Flight From Domestic Space: Men's Roles in the Household." *The Family Coordinator*. October, 1979, p. 599.

Trubo, Richard. "The Consumer's Book of Hints and Tips." Middle Village, N.Y.: Jonathan David, 1978.

Trunzo, Candace E. "Mixing Children and Jobs." *Money*. November, 1980, p. 80.

Turrini, Patsy. "A Mother's Center: Research, Service and Advocacy." *Social Work*. November, 1977, p. 478.

Wagner, Diane. "Two Families Adjust to New Routines." *New York Times*. April 27, 1981, p. C19.

Wakefield, Tom. *Some Mothers I Know: Living With Handicapped Children*. Boston: Routledge and Kegan Paul Ltd., 1978.

Weinberg, Jack. "What Do I Say to My Mother When I Have Nothing to Say?" *Geriatrics*. November, 1974, p.   .

Weingarten, Kathy, and Daniels, Pamela. "Family Career Transitions in Women's Lives: Report on Research in Progress." Paper presented to the American Psychological Association Symposium on Transitional Experiences in Adult Development, Toronto, Canada, August 31, 1978.

Weiss, Joan Solomon. *Your Second Child*. New York: Summit, 1981.

Weiss, Robert S. *Going It Alone—The Family Life and Social Situation of the Single Parent*. New York: Basic Books, 1975.

———— *Marital Separation*. New York: Basic Books, 1975.

Weissman, Myrna M., and Paykiel, Eugene S. "Moving and Depression in Women." *Society*. July, 1972, p. 24.

Wheeler, Michael. *Divided Children*. New York: Norton, 1980.

White House Conference on Families. "Listening to America's Families." Conference Report, 1980.

White, John. *Relax: How You Can Feel Better, Reduce Stress and Overcome Tension*. New York: Dell, 1976.

Whitney, Craig R. "Taking the Kids on a China Tour." *New York Times*. June 29, 1980. Section 10, p. 132.

Wills, Garry. "Against Parenting." *Parents*. January, 1979, p. 115.

Winslow, Joyce. "Help! There's a Child in My Car." *Redbook*. October 1979, p. G2.

Winston, Stephanie. *Getting Organized*. New York: Norton, 1978.

Woman's Day. "A Report on How Working Wives Cope." September 20, 1977, p. 12.

Wolfenstein, Martha, and Mead, Margaret. *Childhood in Contemporary Cultures*. Chicago: University of Chicago Press, 1955.

Wool, Robert. "A Zermatt Ski Holiday With an Infant Daughter in Tow."

New York Times. January 4, 1981, Section 10, p. 5.

Woolfe, Lorin Stephen. "Moving With a Baby or a Toddler. *Baby Talk.* January, 1981, p. 34.

Yankelovich, Daniel. "The New Psychological Contracts at Work." *Psychology Today.* May, 1978, p. 46.

———— *New Rules in American Life: Searching for Self-Fulfillment in a World Turned Upside Down.* New York: Random House, 1981.

Young, Diony, and Mahan, Charles. *Unnecessary Cesareans.* Minneapolis: International Childbirth Education Assn., 1980.

Zussman, Leon, and Zussman, Shirley. *Getting Together: A Guide to Sexual Enrichment for Couples.* New York: William Morrow, 1979.

INDEX

Absolutes, time and task, 188–89
Accident rates, during moving, 123
Accommodations
    for family vacation, 102
    for foreign travel, 110–11
Accounts, joint vs. individual, 207
"Achievement, minimum level of," 154
Adaptation, in marriage, 45
Adolescents, see Teenagers
Adoption, 35–37, 239
Adoption and After (Raymond/
    Dywasuk), 35–36, 37
Adults-only, vs. child-centered, enter-
    taining, 95–97
Adult time, 190
Adversary system, and divorce, 73
Advertisement (newspaper), for care-
    giver, 175
Advertising Age, 198
Advice (unsolicited), 129–31
Affection, in marriage, 45
Affinity, for household chores, 107–08
Age, in work world, 153
Agencies, for caregiver, 175
Air India, 108
Air travel, with small children, 107–9
Alienation, from home, 159
All Our Children (Keniston/Carnegie
    Council on Children), 236
American Academy of Pediatrics, 22
American Bar Association, 74
American Embassy, 111
American Institute of Real Estate
    Appraisers, 200
American Medical Association, 22
American Society for Psychoprophy-
    laxis in Obstetrics (ASPO), 125, 146
Anderson, Bob, 222
Annas, George, 32
Anniversaries, 139

Anthony, E. James, 233–34
Apartment swapping, 103
Appointments, recording, 43
Appreciation, in marriage, 50–51
Arbitration, and single parents, 246
Arm (upper) strengthening exercise, 226
Armstrong, Julie, 17
Assets, types of, 196
Attitude, and communication, 47
Authority, and stepparents, 81, 84
Avoidable expenses, 196

Baby
    adaptability of, 104
    babysitters for, 89
    clothes for, 87–88
    eating out with, 97–100
    and environment, 149–50
    feeding of, 28–30
    as focus of interest, 58–59
    foreign travel with, 110–11
    going out with, 85–88
    handicapped, 34–35
    and individual home care, 179
    and marriage, 49
    and moving, 123
    scheduling of, 185–86
    sensuality of, 60
    sex after, 53–54, 59
    traveling with, 100–4, 105–11
    see also Premature babies; Small
        children
Baby nurses, 13–14
Babysense (Burck), 28
Babysitters, 43, 89–94, 143, 162, 173,
    184, 190
    on family vacation, 103
    fees for, 92
    finding, 90–91

instructions for, 91–92
interviewing, 91–92
and single parents, 75
types of, 90
see also Babysitting coops; Caregiver
Babysitting coops, 92–94
arrangements for, 94
membership in, 93
payment system in, 93–94
Back, see Backache; Groin and lower
back stretch; Upper back exercise
Backache (avoiding), 227–29
driving, 228
lifting, 227
low-back relief, 228–29
posture, 229
sitting and kneeling, 228
sleeping, 228
standing, 228
walking, 227
Backpacks, 110, 227
Bailin, Lotte, 153
Balance sheet, on overload, 160
Banks, Ann, 122
Beer, 215
Being, 238
Benchley, Robert, 100
Benedek, Dr. Therese, 136, 137
Bensman, Joseph, 146
Best's Insurance Guide, 203
Best's Insurance Reports, 203
Better Business Bureau, 202
Between Generations: The Six Stages
of Parenthood (Galinsky), 232, 233
Beverages, 216
Biceps strengthening exercise, 226
Billing (direct), 73
Birth control organizations, 243
Birthdays, 139
Blended families, 80–82, 83
Blood, Margaret, 231
Blood, Robert, 53, 62, 153, 231
Body, synchronized with time, 188
Body composition, 219–20
Body fat, 219–20
Books, for car travel, 105
Borrowing, 197–98
shared, 208
Boswell, Jane, 203
Bottle-feeding, vs. breast-feeding, 28
"Brady Bunch, The" (TV show), 82

Breakables, 140
Breakfast foods, 216
Breast-feeding, 32, 57, 60, 210
vs. bottle-feeding, 28
organizations, 243
Breast measurements, 221
Breathing, while exercising, 224
Brenzel, Heather, 107
Brody, Jane, 214
Brody, Karen, 235
Brothers, Dr. Joyce, 137
Brozan, Nadine, 203
Brunch, 149
Buck passing, and overload, 159
Budgeting, 195–96
Bulkhead seats, and air travel, 107–8
Burck, Frances Wells, 28
Bureau of Labor Statistics, 164
Buses, and traveling with small
children, 107
Business associates, messages from,
162–63
Bust measurements, 221
Butter, 216

Caesarean, 12, 19
organizations, 244
California
divorce in, 71, 73
parent support groups in, 250
Callers (screening), for caregiver job,
176
Caloric content, of food, 215
Caloric substitution chart, 215, 216–18
Car, and traveling with small children,
105–6, 110, 111
Cardiovascular fitness, 220
Career compromise, 153
Career dedication, 153
Careerism, 152–54
vs. family and parenthood, 153
Career switching, 167
Caregiver, 174–79
and agencies, 175
changing, 179
and daycare centers, 182
and family daycare, 181
and individual home care, 179–80
and interviewing applicants, 176–78
and newspaper advertisement, 175

and screening callers, 175–176
and word of mouth, 175
see also Babysitters
Carnegie Council on Children, 236
Car seats, 105, 110, 239
Carter, Jimmy, 74
Cellulite, 221
Census Bureau, 74
Cervical discomfort, after childbirth, 56
Chamber of Commerce, 119, 123
Chanukah, 139
Charging, 208
see also Credit
Chazen, Simona, 65
Cheese, 216
Chest (upper), strengthening exercise, 224
Chicken, 214–15
Child abuse, 247
Childbirth organizations, 240
Child care, 6
facilities, on family vacation, 103
organizations, 240–41
responsibility for, 51
see also Daycare; Nursery schools
Childhood in Contemporary Cultures (Wolfenstein-Mead), 20
Child-rearing literature, 5–6
Children
adopted, 36–37
and babysitters, 92
and caregiver, 178
eating habits of, 212
and entertaining at home, 96–97
fantasies of, 81
friends of, 124
furniture for, 117
guardians of, 205–6
handicapped, 247
hospitalization of, 32–33
lifting, 227
quality time with, 157, 162
and remarriage, 81
in restaurants, 100
rooms for, 115
sick, 174
of single parents, 79–80
society of, 232
see also Hospitalized children organizations; Pre-school children; Small children

"Childrenese," 5
Childspace, 115–17
Christmas, 138, 139
Circulatory system, 220
City community, moving to, 118–19
Classroom, of nursery schools, 184
Cleary, Elliott, 34
Clothes, for baby, 87–88
Cohen, Dr. Martin, 44
Colic, 24–28, 130
responsibility for, 26, 27–28
Colorado, parent support groups in, 250
Color-coding system, and moving, 123
Comic relief, 14–15
Commitment, 3
family, 154
and planning, 42 43
Common sense, value of, 6
Communication
and blended family, 83
after divorce, 76
in marriage, 46–48
and sex, 61
Community
city, 118–19
moving to new, 124–25
in suburbs or country, 119–20
Community newspaper, advertisement in, 175
Commuting, 119, 162
Compassion, in marriage, 50–51
Compassion and Self-Hate (Rubin), 155
Competence, at housework, 170–71
Competition, at work, 153
Compressed time, 164
Compresses, for episiotomy, 56
Condominiums, 201–2
Conflict, in marriage, 44–46, 53
see also Emotional conflict; Rivalries
Conflict avoidance, in distressed families, 135
Congressional Budget Office, 171
Connectedness, and separateness, 232
Connecticut, parent support groups in, 251
Consumer information, 241
product safety, 241
Consumer Reports, 203–4
Continuous service leave, 164–65
Contracts, in marriage, 40–44
Conversation, of mothers, 147, 148

Cooperatives, 201–2
   parent, 182
Co-parenting, 66, 72
COPE, 8
Corbin, Cheryl, 212, 214
Cost of living adjustments, 73
Counseling, professional, 161
   organizations, 242
Country, moving to, 119–20
Couples
   dual-career, 68, 153
   earning power of, 60
   see also Dual-career parents
Credit, use of, 197–98
Credit cards, 198
   separate, 208
Criticism, vs. unsolicited advice, 131
Cross-insurance, 203
Culture of Narcissism, The (Lasch), 64
Custody
   contested, 73
   and dual-career couples, 68
   escalating disputes on, 74–75
   joint, 66, 72, 73
   and mothers, 72
   and single parents, 65–66, 78–79
   "temporary," 71

Daycare, 171–84
   and caregiver, 174–79
   centers, 181-82
   family, 180–81
   individual home care, 179–80
   nursery schools, 183–84
   organizations, 240–41
   parent cooperatives, 182
Day Care Book, The (Mitchell), 155–56
Daycare centers, 181–82
Daydreaming, vs. planning, 186–87
Debts, 197–98
   see also Borrowing
Decision making, 6
   and time, 191–93
Delegating, 154, 187
Denial, as defense mechanism, 34
Dependability, at housework, 171
Depression, post-partum, 17–21
Desserts, 216
Developing family, 230–38
   growing pains and separation, 232–35

and parental self-evaluation, 235–38
power and responsibility transference,
   230–32
Diaper bag, for quick getaway, 87
Diaper changing
   and air travel, 108
   in restaurants, 99
Dick-Read, Grantly, 240
Diet, see Nutrition
Different, fear of being, 154
Dilators, for episiotomy, 56
Disability insurance, 208
Discipline
   and eating out with small children,
      100
   and overload, 160
   and stepparents, 81, 83–84
Discretion, of single parents, 79
Discretionary income, 197
Distressed families, 135
Divided Children (Wheeler), 64
Divorce, 64, 208, 246
   communication after, 76
   and financial support, 72–73, 74–75
   and lawyers, 71, 73
   and other parent, 75
   and small children, 67–68
   and télling family, 68–69
   and third-party mediation, 73–74
   see also Separation
Doctors, phone calls to, 24
   see also Pediatrician
Doing nothing, 187
Do-it-yourself will, 205
Door shutting, 190
Dressing baby, 88
Drinks, and car travel, 106
Driving, 228
Drugstores, 23
Dryness, after childbirth, 57
Dual-career couples, 68, 153
Dual Career Families Re-examined
   (Rapoport/Rapoport), 168
Dual-career parents
   and babysitting coops, 93
   and overload, 160–61
Dywasuk, Colette Taube, 35–36, 37

Early family life, see "What-our
   family-did-to-us" syndrome

"Early Rider" packet, 239
Earning power, of couples, 60
Easter, 139
Easy-to-Make Children's Furniture
    (Stiles), 117
Eating habits, *see* Nutrition
Eating out, with small children, 97–100
Eating personality, 212–14
Eating preferences, 214–15
Economic Recovery Act of 1981, 209
Edmundson, Judy, 17
Effectiveness, vs. efficiency, 186
Einstein, Elizabeth, 80
Emergencies, and foreign travel, 111
Emotional conflict, and hiring caregiver,
    178
    see also Conflict
Employee needs, answering, 163–65
Employer-employee relations, with
    caregiver, 180
Energy levels, and time, 188
Entertaining at home, 94–97
    adults-only vs. child-centered, 95–97
    friends, 148–49
Environment
    and baby, 149–50
    for communication, 48
Episiotomy, after childbirth, 55
    remedies for, 56
Equipment
    for family vacation, 102–3
    for foreign travel, 110
    of nursery schools, 184
Escapism, and overload, 159
Estate taxes, 204–5, 208
Ethnic newspaper, advertisement in,
    175
Europe, traveling in, 109–11
Evans, Nancy, 122
Executive Parent, The (Hersh), 159, 162
Exercise, 218–29
    and backache, 227–29
    before, 221–22
    fitness, 219–20
    spot reducing, 220–21
    strengthening exercises for partners,
        224–27
    stretching, 222
    stretching exercises for partners,
        223–24
Expenses, types of, 196–97

Extended families, 83, 144
Extras, and air travel, 107

Fairchild, Michele, 212
Family, 103, 190
    blended, 80–82, 83
    vs. careerism, 153
    change in, 135–36
    developing, 230–38
    distressed, 135
    extended, 83, 144
    gatherings, 138–39
    and hospitals, 32–33
    loyalties and rivalries in, 136–37
    and marital style, 39–40
    nuclear, 82
    and overload, 161
    practical help from, 12–13
    short-term contracts, 160
    single-parent, 65–66
    support of, 11, 126–41
    telling about divorce, 68–69
    time and, 137, 163
    two dust-rag, 168–71
    and unsolicited advice, 129–31
    visiting rules, 139–40
    "what-our-family-did-to-us" syn-
        drome, 133–35
    and work ethic, 154
    see also Family vacation; Grand-
        parents; Relatives; Surrogate
        family; Two-career family
Family, The (Blood/Blood), 153, 231
Family APGAR questionnaire, 44–46
"Family bed," 130
Family Circle, 5
Family daycare, 180–81
Family Enhancement Program, 8
Family Focus, 8
Family Mediation Association, 74
Family moving survival kit, 123–24
Family reunions, 139
Familyspace, 113–15
Family Ties (Lecker), 134
Family vacation, 101–4
    accommodations, 102
    child care facilities, 103
    child equipment, 102–3
    house or apartment swapping, 103
    with other family, 103

schedule on, 103–4
and togetherness, 104
Farran, Christopher, 27
Farran, Dale, 27
Fat, 214, 219–20
  see also Cellulite
Father, 61
  and breast-feeding, 28
  and hospitals, 33
  newly divorced, 67–68
  organizations, 242–43
  post-partum depression of, 18, 19
  as provider, 60
  separated, 66
  single, with custody, 64
Father-infant bond, 60
"Fathering and Career" (Stewart), 154
Fatigue
  and eating, 213
  and sex, 59
Fat patterning, 220–21
Favors, and new friends, 147
Fees, for pediatricians, 23
Feminist backfire, and returning to
  work, 166
Fever, in babies, 32
Finances, and work, 154, 167
Financial assets, 196
Financial glossary, 196–97
Financial support, and divorce, 72–73,
  74–75
Finkelman, Dr. Martin, 33
First aid kit, for foreign travel, 110
Fish, 214–15, 217
Fish out of water, and overload, 159
Fitness, 219–20
  body composition, 219–20
  cardiovascular fitness, 220
  flexibility, 219
  strength, 220
Fixed expense, 196
Fixed rate mortgage, 199
Flexibility, 96–97, 219
  in planning, 42–43
Flexitime, 164
Floor space, 116
Floor waxing, 169
Florida, parent support groups in, 251
Food, 213
  and air travel, 107
  caloric content of, 215

for car travel, 106
and foreign travel, 109–10
and train travel, 107
Foreign travel, with small children,
  109–11
Forgiveness, in marriage, 50–51
Fowl, 217
Frailberg, Selma, 231
Freed, Dr. Doris Jonas, 72
Free time, 163
Friends, 141–50
  awkward moments with, 148–50
  and baby, 141–42
  changes in, 142–45
  of children, 124
  entertaining, 148–49
  after moving, 125
  new, 145–47
  and obnoxious behavior, 147–48
  old, 147
  practical help of, 13
  of single parents, 75–76
  support of, 11
  as surrogate family, 144
  telling about divorce, 69–70
  visiting, 149–50
  visits from, 150
Fruits, 215
"Fun morality," 20
Furniture, children's, 117

Galinsky, Ellen, 232, 233
Galper, Miriam, 72
Game room (child's), 116
Games, for car travel, 106
Gatley, Richard, 67–68, 70, 71, 74
General Electric, 163
Georgia, parent support groups in, 251
Gifts, 16
  from grandparents, 131–32
Ginott, 5
Giveans, David, 255
Glickstein, Judith, 19, 39
Goals, 156, 186, 187
  and communication, 47
  in marriage, 51–52
  of nursery schools, 184
  and overload, 161
Goal-setting, 6–7

Goal statement test, 190–91
Going abroad, *see* Foreign travel
Going out
  with baby, 85–88
  by yourself, 88–89
Goldstein, Daniel, 109, 110–11
Goldstein, Richard, 109, 110–11
Goldstein, Susan, 109, 110–11
Goodbye House (Banks/Evans), 122
Gorsuch, Blair, 218–19
Grains (whole), 214
Grandparents, 76
  as babysitters, 90
  gifts and spoiling, 131–33
  growth of, 140–41
  practical help from, 12–13
  and small children, 137–38
  telling about divorce, 68–69
Greenleaf, Barbara Kaye, 181
Groin and lower back stretch, 223
Growing pains, 232–35
Guardians, children's, 205–6
Guilt, 5
  and work, 155–58

Habits (changing), and marriage, 49–50
Hamstring stretch, 223–24
Handicapped baby, 34–35
Handicapped children organizations,
  247
Harris, Louis, 198
Health insurance, 208
Health organizations, 243–44
  birth control, 243
  breast-feeding, 243
  Caesarean, 244
  nutrition, 244
Heart, functioning of, 220
Help, for new parents, 239–54
  practical, 12–13
  problems with, 129–31
  for single parents, 75
  see also Paid help
*HELP: A Handbook for Working
  Mothers* (Greenleaf), 181
Hersh, Stephen P., 159, 162
Hiding place (child's), 116
Hinkle, Susan, 183
Hite, Dr. Rodney L., 21
Holidays, 138–39, 184

Holmes, Kay, 31
Home, 111–17, 161–63
  alienation from, 159
  childspace, 115–17
  familyspace, 113–15
  phone messages at, 162–63
  privatespace, 113
  taking work, 160, 162
  work space at, 173
Home-based workers, 173
Home care (individual), 179–80
Home organizations, 244
  house swapping, 244
  moving, 244
Home ownership, 120, 198–201
Home remedies, for colic, 26
Honikman, Jane, 17
Hospital consent, 33–34
Hospitality, 148–49
  see also Entertaining at home
Hospitalized children organizations, 248
Hospitals, 29–34
Hospital for Sick Children (Toronto),
  28–29
Hosting function, 16
Household chores, 167–68
"Househusbands," 151
House swapping, 103
  organizations, 244
Housework, sharing, 168–71
  competence, 170–71
  dependability, 171
  scheduling, 170
  task assessment, 169–70
*How to Get Control of Your Time and
  Your Life* (Lakein), 185
*How to Have a Child and Keep Your
  Job* (Price), 176
*How to Live With Other People's
  Children* (Noble/Noble), 80
Husband-wife role tensions, 157

Idiosyncrasies, and marriage, 49–50
"Illegal" feelings, 82
Ill health, and caregiver, 178
Illinois, parent support groups in, 251
Illness, of children, 174
Illusion, of perfect parent, 5
Image disparity, 156
Immunization, 24

Inadequacy, fear of admitting, 2
Income, 196
    discretionary, 197
Independence Day, 139
Indiana, parent support groups in, 251
Individual accounts, vs. joint accounts,
    207
Inertia, and returning to work, 166–67
Inflation, 60, 208
    and home ownership, 199
Information, vs. prescriptions, 5–6
Initiation, of first-time parents, 7–8,
    10–37
Inner-outer thigh strengthening exer-
    cise, 226–27
Inner thigh stretch, 223
Installment buying, 208
    see also Credit
Insurance, see Disability insurance;
    Health insurance; Life insurance
Insurance cards, 33
Interdependence, in distressed families,
    135
Interest rates, 198
Interference, problems with, 129–31
Internal Revenue Service (IRS), 75,
    205, 208
International Childbirth Education
    Association (ICEA), 125
Interstate Commerce Commission
    (ICC), 120
Interstate movers, 120
Intuition, and caregiver, 178
Investments, 208
    and home ownership, 198, 199
Invitations, 149
Iowa, parent support groups in, 251
Isolation, 7–8, 78, 79
Isometric exercises, 224
Isotonic exercises, 224

Jacobson, Milford, 164
Jane Brody's Nutrition Book (Brody),
    214
Janoff, Ronald, 163–64
Job components, 154
Job division patterns, 167–68
Johnson, Virginia, 57, 60, 62–63
Joint accounts, vs. individual accounts,
    207

Joint custody, 66
    legal, 72
    physical, 72, 73
Joint Custody and Co-Parenting
    (Galper), 72
Jones, Sue, 65–66
Joys and Sorrows of Parenthood, The,
    36, 83, 237
Jumbo aircraft, 107

Kegel exercises, for episiotomy, 56
Keniston, Kenneth, 236
Kneeling, 227–228
Koulack, David, 70, 71

Lakein, Alan, 185, 186, 187
La Leche, 146
Lamaze method, 240
Landers, Ann, 5
Large-circulation newspaper, adver-
    tisement in, 175
Lasch, Christopher, 64
Laundry, 169, 170
Lawyers, and divorce, 71, 73
Leave, continuous service, 164–65
Leboyer method, 240
Lecker, Sidney, 134
Leftovers, 213
Leisure time, 190
Lenz, Elinor, 231–32, 237
LeShan, Eda, 234–35
Let's Lunch (Streich), 100
Levinson, Daniel, 234
Lewis, Nancy, 158
Liabilities, 196
Licensing
    of daycare centers, 182
    of nursery schools, 184
Life Choices: How to Make Critical
    Decisions About Your Education,
    Career, Family, Lifestyle (Miller),
    192–93
Life insurance, 203–4, 208
    and at-home parent, 203
    cross-insurance, 203
    where to go for, 203–4
    and women, 202–3
Lifestyle, 85–125, 211
    babysitters, 89–94

eating out with small children, 97–100
entertaining at home, 94–97
going out, with baby, 85–88
going out, by yourself, 88–89
at home, 111–17
moving, 117–25
traveling with small children, 100–4, 105–11
vacations alone, and alone together, 104–5
Lifting, 227
Lilienfeld, Robert, 146
Liquor, 215
Living in Step (Lofas/Roosevelt), 83
Lofas, Jeanette, 81–82, 83, 84
Logistics, and returning to work, 165–66
Long-distance trains, 107
Louisiana, parent support groups in, 251
Love, 82
and structure, 84
Low-back relief, 228–29
Loyalties, family, 136–37
Luggage, and air travel, 108

McLaughlin, Denise, 195
Madonna/Prostitute Syndrome, 59–60
Magazines (parenting), 245
Magic Years, The (Fraiberg), 231
Maine, parent support groups in, 251
Male sexuality, after childbirth, 59–60
Marital discord, 78
Marital infidelity, 60
Marital style, 38–40
and family context, 39–40
Marriage, 38–53, 235
communication in, 46–48
conflict in, 44–46, 53
contracts in, 40–44
key issues in, 48–53
rating, 45–46
and sex, 53–63
Marriage (Blood), 138
Marriage tax penalty, 209
Massachusetts, parent support groups in, 252
Masters, William, 57, 60, 62
Maternal superiority, and custody, 72
Maternity leave, 165

Mead, Margaret, 20
Meals, balanced, 212–13
Meatless days, 214–15
Meats, 217
"Meetings," on overload, 160
Mental health organizations, 242
Michigan, parent support groups in, 252
Middle age, 234–35
Milestones, in marriage, 48–49
Miller, Dr. Gordon Porter, 192–93
Minnesota, parent support groups in, 252
Minuchin, Salvador, 135
Missouri, parent support groups in, 252
Mitchell, Grace, 155–56
Money, 194–209
and budgeting, 195–96
condominiums and cooperatives, 201–2
credit, 197–98
and financial glossary, 196–97
and home ownership, 198–201
and overload, 160
savings, 197, 208
and two-career family, 206–8
wills, 204–6
Money Book for the '80s (Porter), 201, 204
Money magazine, 206, 207–8
Morris, Dr. Robert, 55, 56, 57
Mortgages, 199–200
for condominiums and cooperatives, 201–2
Mothers, 147, 148
and custody, 72
and hospitals, 33
post-partum depression of, 18, 19–21
returning to work, 165–68
single, 67
Mothers Center, 8
Motivation, for returning to work, 166–67
Moving, 117–25, 244
to city community, 118–19
decision on, 117–18
estimates on, 120–22
moving day, 124
moving in, 124–25
planning, 120–22
preparing for, 122–24
to suburbs or country, 119–20

survival kit, 123–24
Mrstik, Judy, 17
Muenchow, Susan, 77–80
Muscles, strength in, 220

Nassau, Jean, 140
National Council for Alternative Work
    Patterns, 164
National Daycare Campaign Confer-
    ence, 171
National Easter Seal Society, 34
National Institute of Child Health and
    Human Development, 19
Negative net worth, 196
Neighborhoods, 118–19
Neighbors, after moving, 125
Net worth, 196
Neuroses, of childless workers, 166
New Hampshire, parent support groups
    in, 252
New Jersey, parent support groups in,
    252
Newman, Dr. Pamela, 189, 190
Newsletters (parenting), 245
Newspaper advertisement, for care-
    giver, 175
New York, parent support groups in,
    253
New York Times, 72, 161, 203
New York Times Magazine, 83
Night flights, 108
Nine to Five (film), 163
Noble, June, 80, 81, 82
Noble, William, 80, 81, 82
Normality, and parenthood, 2–3
Norman, Michael, 83
Northwestern Mutual Life Insurance
    Company, 163, 164
NOW accounts, 198
Nuclear families, 82
Nursery schools, 183–84
    organizations, 241
Nurses, baby, 13–14
Nursing baby, see Breast-feeding
Nutrition, 210–18
    calorie substitution chart, 215,
        216–18
    eating personality, 212–14
    eating preferences, 214–15
    organizations, 244

and pregnancy, 210
and self-awareness, 212–15
and weight loss, 211, 212
Nutrition (Corbin), 214, 215

Obnoxious behavior, and friends,
    147–48
Occupational malaise, and returning to
    work, 167
Office of Child Support Enforcement
    (OCSE), 74–75
Ohio, parent support groups in, 254
Orgasm, after childbirth, 57
Out of touch, and returning to work,
    166
Overdrafts, 198
Overeating, 213
Overload, 158–61
    buck passing, 159
    coping with, 160–61
    escapism, 159
    fish out of water, 159
    loss of perspective, 158
    panic, 158–59
Over-organization, 186
Overprotection, in distressed families,
    135
Overscheduling, 43, 52–53
Overweight, 213

Packing routines, and moving, 122–23
Paid help, 13
    and overload, 160
Pamphlets (parenting), 245
Panic, and overload, 158–59
Parallel time, 191
Parental Kidnapping Prevention Act, 74
Parental mystique, 3
Parental wellbeing, 4–9
Parent cooperatives, 182
Parent-doctor relationships, 21–24
Parenthood, 237
    attitude vs. technique, 4
    vs. careerism, 153
    in context, 6
    conversation about, 147, 148
    defined, 1
    different styles in, 146–47
    and everyday problems, 3–4

private doubts of, 2–4
and time, 185–87
"typical," 10
Parenthood: Its Psychology and Psychopathology (Anthony/Benedek), 136, 233–34
Parenting, 38
defined, 1
Parent Locator Service, 74
Parents
at-home, 203
bereaved, 247
equality of, 146
family support for, 126–41
first time, 7–8, 10–37
house-bound, 161
perfect, 5
self-evaluation of, 235–38
Parents Are People, 140
Parent sleep rooms, 32
Parents magazine, 27, 31, 77, 204, 237
Parents Resources, 8, 32–33
Parents Resources Newsletter, 21
Parent's Survival Exercise Program, *see* Exercise
Parents' Survival Manual, 11–17
Parent support groups, 8, 21, 146
and colic, 26–27
Parent support groups organizations, 249–54
national, 249–50
by states, 250–54
Partners, 222
in marriage, 45
parents as, 40–44
strengthening exercises for, 224–27
stretching exercises for, 223–24
support of, 11, 14
Passover, 139
Patterns (changing), and marriage, 49–50
Payroll withholding, 73
Pediatrician, 21–24
and colic, 26
hospital affiliation of, 32
and making friends, 146
Peer babysitting exchanges, 91
Peer pressure, 156–57
Pennsylvania, parent support groups in, 254
Personal time, 189

Perspective (loss), and overload, 158
Pets, for adopted children, 37
Phone messages, at home, 162–63
see also Telephone answering machine
Pictures, hanging, 115
Pie, 216–17
Ping-pong effect, 156
Planning, 42–43
vs. daydreaming, 186–87
nutrition, 213
and time, 189–90
Playgrounds, 177
Playgroup, 174
Play room (child's), 116
Pleasure Bond, The (Masters/Johnson), 57, 62
Polishing silver, 169
Porter, Sylvia, 200, 201, 202, 203, 204
Positive thinking, 4
Post-partum depression, 17–21
Post-partum Education for Parents (PEP), 8, 17, 18
Posture, 229
Potatoes, 217
Power, transfer of, 230–32
Pregnancy, and nutrition, 210
Premature babies, 29–30, 248
"Premature Infant, The" (Shosenberg), 29–30
"Preparation D," search for, 20–21
Pre-school children, stepparents of, 83–84
Prescriptions, vs. information, 5–6
Price, Jane, 176
Privatespace, 113
Procrastination, 190
Product safety, 241
Professionals, in child care, 6
Property taxes, 200–201
Protein, low-fat, 214–15
Providers, family daycare, 181
Psyche, and sex, 58–62
Psychology Today, 5, 101, 142, 146, 151, 167
Publications (parenting), 246
Putdowns, after divorce, 77

Quality control at home, 157–58
Quality time, 157, 162

Quinn, Jane Bryant, 202, 207–8

Rapoport, Rhona, 168
Rapoport, Robert, 168
Raymond, Louise, 35–36, 37
Reading nook (child's), 116
Rear shoulders exercise, 225
Reclusiveness, and overload, 160
Redbook, 197
References, for caregiver job, 177
Relatives, 12–13
  as babysitters, 90
Remarriage, 79
  and children, 81
  and stepparents, 82–83
Renegotiable-rate mortgages, 199
Reservation, for air travel, 107
Resolve, in marriage, 45
Resources, for new parents, 239–54
Responsibility, 51
  delegating, 154, 187
  for housework, 168–71
  to self, 8–9
  transfer of, 230–32
Restaurant car, 107
Restaurants, 97–100
Restorative needs, and overload, 160
Reward, food as, 213
Rights of Hospital Patients, The
  (Annas), 32
Right time, for return to work, 166
Rigidity, in distressed families, 135
Rivalries (family), 136–37
  see also Conflict
Role tensions, husband-wife, 157
Rolm Corporation, 165
Romance, for single parents, 77–79
Rooming-in, 31, 32
Rooms, *see* Space
Roosevelt, Ruth, 83
Rosenblatt, Paul, 101
Routines, flexibility of, 42–43
Rubberized suits, 221
Rubin, Theodore Isaac, 155

Safety
  in child's room, 116
  on family vacation, 101–2
  and moving, 123

of nursery schools, 184
on visits, 139, 140
see also Product safety
Sager, Dr. Clifford, 134, 135
Sahlein, Nancy, 142
Salads, 217
Sandwiches, 217
Sauna suits, 221
Savings, 197, 208
Scheduling, 42–43, 187–88
  housework, 170
  nutrition, 213
Schiffman, Suzanne, 161
Scott, Carole Elizabeth, 195–96
Self, sense of, 163–64
Self-awareness, and nutrition, 212–15
Self-evaluation, parental, 235–38
Separated father, 66
Separation, 232–35
  deciding on, 70–74
  and teenagers, 233–35
  see also Divorce
Separation anxiety, 178–79
Separation shock, 71
Sex, 2
  after baby, 53–54, 59
  and communication, 61
  and fatigue, 59
  and marriage, 53–63
  and psyche, 58–62
Sex therapy, 61
Sexual dysfunction, 58
Shared-appreciation mortgages, 199–200
Shoes, and posture, 229
Short-term family contracts, 160
Shosenberg, Nancy, 29, 30
Shoulders exercise, 225–26
Sick children, 174
Silver, polishing, 169
Single Father's Handbook (Gatley/Koulack), 70
Single parents, 64–80, 177
  babysitters for, 90
  and babysitting coops, 93, 94
  and custody, 65–66
  isolation of, 78, 79
  organizations, 245–46
  romance for, 77–79
  tips for, 75–77
Sitting, 227–228

Sitz baths, for episiotomy, 56
Skolnick, Arlene, 5
Sleep, 228
   and car travel, 106
   and foreign travel, 110–11
Sleep-overs, 105
Small children
   adaptability of, 104
   and divorce, 67–68, 73
   eating out with, 97–100
   and foreign travel, 109–11
   and grandparents, 137–38
   and individual home care, 179–80
   and moving, 122
   scheduling, 103–4
   traveling with, 100–4, 105–11
   on visits, 139–40
   see also Baby
Smilkstein, Dr. Gabriel, 44–45
Snacks, 213, 218
   before homecoming, 163
Social context, and marital style, 39
Social secretary responsibilities, 15
Social Security Administration, 180
Sodium, limiting, 214
Soups, 218
Space, see Childspace; Familyspace;
   Privatespace
Spending money, and overload, 160
Spoiling, by grandparents, 132–33
Spot reducing, 220–21
Standing, 228
Stanton, Mary, 115
Stepfamily Bulletin, 80
Stepparents, 80–84
   names for, 84
   organizations, 247
   of pre-school children, 83–84
   and remarriage, 82–83
   weekend, 84
Stewart, David, 154
Stiles, David, 117
Storey, Walter, 163
Streich, Corrine, 100
Strength, muscular, 220
Strengthening exercises, for partners,
   224–27
Stress, and time, 190
Stretching (Anderson), 222
Stretching exercises, 222
   for partners, 223–24

Stride-Rite Corporation, 163
"Stroller hunch," 227
Strollers, 110, 227
Structure, and love, 84
Suburbs, moving to, 119–20
Surrogate family, 144
Swaddling, 130
Sweets, limiting, 214
Swissair, 108

"Talk test," 220
Tampons, 56
Tangible assets, 196
Tape recorder, use of, 106
Task absolutes, 189
Taxes, see Estate taxes; Marriage tax
   penalty; Property taxes
Teenagers, 231
   and separation, 233–35
Telephone answering machine, 15–16,
   163, 190
Telephone manners, 148
Texas, parent support groups in, 254
Thanksgiving, 138, 139
Theory, and contracts, 41–42
Thigh (inner-outer) strengthening
   exercise, 226–27
Thigh stretch (inner), 223
Thigh (rear) stretch, 223–24
Third-party mediation, and divorce,
   73–74
Thomas, Marlys, 206
Throwaways, and moving, 123
Tilling, Thomas, 195, 198–99, 203,
   204, 207
Time, 11, 185–93
   absolutes, 188
   for air travel, 108
   and decision making, 191–93
   and energy levels, 188
   and family, 137, 163
   free, 163
   management, 187–88
   organizing, 189–91
   parallel, 191
   personal, 189
   quality of, with children, 157
   task absolutes, 189
   uninterrupted, 187
   for visitors, 16

at work, 154
  see also Adult time; Compressed
    time; Right time; Scheduling
Tobias, Andrew, 197
Togetherness, 61, 104, 114–15
Touching, 30
Toys, 114, 115–16
  for car travel, 105
Tradeoffs, 7, 41
  and money, 194
  and moving, 118
Traditions, in marriage, 48–49
Train, and traveling with small
    children, 106–7
Traveling with small children, 100–4,
    105–11
  by air, 107–9
  by buses, 107
  by car, 105–6, 110, 111
  on family vacation, 101–4
  foreign travel, 109–11
  by train, 106–7
Travel period, between work and home,
    162
Twins, 248
Two-career family, and money, 206–8
Two dust-rag family, 168–71

Umbrella strollers, 227
Unavoidable expenses, 197
Understanding, and sex, 61
Uniform Child Custody Jurisdiction
    Act, 74
Upper arm strengthening exercise, 226
Upper back exercise, 225
Upper chest strengthening exercise, 224
USDA (Uniform Simultaneous Death
    Act), 204–5
U.S. Department of Health and Human
    Services, 181
U.S. government, 163

Vacations alone, and alone together,
    104–5
  see also Family vacation
Vaginal Birth After Caesarean Section
    (VBACS), 31
Vaginal discharge, after childbirth, 57
Vaginal discomfort, after childbirth, 56

Vaginismus, after childbirth, 56
Variable expenses, 196
Variable-rate mortgage, 199
Vegetables, 215, 218
Virginia, parent support groups in, 254
Virtue, and guilt, 155
Visitation rights, 72
  of grandparents, 69
  and single parents, 76
Visiting, 139–40
  friends, 149–50
  nursing schools, 184
Visits, 15–17
  from friends, 150

Walking, 227
  and posture, 229
Wall space (upper), 116
Water, in foreign countries, 111
Waxing floors, 169
Weekends, 43
  stepparent, 84
Weight, 211, 212, 215
Weissbourd, Bernice, 8
Welcome Wagon, 125
Welles, Sara, 195
"What-our-family-did-to-us" syndrome,
    133–35
Wheeler, Michael, 64, 73
White, Barbara, 70
Whole grains, 214
Wills, 204–6
  children's guardians, 205–6
  do-it-yourself, 205
  and USDA, 204–5
Wills, Garry, 237–38
Window washing, 169
Wisconsin
  divorce in, 71
  parent support groups in, 254
Withholding (payroll), 73
Wolfenstein, Martha, 20
Woman's Day, 169–70
Women, 64
  and life insurance, 202–3
Women's groups, 248–49
Wonderful Crisis of Middle Age, The
    (LeShan), 234–35
Work, 151–68
  basic questions in, 152

careerism, 152–54
  and home life, 161–63
  options, 163–65
  organizations, 249
  and overload, 158–61
  and parental guilt, 155–58
  readjustments in, 151
  returning to, 165–68
Work ethic, 154
Work frustrations, and overload, 160
Working Mother, 241
Work options, 163–65
  compressed time, 164
  continuous service leave, 164–65
  flexitime, 164
  work sharing, 149, 164
Work sharing, 149, 164
Work space, 173
  child's, 116

Xerox Corporation, 163

Y services, 89, 146
Yale University Health Services Parent
  Support Group, 219
Yankelovich, Daniel, 151
"Your Child Has a Future" (Cleary),
  34, 247
*Your Financial Plan: A Consumer's
  Guide* (Scott), 195–96
"Your Rights and Responsibilities When
  You Move" (booklet), 121
Youth, and work, 153

Zoning, and home ownership, 201
Zussman, Dr. Shirley, 58–62